OUR COSMIC ANCESTORS

Maurice Chatelain

OUR COSMIC ANCESTORS

MAURICE CHATELAIN

Cover Art "The Astronaut" and Illustrations
Thierry Chatelain

Foreword
Charles Berlitz

Temple Golden Publications
Sedona, Arizona

CONTENTS

FOREWORD

by Charles Berlitz

As the Earth approaches what we might term planetary maturity, perhaps recognizable by the capacity of its inhabitants to discover and contact the elemental forces of the universe, intelligent forces from other parts of the cosmos seem to have discovered, and to be observing, Earth.

These observers, commonly referred to for the last thirty years as UFOs, which may previously have been visitors to our air space for thousands or millions of years before their increased visitations in the present period, have in the past been afforded a variety of explanations by those who saw them. They were gods, dragons, ghosts, devils, signs of doom and portent, or messages and even messengers from God. Prophets from Earth have thought that they had conversed with such messengers and relayed their warnings to their people.

Since the 1950's, a cresting new wave of unidentified earthly visitations has been reported in the skies, in the seas, and on the lands of almost all areas of Earth. Despite the ironical reporting of such phenomena in the local press and tendencies to discredit or a reluctance to follow up initial reports, both of which suggest a form of censorship from official sources, the actuality of these unidentified visitations will not vanish. No one among the millions who have personally observed UFOs will forget their convincing presence, and these include heads of state, astronomers, air force and navy personnel of many countries, civilian pilots, ship captains, police investigators, and countless other observers who would normally hesitate, because of their professional careers, before reporting a UFO. These witnesses are likely not to be swayed by superstition or popular emotion.

As public credence begins to accept the invasion of UFOs in the skies of Earth, the frustrating question continues to pose itself with increasing frequency as to what those who direct the flights of UFOs desire from this planet. Are they looking for planetary living space?

1

For minerals? For water? Or, perhaps for food? Or are they looking or waiting for something that is not yet clear to us?

UFOs, while demonstrating considerable curiosity about activities on Earth, especially atomic, space research, communication centers, and war zones, have not yet sent messsages to representatives of the powers of Earth that we have been able to perceive; and, as there have been well-authenticated cases where UFOs have been fired upon in flight or even after landing by the local military, it is unlikely that those who send them, unless they are bent on conquest, will continue to risk the danger of direct contact with the suspicious and warlike inhabitants of Earth.

However, landings continue to be made, many in isolated areas. The most recent count lists I925 cases in 66 countries where physical traces of observed landings have been found imprinted or burned on the ground. More than 20% of these landing reports have included the sighting of crews or "humanoid creatures" from the UFOs by human observers.

A notable observer of the UFO phenomenon, Maurice Chatelain, space scientist, a designer of the Apollo space craft, NASA Chief of Communications for the Apollo lunar missions, is of the opinion that there are messages to be read, for those able to read them, within the UFO landing patterns themselves and within the traces left by UFOs on the ground.

Maurice Chatelain, working with other French researchers, has developed, with typical French dedication to innovative theories, convincing proof that advanced mathematical information is contained within the patterns of landing and also the imprints on the earth left by UFOs at the time of landing. It is their theory that this information is an opening gambit offered to the inhabitants of Earth for future communication. This information, when run through computers, has surprisingly and correctly given basic mathematical ratios which indicate a knowledge and sophisticated use of advanced mathematics.

A message left by space visitors using mathematics as an international or interspacial language has a certain logic, since a knowledge of mathematics would be a necessity for space travel and would be recognized by some member of a planetary population such as ours,

2

just now preparing for the exploration of the cosmos. Maurice Chatelain, with his unique experience in space communications and data processing, is ideally suited to recognize such messages and their importance. The engrossing book that he has written traces a pattern of attempted contact by space travelers on what must seem to them the unfriendly surface of a minor planet, whose inhabitants have constantly misunderstood their motives and considered them enemies to be feared. Therefore, instead of direct contact, a series of mathematical messages are being offered to the people of Earth. If these messages are recognized and answered, it may prove to be the first step to finding intelligent allies in what many of us have feared to be an empty universe -- perhaps with as much reason as Europeans considered, before Columbus, that travel westward would lead to a pouring precipice of the waters over the flat edge of the world.

Communications with UFOs may be more important than we presently realize, since there seems to be a continuing effort on their part to tell us something, if a key can be found to understanding them. Almost two centuries ago a key was discovered in Egypt, the Rosetta Stone which, through the efforts of Champollion, another Frenchman, unlocked much of the mystery of the distant past and opened the door to the surprising civilization of ancient Egypt. The key that will unlock the secret of extraterrestrial civilizations will undoubtedly open up information that will be even more surprising and considerably more important, since it will deal not with a segment of our past, but with the future of the world, and will concern us all.

Charles Berlitz

INTRODUCTION

Most American space flights, from Mercury and Gemini to Apollo, were followed by unknown spacecraft that could have come from another civilization in outer space and have already established bases on the Moon.

The recent decoding of strange radio signals received from outer space seems to indicate that astronauts from Epsilon Bootis could have been in orbit around the Earth, at the same distance as the Moon, for the last 12,600 years.

A clay tablet covered with cuneiform script and discovered in the ruins of Nineveh shows a huge number, 195,955,200 millions, which represents expressed in seconds, an enormous period of time of 2268 million days or 6.3 million years.

This period of time, which seems to have been computed 64,800 years ago, is an exact multiple of any astronomical cycle known so far and must, therefore, have been an astronomical constant of the universe.

Mayan astronomers, whose chronology appears to go back to 49,611 BC, had computed enormous periods of time of 93 and 403 million years corresponding to cosmic cycles that we have just recently discovered.

They had computed a long calendar of 5163 years based on the conjunctions of Jupiter and Saturn, and a shorter one of 104 years based on Mars and Venus. They knew that these conjunctions occurred exactly behind the Sun every 2,383 years, and that the same solar eclipse happened every 521 years on the same day of the year and the same point on the zodiac.

The Mayan calendar of 14,040 days or 39 years was based on the coincidence of Mercury years of 117 days, sacred years of 260 days, solar years of 360 days, Venus years of 585 days, Mars years of 780 days, and Mars-Uranus conjunction cycles of 702 days.

5

The Great Pyramid was built according to the two mathematical factors Pi of 22/7 and Phi of 89/55. Its volume and weight were exact fractions of those of the Earth, and all of its dimensions are related to astronomical cycles and conjunction periods. With the Sphinx and the other two pyramids, it clearly indicates the exact point where the treasure of the Pharaohs could be located.

The Egyptian calendar, which seems to be related to the Mayan one, was established in 49,2l4 BC. It was based on the coincidence of solar years of 365 days, with Sirius years of 365 1/4 days every 1460 years and with Venus years of 584 days every 2336 years.

A huge Maltese Cross made of thirteen ancient Greek temples and covering 540 kilometers across the Aegean Sea, has recently been discovered. It shows the perfect division of a circle into 28 equal sectors.

On the floor of the Chartres cathedral, a circle, a square, and a rectangle, each cover an area which is exactly one hundredth of that of the base of the Great Pyramid. Ten French cathedrals are located on the map in the same relative positions as ten stars of the Virgo constellation in the sky. On a map of France, a triangle made by three very ancient monuments represents the exact cross-section of the Great Pyramid, but fourteen million times larger.

An astronomical calculator, discovered at the bottom of the Aegean Sea and certainly several thousand years old, could compute eighteen different astronomical cycles derived from the ancient Egyptian lunisolar cycle of 76 years, by means of a differential and various bronze gear trains.

Our ancestors could cross the oceans and navigate around the world by using the circular winds and currents. They knew their latitude from the height of the polar star and their longitude from the interval between sunset and moonrise which is different for every point on any particular day.

Modern calculation of ancient eclipse and conjunction dates shows that everything that is written in the Bible is the true story of historical events that really happened in the past but have been slowly distorted by many successive writers, translators, and interpreters who

6

could not find the right words for events or objects which they had never seen before.

For example, there seems to be no doubt that the word ELOHIM, which is a plural in Hebrew, should have been translated as astronauts, that Adam and Eve also could have been astronauts, and that the Garden of Eden could have been an enormous spaceship in orbit around the Earth.

Is astrology an exact science or an enormous impostor? Sumerian astrologers invented 9700 years ago a zodiac with twelve signs, but the Mayas computed a more precise one with 13 signs which is now used by some modern astrologers.

The Earth poles and continents have shifted many times in the past. Our polar ice caps were once tropical jungles while our deserts were at the bottom of an ocean. This is why we never find ruins of ancient civilizations that are older than a few thousand years. The vestiges of the first human cultures must be now under the polar caps or at the bottom of the oceans.

There are many megalithic computers around the world, like Stonehenge and the Medicine Wheel of Wyoming. They all indicate a fantastic astronomical knowledge which could only have been obtained after tens of millenia of observations and recordings, or by the intervention of astronauts from another civilization from another world in outer space.

The Earth had three different moons in the past before the present one. The last moon was much larger and much closer than ours, which resulted in a huge tidal belt around the equator as well as frequent eclipses, lunar years of 264 days and solar years of 288 days.

The same numbers 264 and 288 were found in the dimensions of the Tower of Babel whose volume was l/6 of that of the Great Pyramid and six times that of the Ziggurat of Ur in Mesopotamia.

There is now little doubt that the mysterious continent of Atlantis was a part of the American continent, a huge plateau between Cuba, Florida, and the Bahamas, which has now been submerged for l2,000 years, and where the ruins of enormous constructions and a huge pyramid have recently been discovered.

On the other hand, the numbers of flights and landings of alien spacecraft have been increasing recently, as well as mysterious messages received from outer space; and it seems that the time is not far when we will finally meet our cosmic cousins, the descendants of our ancestors from outer space.

Maurice Chatelain

THE APOLLO SPACECRAFT

Thirty years ago I was living in San Diego, California. I had come there from Casablanca in 1955 with my wife and my three sons at the time when Morocco was becoming independent. After seven marvellous years in Casablanca, I had no wish to return to my native France.

One lived well in Morocco, and we had many friends there. Among them were a few intimates who worked hard in the daytime and lived it up at night. That was exactly the kind of life that appealed to me. I worked ten hours a day and had five businesses going simultaneously, including a venture in television that really interested me. We spent seven years in Casablanca, and all went well when suddenly, under pressure from the United States, France decided to pull out of Morocco and grant it independence.

In just a few weeks a well-organized and prosperous country was turned into unimaginable social and economic chaos. Even the most secure businesses went bankrupt because no one paid what was due, and it wasn't even possible to send children to school because they could have been killed in the streets. Disgusted and sorry about being a Frenchman, I thought it better to leave, and the sooner the better. But first we had to know where to go.

One of our best friends in Casablanca at that time was an American of Greek ancestry, who, as the president of the United States Chamber of Commerce in Morocco, had helped me a great deal in the past. He was to be even more helpful now, since he was also the American vice consul in Casablanca.

I went to see him and asked for advice. He said I should have my head examined if I ever dreamed of returning to France, already crowded with refugees from Indochina and North Africa. His advice was to go to the wide, open spaces of California. A mutual friend, now residing in Beverly Hills, would certainly be glad to sponsor me and my family and give the necessary guarantees to the United States immigration authorities.

I was tempted to follow his advice; I spoke English well enough. However my wife, who had for some strange reason studied German as a second language in school and had three small boys, was not so easily persuaded. I finally prevailed, and the very next morning all of us went to the American Consulate to sign the immigration papers and to receive warm recommendations given to our family by my Greek-American friend.

My decision to move to America proved to be right. For the next twenty years I worked for a number of aerospace organizations and industries and was supported by the United States Navy, the United States Air Force, and NASA. I was even reimbursed by the United States Government for the cost of moving my family to the United States, though it took a while to achieve that. If ever I regretted coming to the States, it was never for professional reasons; because working in California is so much more agreeable than it is in France, where I would never have succeeded as I have here.

After having lived in Beverly Hills for about a month and having found that it wasn't too difficult to find work in the electronics industries, I decided to look for a home in San Diego, where the rents were more reasonable and the landscape reminded me of the Cote d'Azur of southern France.

My first job was a three-year stint as an electronics engineer with Convair Astronautics. Convair was then building the delta-wing F-102 and F-106 fighter planes and the Atlas intercontinental ballistic missile for the military, which were successes, as well as a commercial passenger plane that was not, even after its name had been changed several times.

I started working in telecommunications, which I knew well, and was soon shifted to telemetry, which I knew little about, until finally all my work was with radar, which I didn't know at all. After three years I had become an expert in each of these fields and was making a name for myself.

I had published some technical articles and had given a lecture. But then Convair's business turned sour. Its commercial airplane still did not sell and the Air Force started cutting contracts. Luckily for me, a competitor of Convair, the Ryan Aeronautical Company, that had built Charles Lindbergh's airplane in 1927, decided to start an electronics division and began luring specialists away from Convair.

As a result, in 1959, I landed at Ryan Electronics as head of an electromagnetic research group in charge of developing new radar and telecommunications systems. It was there that I finally had a chance to use my imaginatioin and create new communication systems for which I received eleven patents. That was the great era of electronics, a time that will never come again.

Ryan was actually a small company and did not build airplanes or missiles. It specialized in building drones, small pilotless airplanes that were a big success. The Air Force used these drones for fighter pilot training and shot them down faster than we could build them. At a certain time we even started repairing the least damaged drones, quite contrary to certain principles of American business.

Ryan was also building the world's best radar navigation systems, which gave the most precise readings of aircraft position. One of these flight instruments enabled a military airplane to fly on automatic pilot from San Diego to Washington, DC, missing its target by less than two hundred yards.

Thus I turned out to be a specialist in electronic navigation. One of my patents - an automatic radar landing system that ignited retro rockets at a given altitude - was used in Ranger and Surveyor flights to the Moon, the latter spacecraft making soft landings without suffering damage.

But even Ryan didn't do well financially. The drones sold like hot cakes but the Air Force needed more than we could supply them; so Ryan lost one contract after another within only a few weeks, something that is typical of the American way of business. As a result Ryan was in financial difficulty. It became clear that I would have to look for another job. Since Convair, the only aerospace company in San Diego besides Ryan, by now faced even greater economic difficulties, I had to go up to Los Angeles to find a suitable position.

The job situation was much better there, but I did not want to move nearly a hundred miles north to Los Angeles for several reasons.

First of all, Los Angeles is not a city like San Diego. Los Angeles is a chain of industrial suburbs stretched in line over sixty miles and nobody likes to live there if he can help it. In addition, we had just bought a brand new home in San Diego, with a magnificent view of the bay, and we had no wish whatever to go and live in the notorious smog of LA.

So it was decided that my wife and my three sons, together with our huge Newfoundland retriever, Katanga, would stay in San Diego; and I would drive to Los Angeles on Monday and return on Friday, as many of my friends had been doing. It was far from my ideal way of life, but what else could I do?

It so happened that at that precise moment when Ryan and Convair were having their great difficulties in San Diego, North American Aviation was building a new, gigantic aerospace plant for 30,000 employees in Downey, a southern suburb of Los Angeles, in the hope that it would receive the Apollo development and construction contract from the United States Government, the space project whose goal was to land a man on the Moon.

To start building such vast production facilities before receiving a contract seems foolhardy but very American; because how could you hope to get the contract if you didn't have the factory first to show the customer? But North American had no doubts that it would get the bid. The company had cemented its relations well with Lyndon Johnson, at that time the Vice President of the United States and in charge of the space program.

At the very time when the new Downey plant was completed, it was announced that North American had submitted the best technical proposal for both development and production of the Apollo spacecraft and therefore had been awarded the contract. It was worth billions of taxpayers' dollars, but nobody complained about it at the time. The only question was who would be first to land on the Moon - the Russians or the Americans?

All that was left to be done was to build the Apollo. First it had to be decided how to do it; and no one as yet had a clear idea of what, in reality, this project required. Engineers, thousands of the best engineers available, were needed. To make these engineers want to come and work in a dairy suburb of Los Angeles populated by over a million cows, the pay had to be good. But that was no problem; the money was there.

I was among the very first men who presented themselves to North American; and since I was already known in the industry as a radar and telecommunications specialist, I was immediately offered the task of designing and building the Apollo communication and data-processing system. Nobody specified my duties or functions, because no one at that time knew what these systems would be like. But that, again, was of no importance in view of the rush to land on the Moon!

I took my leave of Ryan, and within two weeks I was working at North American on the Apollo project at nearly double my Ryan salary and began to endure the endless commuting of over a hundred miles between San Diego and Downey. Fortunately, there was a magnificent four-lane superhighway almost door to door and it took me only an hour and a half to cover the distance for less that five dollars' worth of gasoline per round trip.

At that time I had the best car I ever owned - a pale green Chevrolet convertible with a powerful motor and a white top. For me, who always like to drive, even from Paris to Casablanca, this drive to work along the seashore was a sheer delight. In the fresh air of the early morning, I had lots of time to think about many things that had nothing to do with the space program.

For the first few months I left San Diego every Monday morning and returned Friday night at suppertime. In Downey I stayed in the Tahitian Village motel, which had been built at the same time as the new plant. The motel was charming, with waterfalls and tropical vegetation; but I did not have much time to appreciate all this. I worked twelve hours a day with little time to eat and sleep. Later, when my work became organized and I put in only eight hours a day like the rest of my colleagues, I would go home to San Diego everyday.

When the Apollo project started, there was no communication equipment powerful enough or sensitive enough to make voice transmission possible from Earth to the Moon, not to mention transmission of television pictures over that distance. Such things had to be invented, perfected, and built. Relay stations had to be installed all

13

around the globe in the Tropics with parabolic dish antennas, some over 200 feet in diameter, in such a way that one or two of them would always be in contact with any Apollo spacecraft orbiting around the Moon. All these stations had to be in contact with each other and all of them had to report to the Apollo Space Flight Center in Houston, Texas. All the new equipment, built by some twenty different suppliers from all parts of the United States, had to be coordinated and made compatible.

How I was put in charge of all of this within a few months after I had started my new job at North American, I will never understand; but that is of no importance now. The only thing that really counts is that everything went well. Everything functioned much better than we thought it would at the beginning, or even better than we ever expected. I think that it must have happened because of some divine influence, not by human intelligence alone. Since that time I firmly believe in benevolent intervention of the gods into human affairs.

In April 1963 some technical publications announced the convocation of an international astronautical congress in September in Paris, and specialists were invited to submit papers for presentation at the conference. I did not want to pass up such an opportunity; in addition, I badly needed a vacation. Without telling anyone, I sent to Paris the text of a lecture about the communications system of the Apollo spacecraft, by that time very well known to me. In a few weeks, to my surprise, there was a letter from Paris comfirming that my lecture had been accepted. They promised to let me know soon the exact day and hour when I was to deliver my presentation at the congress.

That was the exact moment when my troubles began. First, I was not supposed to submit any lecture about Apollo on my own. I should have asked for an authorization to do so from NASA. Secondly, I could not be given a vacation, because I was needed all the time at the Apollo project, not even if this vacation could be squeezed in during the congress in Paris. Thirdly, and most seriously, North American unbeknown to me had already assigned a few other men, with less to do and more backing than I had, to go to Paris and talk about Apollo.

But then again, the gods smiled upon me. A miracle happened that I can only describe as benevolent divine intervention. Suddenly somebody found out that during the projected Apollo Moon flights,

14

sunspot activity would be at its peak. Sunspots can severely impede and even completely disrupt radio space communication. It should be pointed out here that, considering the number of people involved in Apollo, this discovery certainly could have been made somewhat earlier.

Naturally, once it was discovered, a new countdown schedule - a new sort of horoscope - had to be established without delay, in order to take into account solar radiation from sunspot activity. This activity had to be calculated years in advance of the projected flights to the Moon. The missions had to be rescheduled for the most opportune periods of minimal sunspot interference.

No doubt it was sheer coincidence that at the time the most qualified observatory for sunspot predictions was at Meudon, France, near Paris, where the astronautical congress was to convene. It would have been useless to discuss sunspot activity with French astronomers who spoke little English. Somebody was needed who could speak French, had at least some knowledge of astronomy, and knew everything there was to know about space communications.

Believe it or not, of all the people at North American Aviation there was only one person with all of these qualifications; and so it was decided that I would spend four weeks in France after all - two in Paris with expenses paid by NASA and two on the Cote d'Azur at my own expense. Remembering the many long faces at North American, I think that was the day I lost quite a few friends.

That is how, on one beautiful afternoon in August 1963, I arrived in an Air France Boeing 707 at Orly airport and an hour later was in a Renault convertible, dashing down the Autoroute du Sud on my way to St Tropez, without taking one look back at Paris. There would be time enough for Paris later on. First I had to get to St. Tropez. Why St Tropez? For several reasons, although not all of them shall be discussed here. St Tropez is the home of my friend Robert, who owns one of the most famous restaurants on the Moorea beach in nearby Pampelone, and is my best friend in France.

Although I was born in Paris, every time I go to France I feel more at home in St Tropez, and that is where I spend most of my vacation time. The Paris that I knew as a young man does not exist any more; and so far I have not had enough time to acquaint myself with the new Paris, so I go to St Tropez, where I know everything and everybody.

I was back in Paris only two days before the congress of astronautics began when I received a telephone call from someone I had never heard of and whose name I will not mention here. He informed me that he was greatly interested in space communications and extraterrestrial life and that he would be glad to meet me for dinner to discuss these topics.

Since I had nothing else to do that day and since this man intrigued me, I accepted the invitation. It was a fascinating evening. After I had told him just about everything that I knew about Apollo, I learned from him a lot of things of which I had no knowledge whatsoever - like ancient civilizations that probably had been brought here by astronauts from space many, many thousands of years ago.

My presentation at the congress went very well. I lectured on space communications in general and about the Apollo systems in particular and was swamped with questions not only about the spacecraft communications, which I expected, but also about the possibility of contacting extraterrestrial civilizations and the consequences that these contacts would produce. For that I was not quite prepared.

The congress should have been primarily interested in questions concerning the Apollo spacecraft and the exporation of the moon; but the most lively discussions developed about the possibilities offered by the huge antennas of radio telescopes to explore the universe. The Russians were all well versed in these matters because their government supported such exploration; but some American scientists, who knew how badly such scientific endeavours were received in Washington, tried to strike a pose of indifference.

Reminding myself that I was an American, too, I tried to avoid these taboo topics; but I couldn't suppress entirely my curiosity, and kept discussing galactic theories with some Russians privately. A great deal of new information and stimulation to explore intelligence in space came from my Russian colleagues. I cannot give their names here, but without their help I possibly would never have written this book.

As for the Apollo spacecraft itself, I should mention here that, as everybody knows by now, it consisted of three main parts. First there was the command module, a truncated cone about 8 feet high, 13 feet wide at the base, and over 3 feet wide at the top, where the landing parachutes and the radio antenna to be used after the splashdown were snugly stowed away. A tunnel provided passage to the lunar exploration capsule. The service module, to the rear of the command module, was nearly 17 feet long and also 13 feet wide and contained all the life-support systems.

Another truncated cone contained the lunar exploration module and its moon vehicle, the lunar jeep, ready for man's first ride on the Moon. The jeep was abandoned on the Moon, the lunar module left in orbit around the Moon, and the service module discarded in orbit around the Earth. Only the command module, with the heat shield at its base, could withstand the tremendous temperatures caused by friction during descent through the atmosphere; and the three astronauts and everything that they had taken with them from the Moon returned to the Earth in it.

Magazines all over the world have described the Apollo spacecraft and all that it contained, but there are still a few interesting things that have not been mentioned. The fuel cells were the source of both electric current and water supply for the Apollo. These ingenious cells, developed for the Moon mission, combined liquid hydrogen and oxygen to produce both electric current and water in one operation. It was a simple idea, but somebody had to think of it.

The navigation system was not complicated either. A platform stabilized by three gyroscopes was supporting a sextant and a telescope and was connected to an electronic computer in permanent contact with Earth. It was enough to turn either the telescope or the sextant and take aim of certain points of the Moon's surface or some star - Canopus, for example - and the computer would transmit the exact angles of the sightings with the three axes of the stabilized platform to Earth with all the necessary information.

The distance from Earth or Moon was measured simply by taking the angular reading of the Moon's disc or the two sides of the Earth. To take these readings, the capsule had to be moved on all three principal axes, and this was achieved by firing small rockets placed all around the service module. To avoid overheating, Apollo had to be rotated constantly so that one side would not be exposed all the time to the Sun.

What were the means of communication between Apollo and the Earth? At close distances, the exact position of Apollo was measured by tracking radar from Earth in the C band between 5,715 and 5,815 MHz (megahertz, a unit of frequency). The radar signal was received and amplified by a transponder and retransmitted by Apollo back to Earth. The coded messages from Houston to Apollo were transmitted in ultrahigh frequencies (UHF) on the 450-MHz band, on one direction only. Voice and telemetry were carried on very high frequencies (VHF) on the 259- and 296-MHz bands.

When Apollo arrived within proximity of the Moon, the communications systems previously used could not reach that far; so all communications went through one single, very powerful, transmitter with a directional antenna in the S band, between 2,106 and 2,287 MHz, with a great number of channels, each transmitting several signals at the same time through multiplexing. For instance, there were seven channels to feed medical information about the physical condition of the astronauts, nine to retransmit the stored telemetry data from the passage behind the Moon that could not be beamed directly. The communication systems were improved from one Apollo mission to the next, especially the television system.

Today the Apollo program has long been terminated and nearly forgotten. So perhaps it would be useful to recall these eleven sensational missions in the order that they were launched. Altogether there were twenty Apollo modules built, of which twelve were supposed to be launched. The rest were to be tested for endurance, heat resistance, buoyancy, and many other qualities.

The first of the dozen modules intended for launch, named Apollo 6, burned up in a flash during a practice countdown on the ground on 27 January, 1967, killing all three astronauts on board - Virgil I. Grissom, Edward H. White II, and Roger B. Chaffee. The whole Apollo program was interrupted until the command module could be redesigned and rebuilt so that an electrical fire in the oxygen-laden atmosphere inside the module could not occur again.

Apollo 7 with Walter M. Schirra, Jr., Donn F. Eisele, and R. Walter Cunningham stayed in orbit around the Earth for eleven days, 11-22

18

October, 1968, for a breakdown test. All worked well. Apollo was ready to fly to the Moon.

Apollo 8, with three astronauts, Frank Borman, James A. Lovell, Jr, and William A. Anders aboard made man's first Moon orbit, at an altitude of about sixty miles above its surface, the first time the hidden face of the Moon had ever been seen by man himself. This first Moon mission lasted 21-27 December, 1968.

Apollo 9, carrying the lunar module for the first time, with James A. McDivitt, David R. Scott, and Russell L. Schweickart aboard, hung ten days long in orbit around the Earth 3-13 March, 1969, to test the separation and rendezvous of the command module and the lunar module. Schweickart went outside the command module and took a spacewalk, attached to the ship by an umbilical cord.

The Apollo 10 mission took place 18-26 May, 1969, with Thomas P. Stafford, John W. Young, and Eugene A. Cernan aboard. Young stayed in the command module in orbit around the Moon, while Stafford and Cernan descended in the lunar module to less than ten miles above the surface and then rejoined the command module in orbit.

Apollo 11, with Neil A. Armstrong, Michael Collins, and Edwin E. Aldrin, Jr. aboard, was the first Apollo flight to reach the goal. While Collins flew in orbit around the Moon in the command module, Armstrong and Aldrin descended in the lunar module, landing in the Sea of Tranquility at 4:17 pm, 20 July, 1969, after a flight of 102 hours 45 minutes from the Earth. After 6 1/2 hours of rest, Neil Armstrong opened the door of the module and climbed down, the first man ever to walk on the moon. The time was 10:55 pm EDT. Aldrin followed him after a few minutes. The Americans were first on the Moon! All returned to Earth safely on 24 July.

Apollo 12 carried Charles Conrad, Jr., Richard F. Gordon, and Alan L. Bean through thunderclouds right at the start, experiencing an electrical discharge of short duration that did not hamper the flight. The mission, lasting ten days, 14-24 November, 1969, took Conrad and Bean to the Sea of Storms, right next to Surveyor 3, which had landed there two and a half years before. Some of the more important parts from Surveyor 3 were brought back in remarkably good condition.

Apollo l3, with James A. Lovell, Jr., Fred W. Haise, Jr., and John L. Swigert, Jr., aboard, ran into trouble, seemingly confirming the superstition tied to this number. The mission which took place ll-l7 April, l970, was already halfway to the Moon when one of the oxygen tanks exploded, knocking out some instruments. The question was no longer how to land on the Moon but how to get back to Earth as soon as possible. It was decided that the best solution was to continue the flight to the Moon, make a loop around it, and come straight for a splashdown, all the time saving as much oxygen as possible. Everything went as planned, and Apollo l3 returned safely without further complications. The cause of the explosion was never determined, although several official explanations were given.

Apollo l4, with Alan B. Shepard Jr., Stuart A. Roosa, and Edgar D. Mitchell aboard, went to the Moon from 3l January to 9 February, l97l, landing in the hills of Fra Mauro, and using a cart to transport the scientific instruments.

Apollo l5 took David R. Scott, Alfred M. Worden, and James B. Irwin, 26 July - 7 August, l97l to the Apennine Mountains of the Moon. It carried a 'lunar rover', an electric vehicle that made it possible for Scott and Irwin to take several trips on the Moon's surface, covering nearly twenty miles. This Moon 'jeep' also made it possible for people on Earth to see the takeoff blast of the lunar module on live television, since the rover and its television camera and transmitter were left behind on the Moon.

Apollo l6, with Charles M. Duke, Thomas K. Mattingly, and John W. Young aboard, landed in the Descartes Highlands. The mission, l6-27 April, l972, brought back the most extraordinary photographs in ultraviolet light of the Earth's atmosphere, interplanetary gases, and many stars, constellations, and galaxies.

Apollo l7, with Eugene A. Cernan, Ronald E. Evans and Harrison H. Schmitt aboard, flew to the Moon on 7 December and returned on l9 December, l972. The landing spot was in the Taurus-Littrow Valley. This Apollo mission was the longest both in time and in distance covered and also brought back the biggest load of Moon rocks. In addition, Schmitt, a geologist, was the first civilian to visit the Moon, all the other astronauts having been military men. With Apollo l7 the program, which had started in the l960's with so much enthusiasm, ended amid growing indifference and even some hostility from many

Americans who were shocked to find out how high the cost of the landing on the Moon really was. Some even complained that the live television coverage of the Moon missions had pre-empted their cherished football games.

During these missions several strange things happened. Some still cannot be talked about; and some I will mention without revealing my sources of information and with the utmost reserve, because I personally was not there when the incidents allegedly took place. It could be, for example, that both the American and the Russian space programs did bring back discoveries that were not anticipated.

The American space program was an extraordinary success, but it should not be assumed that everything went smoothly all of the time. There were many technical difficulties to be dealt with in flight, but with the means aboard, the crews could solve them all in short time. Some breakdowns required consultation with and advice from the controllers and technicians in Mission Control at the Flight Center in Houston.

Difficulties started as early as the first flights of the Gemini program, the second phase in the American push to reach the Moon. (The first was the single-man Mercury program.) Gemini 3 blasted off 23 March, 1965, with astronauts Virgil Grissom and John Young aboard. It made three orbits around the Earth and was supposed to re-enter the atmosphere at a very precise angle in order to achieve the greatest possible slowdown before landing. But the spacecraft's guidance computer did not work properly and it landed nearly sixty miles short of the target area where a US Navy carrier was waiting to pick it up.

Gemini 4 was launched on 3 June, 1965, with James A. McDivitt and Edward White aboard, and achieved an elliptical orbit between 100 and 170 miles above Earth. With McDivitt photographing him, White went for a 'space walk', but when he returned to the craft, the door of the capsule would not close. It took some time to fix that. In all, Gemini 4 made sixty-two Earth orbits, returning 7 June. As on the previous flight, its landing computer malfunctioned and the splash-down was again sixty miles short of the pick-up carrier.

When, on 21 August, 1965, Gemini 5 put L. Gordon Cooper, Jr., and Charles Conrad into orbit between 100 and 160 miles up, the heater

21

for the oxygen malfunctioned and then the stabilizing rockets became erratic and other trouble cropped up. Mission Control gave the order to descend, which the craft did on 29 August, after a record eight-day flight.

Gemini 6, with Walter Schirra and Thomas P. Stafford aboard, wouldn't lift off the launching pad and the rocket motors had to be stopped - always a very dangerous process. Gemini 7 was supposed to make a rendezvous with Gemini 6 in space, but Mission Control decided to launch Gemini 7 first.

Gemini 7 was launched on 4 December, 1965, with Frank Borman and James Lovell aboard, and was placed in a circular parking orbit of less than 200 miles altitude, where it waited until 9 December, when Gemini 6 finally was able to lift off. Gemini 7's flight set a new endurance record of fourteen days and the planned rendezvous of the two spaceships took place without further complications.

Gemini 8 was launched on 16 March, 1966, with Neil Armstrong and David R. Scott aboard, and after only five revolutions around the globe succeeded in catching up and docking with an unmanned 3-ton Agena rocket that was already in orbit. But exactly 28 minutes after the successful docking there was real trouble. For no apparent reason, the two linked spacecraft began to spin. The astronauts in Gemini 8 decided to free themselves from the Agena, but the Gemini capsule continued to rotate faster and faster.

The astronauts themselves found the source of the trouble. One of the stabilizing rockets had failed to turn off and was causing the spin. All fifteen remaining stabilizers had to be reignited in turn to counteract the momentum caused by the spinning and to bring Gemini back to normal attitude. When this was finally achieved, only a quarter of the rocket fuel remained. Instead of the planned three-day flight in orbit, the mission had lasted only seven hours when Mission Control ordered Gemini 8 to return to Earth immediately.

Gemini 9, with Thomas Stafford and Eugene Cernan aboard, also had to carry out docking with another Agena rocket in orbit 180 miles up; but the Agena wouldn't start as planned on 17 May, 1966. Another Agena rocket was lauched on 1 June, but some trouble on the launching pad delayed the start of Gemini 9 for two days. Finally, on 3 June, Stafford and Cernan lifted off and caught the Agena after only three orbits. However, they could not dock properly because the locking system wasn't fully opened.

On the second day of the Gemini 9 mission Cernan stepped out into space but had to come back in a hurry. He was using up his energy four times faster than had been expected and had difficulties with orientation. Finally he could not see anything, because his helmet fogged up completely. The planned experiment with an individual rocket propulsion system for the astronauts floating in space had to be abandoned, and the whole mission lasted only three days.

Gemini 10 was launched on 18 July, 1966, with John Young and Michael Colliins aboard, 101 minutes after an Agena rocket had blasted off in a wrong orbit, again because of a computer error. The astronauts had to use up sixty per cent of their fuel before they caught up with the Agena and docked. The two linked ships then used the big Agena rocket motor to reach an orbit 480 miles up and find the other Agena (of Gemini 8) that was orbiting the globe. The first triple rendezvous in space was accomplished.

Gemini 11 took off on 12 September, 1966, with Richard Gordon and Charles Conrad aboard, 1 hour 37 minutes after lift-off of an Agena rocket. It took them only 94 minutes to catch it and dock, an important achievement in fuel economy. The next day Gordon took a walk in space detaching a cable from the Agena and fastening it to Gemini. This operation was scheduled to last for 107 minutes, but Gordon (like Cernan before) had trouble with his respiration, tired fast, and ran out of breath in 38 minutes. He had to return to the Gemini capsule, whereupon both astronauts started up the big Agena motor and lifted themselves to a new altitude record of 850 miles above Earth. In this new orbit Gordon made another space walk without difficulties.

Gemini 12, the last of the series, had its lift-off on 11 November, 1966 with James Lovell and Edwin Aldrin aboard. It made the link-up with its Agena on the third orbit. Three space walks were planned, but Mission Control discovered some instability in the linked-up pair and refused permission to use the big Agena motor. Instead the astronauts had to climb to a higher orbit using only the small auxiliary motors. That was accomplished and Aldrin had his three walks without incident.

As we see now, not one of the ten Gemini flights was free of troubles or obstacles, but all missions were accomplished approximately on time and without any loss of life. That was possible mainly because of the composure and the extraordinary technical competence of the astronauts. The European astronautical engineers should learn a lesson from these experiences of the American space program. They are not, as they think, the only ones with troubles. Three of the most capable American astronauts died when the real drama started, in the fire on the ground in the Apollo 6 capsule during the very last test before the flight.

But the astronauts were not limited to equipment troubles. They saw things during their missions that could not be discussed with anyone outside of NASA. It is very difficult to obtain any specific information from NASA, which still exercises a very strict control over any disclosure of these events.

It seems that all Apollo and Gemini flights were followed, both at a distance and sometimes also quite closely, by space vehicles of extraterrestrial origin - flying saucers, or UFO's (unidentified flying objects), if you want to call them by that name. Every time it occurred, the astronauts informed Mission Control, who then ordered absolute silence.

I think that Walter Schirra aboard Mercury 8 was the first of the astronauts to use the code name 'Santa Claus' to indicate the presence of flying saucers next to space capsules. However, his announcements were barely noticed by the general public. It was a little different when James Lovell on board the Apollo 8 command module came out from behind the moon and said for everybody to hear: 'We have been informed that Santa Claus does exist!' Even though this happened on Christmas Day 1968, many people sensed a hidden meaning in those words that were not difficult to decipher.

James McDivitt was apparently the first to photograph an unidentified flying object, on 4 June, 1965, when he was over Hawaii aboard Gemini 4. Frank Borman and James Lovell took magnificent photographs of two UFOs following Gemini 7 on 4 December, 1965, at a distance of a few hundred yards. The UFOs looked like gigantic mushrooms with their propulsion systems clearly showing a glow on the underside.

24

The following year, on 12 November, 1966, James Lovell and Edwin Aldrin in Gemini 12 also saw two UFOs at slightly over half a mile from the capsule. These were observed for quite some time and photographed repeatedly. The same happened to Frank Borman and James Lovell in Apollo 8 on Christmas Eve 1968, and to Thomas Stafford and John Young aboard Apollo 10 on 22 May, 1969. The UFOs showed up both during the orbit around the Moon and on the homeward flight of Apollo 10.

Finally, when Apollo 11 made the first Moon landing on the Sea of Tranquility and, only moments before Armstrong stepped down the ladder to set foot on the Moon, two UFOs hovered overhead. Edwin Aldrin took several pictures of them. Some of these photographs have been published in the June 1975 issue of *Modern People* magazine. The magazine did not tell where it got them, vaguely hinting at some Japanese source.

There was even some talk that the Apollo 13 mission carried a nuclear device aboard that could be set off to make measurements of the infrastructure of the Moon and whose detonations would show on the charts of several recording seismographs placed in different locations. The unexplained explosion of an oxygen tank in the service module of Apollo 13 on its flight to the Moon, according to rumors, was caused deliberately by a UFO that was following the capsule to prevent the detonation of the atomic charge that could possibly have destroyed or endangered some Moon base established by extraterrestrials. Well, there was a lot of talk and there still is.

It was also said that during their flights, our astronauts frequently felt as if some external forces were trying to take over their minds. They experienced strange sensations and visions. What seems almost certain is that some of the astronauts did have psychological problems and changes of personality after their missions in space. Some turned deeply religious, some seemed to develop mental trouble - facts that, of course, could be ascribed to pure coincidence without particular significance.

The experiments in telepathy carried out in space by some astronauts have been discussed and even published. Special symbol cards of geometric figures were used to transmit thought from the participant in orbit around the Moon to the correspondent on the surface of the Earth. Most of these experiments were successful, much more so than similar telepathic experiments conducted on Earth, which generally had a lower score.

Then there is the case of astronaut Gordon Cooper that arouses curiosity for more than one reason. He was the pilot of Mercury 9 in l963 and of Gemini 5 in l965. He was unquestionably one of our most skilled space pilots, yet he never flew an Apollo. Gordon Cooper, now manufacturing skydiving parachutes after having quit the space program, has never told anyone outside of NASA what he saw in space. But there are those who think NASA may have removed him from the Apollo flights because he had seen too much.

It is also curious that this man, who is not only an astronaut but also a scientist, has now become a firm believer in extraterrestrial life and civilizations and is convinced that space visitors to Earth have been around for a long time, from the most distant past up to this very day. Not long ago Gordon Cooper participated in an archaeological expedition to South America that discovered the remnants of a very old and very advanced civilization dating back more than five thousand years. Pottery, sculptures, and hieroglyphs very similar to Egyptian artifacts of the same period were discovered, confirming once more the theory the Egyptian and American cultures had a common origin.

It is quite natural for a famous astronaut to be interested in ancient astronauts, but one may still wonder whether Cooper did not acquire his sudden interest in extraterrestrial civilizations by seeing for himself in space, things that he did not have the right to tell us.

THE CONSTANT OF NINEVEH

For thousands of years, astrologers and mathematicians have been greatly impressed by the majestic regularity of the stars moving in the skies. For millennia they tried hard to discover the secrets of this marvellous clock. These skywatchers realized that a very long period of time, one probably encompassing millions of years, had to exist that would represent in even numbers, the revolutions of all the celestial objects. At the end of such a constant period, all the bodies of the firmament would again find themselves in their original positions on the band of the zodiac.

These astrologers and mathematicians called this time span the 'great constant' or the 'great year', but did not know that indeed this number existed and had been calculated tens of thousands of years before their time to be used by early civilizations, but then lost and forgotten as cataclysmic natural disasters and wars destroyed one civilization after another. The astrologers tried in vain to find the great constant and finally gave up. But now, by a chain of strange coincidences, this magic number has been found on an old clay tablet from Nineveh.

Around the middle of the nineteenth century there was a French consul, Paul Emile Botta, in Mosul, in what is now Iraq, who had very little to do. To kill time Botta took long horseback rides into the desert and the hills surrounding the city. He noticed that some of the mounds had so perfectly rounded forms that they could not have been made by nature. Also, old pottery shards were found on many of these hills, indicating that these sites were ancient human habitations.

One day in 1840 Botta gave into his urge to dig up one of the round mounds to see what was inside. He started excavating the Kuyunjik hill on the Tigris River, just outside of Mosul. Besides the usual broken pottery he found a great number of clay tablets in different sizes, but mostly measuring uniformly 17 by 22 centimetres or, as

27

was discovered later, 12 by 16 Sumerian fingers of 14 millimetres each. These tablets were covered with cuneiform characters, produced with an angled stylus. At the time there was much talk about and interest in this form of writing, but no one had deciphered it yet.

Cuneiform inscriptions had been discovered for the first time during the fifteenth century in the ruins of Persepolis, in Persia, the ancient capital of King Darius I. In 1472 the ambassador of Venice at the Persian court, Giosophat Barbaro, described these tablets, as did in 1602 Antonio de Gouveia, the ambassador of Portugal at the same court and the explorer Pietro della Valle, who brought the first samples of cuneiform tablets back to Europe.

Luckily no one at that time could understand these writings; because if the Pope had read their message and discovered that it was the Earth that turned around the sun, or that the biblical version of the Flood was nothing but a pale reflection of the saga of Gilgamesh, or that a great part of Genesis was inspired by Sumerian legends, it is not difficult to imagine what would have happened to the old clay tablets and to the people who found or read them.

Consul Botta tired fast from his efforts to collect broken pottery and clay tablets and started to lose interest, when he met in Mosul in 1842, a young Englishman by the name of Henry Layard. They became good friends, smoking opium and hashish together; but fortunately Layard had to give up drug smoking because it made him very sick.

Botta told him about his excavations and Layard became very interested. Together they climbed the Kuyunjik hill and Layard was convinced right away that this was a very interesting archaeological site worthy of serious exploration. But Layard had to go to Istanbul on a diplomatic mission, and neither he nor Botta had the means for serious digging. Nothing came of this first project, but that did not discourage Botta.

In 1843 he received a grant and started to dig up the Khorsabad hill next to Kuyunjik. He found the first Assyrian palace ever discovered, that of King Sargon II, who built this edifice as his summer residence in the vicinity of Nineveh in 709 BC, after he conquered Babylon. This palace yielded a very rich reward of artifacts, bas-reliefs in huge quantities, statues of winged lions and winged bulls, and more. Most of it landed in the Louvre Museum in Paris, with the exception of a boatload of treasures that sank in the middle of the Tigris when the current tore a large barge from its moorings.

No matter how many fabulous finds were later made by his successors, Botta will be remembered forever as the discoverer of the Assyrian civilization. He also enabled Layard to find Nineveh and the palace of King Assurbanipal, with its tens of thousands of clay tablets. When Botta left Mosul in l846 he asked the new French consul, an architect by the name of Victor Place, to continue digging for treasures along the Tigris and to send all the loot to the Louvre.

When Layard returned to Mosul, he started to lay bare the mound of Nimrud (ancient Calah) where he found a considerable quantity of bas-reliefs and statues, which he shipped to the British Museum in London. But Layard's success at Nimrud hill did not make him forget his primary interest - the site of Kuyunjik, where he hoped to find Nineveh, the ancient capital of Assyria. So he went digging there again. First he sank an l8-foot-deep shaft straight down until he hit a solid layer of brick. From there Layard ordered tunnels dug in several directions. He found a grand hall with a massive portal flanked by two winged bulls. After a month of terracing at Kuyunjik, Layard discovered nine great chambers of the palace of Sennacherib, who reigned from 704 to 68l and who was one of the most cruel and powerful kings the Assyrians ever had.

Each day brought new finds, statues, bas-reliefs, whole walls covered with magnificent glazed brick, mosaics of cuneiform signs in dazzling white on turquoise blue. It was there that Layard's crew found the famous alabaster bas-relief of the wounded lioness which is now in the British museum. But even all these priceless artifacts from the palace of Sennacherib would not have given Layard his proper place in history. What made him really famous was a discovery made later at the same site with the help of his assistant Hormuzd Rassam.

The French and the English were not at that time on very good terms, especially in the Arab lands. To avoid friction, Botta and Layard drew a vague line of demarcation across the Kuyunjik excavation site and each worked on his side. But one day, when his French colleague was not around, Rassam, assisting Layard, decided to start a tunnel from his side straight into French territory. By the greatest of coincidences he hit the library of Assurbanipal, the Assyrian king who had reigned from 669 to 626 BC. The library contained over thirty thousand cuneiform clay tablets and was a collection of all the science and history known at that time, assembled from several previous civilizations.

In 1846 an Englishman, Henry Rawlinson, had broken the cuneiform alphabet by using a text that was engraved in three different languages on a slab of stone at Behistun, in Persia, at the time of Darius I, 2,500 years earlier. In Mosul nobody could read the newly discovered clay pages, so the tablets were all sent to the British Museum, where for twenty years they rested in the basement storage rooms.

Rassam had found the tablets in Kuyunjik in 1850. Twenty-two years later, in 1872, a young English Assyriologist, George Smith, began to translate them. Again by chance and sheer luck, he soon found the fantastic tale of the Sumerian hero Gilgamesh, his friend, Enkidu, and Utnapishtim, the friend of the gods, who had been warned about the coming deluge, built an ark, escaped the Flood, and landed on the mountain Nizir. Smith had the impression that he had read this story before, someplace in the Bible, but with other names.

What disturbed him even more was the fact that the cuneiform tablets he was translating were written in 700 BC and told stories about events that took place three thousand years before the actual imprinting of the clay tablets. The saga of Gilgamesh and his friends was older than the Bible; so the Hebrews who wrote the Holy Book had taken their inspiration from the Sumerian legend and invented the story of Noah and his Ark, embellishing it with a few minor details.

Unfortunately there was a chapter missing from the story of Gilgamesh. One clay tablet was not to be found in the storerooms of the British Museum. Most likely, it had been pulverized to dust long ago, but Smith had a great urge to go to Nineveh and was trying to persuade everyone that the missing cuneiform page still had to be in the ruins of Kuyunjik. All that had to be done was to find it.

Smith convinced some important people who were curious to read the final chapter of the Gilgamesh saga, and the necessary funds were collected. Smith arrived in Mosul in 1873. It took him only a few days digging at Kuyunjik to find the missing tablet. The benevolent intervention of the gods was demonstrated once more.

Smith continued to search and found about 3,000 more clay tablets at a lower level of the burned-down palace. All were marvellously well preserved; and Smith understood that the heavy wooden floors of the palace, when the conflagration took place, had fired the soft clay as if it was a kiln, thus keeping it from disintegrating over thousands of years.

His mission splendidly accomplished, Smith returned to London, translated and published the missing chapter of his continuing story of the hero Gilgamesh, and discovered several other interesting stories in the new tablets that he brought home.

One inscription of one hundred and fifty-two lines told about the six-year war conducted by Sennacherib, how he defeated Hezekiah, the King of Judah, how he defeated forty-six of his cities and gave the ruins to his allies, the kings of Gaza, Hebron, and Ascalon. It also told how King Hezekiah saved his life by paying a ransom of three hundred talents of silver and thirty talents of gold, the equivalent in our present-day weight system of 18,000 pounds of silver and 1,800 pounds of gold. This document is the only one that directly authenticates the same events told by the Bible.

Smith also discovered that King Assurbanipal, known in history only as one of the most cruel tyrants, was in reality a sort of a genius of his time, who had learned and assimilated all the known sciences of that period, mainly astronomy and mathematics.

Assurbanipal did not act as later Christian conquerors did. He did not destroy a single document that fell into his victorious hands. All materials were carefully preserved and brought to Nineveh, where the king's scribes translated and classified them to be deposited in the library. We can say now that Assurbanipal created the first 'Encyclopedia Assyriana' and indeed his statue should be standing in halls of higher learning, replacing those of the ignorants who, not so long ago, believed that the Sun revolves around the Earth.

Among the tablets translated by Smith was a certain quantity that contained nothing but numbers, fantastically huge numbers, apparently derived from very complicated calculations. But in 1875 archaeologists did not care for numbers any more than they do today, and so these tablets with the mathematical signs were put aside and forgotten.

I have not been able to find out to this day when and where somebody decided to study these mathematical tablets again; but the translation into our decimal system was finally published a few years ago, and one number stood out. It consisted of fifteen digits: 195,955,200,000,000. That represents nearly 200 million million, more than the distance from the Earth to the Sun, if somebody were eccentric enough to measure this astronomical distance in millimetres! Many specialists in different countries tried to find out what this fantastic number could have meant three thousand years ago to the Assyrians, who were not known to be great mathematicians or astronomers. It seemed that Assurbanipal must have found this number somewhere, probably in Egypt, or Chaldea, or even in Persia.

I personally discovered the existence of the number in 1955, when I had just arrived in California. I found it in a recently published book and did not at that moment pay any particular attention. Then in 1963 in Paris, when I was told about the calendar of the Mayas, who also calculated with enormously high numbers, I remembered this number from Nineveh and began suspecting that it somehow could prove there was a tie between the Assyrian and the Mayan civilizations. At that time I made some calculations which showed that the Nineveh number could also be expressed as 70 multiplied seven times by 60.

Then one day I remembered that the Sumerians, who were the ancestors of the Babylonians, who in turn were invaded by the Assyrians, used calculations based on multiples of sixty more than three thousand years ago. We still do not know for sure who the Sumerians were and where they came from; but we have found out that they were truly great astronomers who knew the revolution periods of all the planets of the solar system, including Uranus and Neptune.

They were the ones who divided the day into 86,400 seconds with 24 hours of 60 minutes of 60 seconds each. Immediately the realization came to me that the number of Nineveh represented a very, very long period of time expressed in seconds! It did not take long to cal-

Ancient astronomical cycles derived from the Nineveh constant of 2268 million days

name of the cycle	number of cycles	solar days	tropical years
Sidereal Mercury	25,781,931	87.968585	0.240849997
Sidereal Venus	10,093,427	224.700689	0.615210077
Sidereal Earth	6,209,338	365.256328	1.000038651
Sidereal Mars	3,301,404	686.980448	1.880890070
Sidereal Jupiter	523,475	4,332.585128	11.862224557
Sidereal Saturn	210,796	10,759.217442	29.457760109
Sidereal Uranus	73,912	30,685.139084	84.013123715
Sidereal Neptune	37,681	60,189.485417	164.793344125
Sidereal Pluto	24,998	90,727.258181	248.402992239
Mercury–Venus	15,688,504	144.564453	0.395804342
Venus–Earth	3,884,089	583.920708	1.598721862
Earth–Mars	2,907,934	779.935170	2.135391656
Mars–Jupiter	2,777,929	816.435553	2.235326389
Jupiter–Saturn	312,679	7,253.445227	19.859274208
Saturn–Uranus	136,884	16,568.773560	45.363797084
Uranus–Neptune	36,231	62,598.327399	171.388534680
Neptune–Pluto	12,683	178,822.045257	489.598517701
Nodal lunar month	83,344,907	27.212221	0.074504588
Sidereal lunar month	83,011,059	27.321661	0.074804226
Ecliptic lunar month	78,518,232	28.885011	0.079084537
Synodic lunar month	76,801,721	29.530588	0.080852068
Ecliptic lunar year	6,543,186	346.620133	0.949014440
Tropical solar year	6,209,578	365.242211	1.000000000
Sothic solar year	6,209,434	365.250681	1.000023190
Sidereal solar year	6,209,338	365.256328	1.000048315
Saros cycle	344,390	6,585.557072	18.030657104
Lunar precession	333,848	6,793.510819	18.600015576
Lunar standstill	333,608	6,798.398120	18.613396561
Meton cycle	326,818	6,939.642247	19.000110153
Celtic cycle	110,885	20,453.623123	56.000162330
Egyptian cycle	81,703	27,759.078614	76.001835918
Mayan cycle	66,769	33,967.859336	93.000913598
Climatic cycle	300	7,560,000.00	20,698.59333
Solar precession	240	9,450,000.00	25,873.24166
Sothic–tropical	144	15,750,000.00	43,122.06944
Sothic–sidereal	96	23,625,000.00	64,683.10416

culate that the number of Nineveh with its fifteen digits was equal to 2,268 million days of 86,400 seconds each.

That was a good start but did not answer the main question - what did this huge time span of more than six million years stand for? It was certainly longer than the age of man on Earth. Then the thought flashed into my mind that the clever Sumerians were familiar, among other things astronomical, with the precession of the equinoxes - the turning of the terrestrial axis of rotation around the pole of the ecliptic. This movement has a cycle of 9.450 million days or about 26,000 years.

When I divided the Nineveh number by the cycle of the precession of the equinoxes, also called the Big Year, I had the greatest surprise of my life! The sacred number of Nineveh divided exactly into 240 Big Years of 9.450 million days each. I saw that the fifteen digits on the clay tablet from Nineveh represented for the Sumerians two hundred and forty rotations of the seasons around the zodiac, expressing time in seconds, not days or years as our astronomers would do today.

Then came my conclusion that this enormous number of Nineveh could very well be the long lost magic number called the 'great constant of the solar system', the number that alchemists, astrologers, and astronomers had been looking for for a very long time, while their ancestors were familiar with it more than 3,000 years ago.

Naturally, I had to prove first that I was right, but that did not seem so difficult any more. If the number of Nineveh really was the great constant of the solar system, it had to be an exact multiple of any revolution or conjunction period of any planet, comet, or satelite of the solar system. It took some time to do this work and lots of numbers; but, just as I had expected, every period of revolution or conjunction of all the solar system bodies calculated with the constant of Nineveh corresponded exactly down to several decimal points with the values given in the modern tables of United States astronomers, and nearly so with the French tables which gave slightly different numbers for the planets Uranus, Neptune, and Pluto.

I have not been able to find even a single period of revolution or conjunction of a solar system planet or satellite that would not be an exact fraction down to the fourth decimal point of the great constant of the solar system. For me that is sufficient proof that the Nineveh constant is a true solar constant and has full validity today as it had when it was calculated many thousands of years ago.

However, there is one case where a slight discrepancy shows up at the sixth decimal place if the Nineveh constant of 2,268 million days is divided into tropical years. The difference equals twelve millionths of a day per year, so slight that it took me quite a while to discover it; but it does not detract a thing from the full validity of the Nineveh number. On the contrary, this discrepancy gives us a marvellous opportunity to calculate exactly when the Nineveh constant was created. Modern astronomers and their caesium atomic clocks have told us that because of an infinitesimal slowing down of the Earth's rotation, the tropical year is getting shorter by sixteen millionths of a second per year.

This helped me to calculate the true age of the Nineveh constant and led to the discovery that the great constant of the solar system accidentally found in the ruins of the royal library of King Assurbanipal must have been computed 64,800 years ago, give or take a few years. Effectively, the discrepancy of 1.0368 seconds divided by the annual decrease of the tropical year of 0.000016 seconds gives us the crucial number of 64,800 years, the true age of the Nineveh constant.

In light of this discovery, the distant past of 27,000 years ago, when Cro-Magnon man painted the caves of Lascaux in France or the temples of Tiahuanaco were built in Bolivia, not to mention the disappearance of Atlantis a mere twelve thousand years ago, indeed look like recent history. Even the oldest legends telling us about the Egyptian chronology dating back to 49,214 BC, or the Mayan calendar starting in 18,633 BC, or the Mahabharata Hindu calendar in 7116 BC, or the more recent Byzantine or Scandinavian beginnings of time counting in the years 5509 BC or 4713 BC, now seem very believable and most likely true.

One of the recent discoveries allowing us a glimpse of early man was made in the cliffs of Del Mar near San Diego, California. The skull of a *Homo sapiens* or Cro-Magnon man was found and dated by Dr. Rogers, director of science at the Museum of Man in San Diego, and Dr. Bada, professor of marine biology at the Scripps Institute of Oceanography, as more than 50,000 years, and maybe even 65,000 years old.

Both scientists agreed that the brain in this skull had been large enough for the highest intelligence and that this individual could have been capable during his lifetime of observing and registering astronomical cycles. Possibly he could even have made mathematical calculations as complex as the constant of Nineveh. But unfortunately we will never know if this man was born on Earth or came here as a visitor from another space civilization. Our only certitude is that there were very intelligent men on Earth more than 50,000 years ago, a fact that topples all our present scientific theories about the evolution of man.

The discovery that our ancestors of 65,000 years ago knew as much and probably more than we do about the solar system is really baffling. First of all, the birth date of the Nineveh constant coincides precisely with the sudden arrival on Earth of Cro-Magnon man, the first human with a brain volume equal to ours, the first successful result in a program for the improvement of the human race.

The primitive man before him had no more than 800 cubic centimetres of brain. The modern man in today's civilized countries averages about 1,600 cubic centimetres. But if people living on Earth 65,000 years ago were the primitive Stone Age humans, who, as the anthropologists think, could hardly fashion a flintstone, they could not possibly have calculated the Nineveh constant based on the precession of the equinoxes - a slow westward drift of one degree in seventy-two years, and the revolution periods of the planets, three of which, Uranus, Neptune, and Pluto, are totally invisible to the naked eye.

The only logical conclusion, no matter how much it will make establishment scientists frown, is to assume that astronauts from another solar or galactic civilization visited our ancestors 65,000 years ago and started the sudden evolution of man by improving his intelligence through insemination and mutation and then by initiation into the knowledge of astronomy, mathematics, metallurgy, and other secrets of civilization. All this could have happened during the interglacial period between the first and second Wurm ice ages, when the polar star was Vega and the climate on Earth was just about the same as it is right now, if we want to believe the 21,000-year climatic cycle that has been discovered in the geological carboniferous strata. It was an ideal time to create and educate a new and superior human race. But how can we prove this?

About sixty years ago, in 1928, European radio operators in France, Germany, Norway, and Holland noticed a strange phenomenon. When they transmitted in all directions a series of signals, they received two series of echoes instead of one. Normal echoes, after circling the Earth by bouncing several times on the ionosphere, always came back after a normal delay of one seventh of one second.

On the contrary, abnormal echoes always came back after an interval varying from 3 to 15 seconds, as if they had bounced from some object located at a distance from Earth of 450,000 to 2,250,000 km, but always a little bit farther than the Moon. As usual, this discovery was kept as secret as possible, and, after several years, it was even completely forgotten.

Then a few years ago, a young Scottish astronomer by the name of Duncan Lunan had a bright idea. He thought that these signals could very well have come from an alien spaceship orbiting the Earth at about the same distance as the Moon and that the variable intervals between the transmission of signals and reception of echoes might represent an intelligent coded message representing geometric figures or even the map of a constellation, as Bracewell had already suggested in 1968.

With the usual television technique of so many dots per line and so many lines per frame, Lunan transferred the various intervals on a chart as he would have done on a television screen. He then successively obtained several different drawings of the same constellation, with different orientations, but with the same star always at the centre.

As Lunan says in his book *Man and the Stars*, as an astronomer it did not take him long to recognize the constellation as that of Bootes and the star as Epsilon Bootis, which our ancestors called Izar and which is located at about 103 light-years, or 975 million million km, from the Earth.

One of Lunan's important discoveries was that the configuration of the Bootes constellation shown on his charts was not exactly the same as that which we can see today from the Earth, and he found an explanation. The big star Alpha Bootis, or Arcturus, is one of the fastest moving stars in our skies. It has an angular motion of 2.29 seconds of arc per year in a southwest direction, and its position in the sky moves by an apparent diameter of the Moon in only 800 years.

According to Lunan, Arcturus now appears to us about seven degrees apart from where it appears on the chart, which means that the map could have been established and transmitted 11,000 years ago. However, Arcturus does not move with a constant apparent velocity, and taking an average of only 2 seconds of arc per year, we obtain a date of 12,600 years ago which corresponds to those of the other stars of the same constellation.

As a consequence, assuming there is an alien spacecraft presently orbiting the Earth, it arrived in its present position about 13,000 years ago; and, after observing the configuration of their native constellation of Bootes as they saw it from their orbit around the Earth at that time, the astronauts on board have been continuously transmitting signals since then, waiting for human astronomers to become intelligent enough to understand them.

Finally, around 1900, the first radio signals were transmitted from the Earth by Marconi, Tesla, and others, and the Izarian astronauts knew they were now in business. They started retransmitting the earth signals, with various intervals representing a code, and the code represented a map of the constellation of Bootes with the star Izar at the centre.

For me, however, the most extraordinary and the most controversial part of the story is not so much the constellation map as the intervals between the different signals from the alien spacecraft. These intervals are always an exact number of seconds of time and, as you know, our second of time is supposed to be a human invention. Up to now, the Sumerians have been credited with the fantastic idea of dividing the solar day into 86,400 equal parts they called seconds.

In other words, these alien astronauts from a distant planet in outer space, who had been orbiting our planet in a spacecraft for 13,000 years, knew from the very beginning that the human race divided the solar day into 86,400 seconds of time. And how could they know it

38

unless they made the division themselves and landed on the Earth to teach the humans how to use the second to measure the passing of time?

And then everything becomes clear. Seven and nine have always been sacred numbers. Their product multiplied by l00,000 gives us 6.3 million years. Multiplied then by the 360 days of the year and by the 86,400 seconds of the day, we obtain the mysterious Nineveh number of l95,955,200,000,000 seconds of time. And since we know that the Nineveh constant corresponds to the exact length of the sidereal and tropical years as they were 64,800 years ago, this seems to indicate that the landing on Earth of the alien astronauts from Izar did actually occur about that time or maybe a little bit later.

What happened next, we can only guess. It is quite possible that, after inseminating and educating the human race, they went back to their home planet to report on the results of their mission and returned to our solar system only l3,000 years ago when they thought the human race had become civilized enough. As a strange coincidence, this was the time of the advanced civilization of Atlantis, l,000 years before its destruction by a cosmic cataclysm; and it could very well be that survivors from Atlantis or their descendants are still in orbit around the Earth, visiting us from time to time.

There is, however, something else in the discovery of Duncan Lunan that seems to have escaped his brilliant mind. As I said before, the ancient human year of 360 days does not make any sense on the Earth where it does not correspond to any astronomical phenomenon. But it could mean something for alien astronauts orbiting the Earth.

During a terrestrial solar year of 365 l/4 days, their spacecraft would be sometimes closer and sometimes farther from the Sun. We shall see later that a solar year of 360 days would correspond to a distance from the Sun l.00968 times shorter than the present distance of the Earth. Assuming for the Earth an average distance of l49.60 millions of kilometres and a 360-day orbit for the minimum distance of the Izarian spacecraft, we obtain for that spacecraft a minimum distance from the sun of l48.l65 millions of kilometres, and a maximum distance of l5l.035 millions of kilometres corresponding to a solar year of 370 l/2 solar days.

39

This would represent for the Izarian spacecraft an average distance from the Earth of 1.35 millions of kilometres for a circular orbit, but it is very likely that the spacecraft transferred from time to time into an elliptical orbit around the Earth to get a closer look at the human race or even land and visit them. In that case, its minimum distance from the Earth could be as low as 450,000 kilometres, which is about the distance of the Moon and corresponds to the minimum delay of the echoes.

There seem to be a number of other conclusions that could be derived from the discovery of Duncan Lunan; but I have no room left here to discuss them and they will be the subject of another book. Let us just say for the time being that the discovery of the Izarian spaceship seems to explain the origin of the constant of Nineveh.

One may ask why the constant of the solar system should have been calculated 64,800 years ago, and the answer may be that it was the time of a special configuration of the planets in our solar system. If my calculations are right, there was at the time a five-fold conjunction of five of the outer planets - Mars, Jupiter, Saturn, Uranus, and Neptune - an exact alignment of these planets with the sun which is so rare it takes place only once every 4,627 years. Personally, I like this number '64,800' because it is exactly six times the number 10,800 that was the sacred number of the Chaldean and Hindu astrologers; so the number 64,800 must have been the sacred number of cultures long before the Hindus and the Chaldeans.

The number 360 and its different multiples like 10,800, 86,400, and 432,000 are found in many sacred texts and legends of the distant past. Why did the Mayas, the Sumerians, the Chaldeans, the Babylonians, and the Egyptians use in their calculations enormous periods of time that were all multiples of 360 days or 360 years? Their choice must have had some reason and I can see only two possible explanations. Either the number 360 was given to their ancestors by astronauts or at that time the solar year was exactly 360 days long. The first explanation is very possible, the second one less so - but not totally impossible.

The laws discovered by Johannes Kepler say that for the solar year to be exactly 360 days, the distance of our planet Earth from the Sun would have to be 1.009684 times shorter than now. That seems to be impossible at first glance, but less so if one remembers the theories of the planet Venus being a planet that wandered into our system at some time in the past and was captured by our Sun. Earth certainly had its part in this capture and was possibly pushed farther out from its original orbit, giving us a longer year.

So it is possible that our year was exactly 360 days long ago and that the constant of Nineveh represented at that time exactly 6.3 million years of 360 days of 86,400 seconds each. As we will see later, there is another possibility, namely, that of a longer day of 24.35 hours as the result of a stronger pull of the Moon which was at some time much closer to our planet. That could also explain why the constant of Nineveh was calculated in stable seconds instead of days which could vary slowly over the ages.

When after a while one gets used to the idea that all that takes place in the solar system is regulated by one constant, the mind is ready to start understanding one of the great mysteries of human history, namely, the regular returns of ice ages, that have played a very important part in the existence of the primitive man and in the development of our present civilization.

We are nearly certain now that the periodic invasions of ice from the polar caps are caused by several overlapping astronomical cycles. Some of these cycles are well known while others are objects of heated debates and therefore of particular interest to me.

The first of these cycles is the precession of equinoxes, or the rotation of the axis of our planet around the pole of the ecliptic. The duration of this cycle is about 26,000 years. The second cycle is that of the variation of the eccentricity of Earth's orbit around the Sun. Its duration is about 104,000 years. The third cycle is the combination of the first two and causes changes of temperature and humidity on our planet. This third cycle is about 21,000 years. The fourth cycle is that of the variable obliquity of our Earth's rotational axis in relation to the ecliptic and its duration is about 42,000 years. The fifth cycle, a combination of all previous cyclic changes and possibly one or two more unknown factors, is that of the ice ages. This is the cycle that no two scientists explain in the same way. Each geologist has his own theory and refuses all the others.

I am not a geologist and therefore can say what I think. Let me just state that the glacial periods repeat themselves every 126,000 years

41

or so, with a shorter warm period of about 42,000 years in between the two severest periods of ice, and then a longer and warmer period of about 84,000 years with a slightly colder period in the middle. It would take five such periods or about 630,000 years for the whole chain of events to be repeated.

The theory is in harmony with the constant of Nineveh. You have possibly noticed already that all the above cycles are approximate multiples of a common factor - a time span of 5,175 years that I call the 'building block' of ice ages. When we divide the constant of 2,268 million days by 1,200, we obtain a construction block of 1,890,000 days or 5,174.648 years. This is very close to 5,175 years and also noticeably close to the Great Cycle of the Mayas that was equal to 5,163 years. So our ice age block is close enough to simplify it to 5,175 years; and if we use it, we obtain results that, except for the Mulberg and Wurm glaciations, are very close to the dates given by certain geologists that I do not want to name here.

Of these two, the Mulberg glaciation shows only one glacial period, while the Wurm has three. That seems difficult to explain unless the great glaciation cycle of 630,000 years is accepted with alternate very warm and very cold periods every 315,000 years. That would have precluded the first ice age of the Mulberg from occurring 350,000 years ago and would have caused the third ice age of the Wurm that ended only 20,000 years ago and caused the Great Deluge by sudden melting of the ice sheet.

We can calculate then, under these conditions, that the peak ice ages occurred in the following approximate numbers of years ago: Gunz - 599,600 and 558,200; Mindel - 475,400 and 434,000; Mulberg - 309,800; Riss - 227,000 and 185,600; Wurm - 102,800, 61,400, and 20,000. If this chronology is correct and nothing changes in our solar system, we do not have to worry much at present about the two next ice ages. These should come 21,400 and 62,800 years from now, allowing us plenty of time to prepare and to emigrate to tropical zones, if it becomes necessary.

The constant of Nineveh has many more surprises to offer and I cannot cease to marvel about it. One example is the case of the planet Pluto. Its orbit has an inclination of 17 degrees from the ecliptic where the orbits of other planets are. It was discovered in January 1930 by the astronomer Clyde Tombaugh only because it crossed the eclip-

42

tic at that time - an event that will occur again only in the year 2048 when this planet will return to the southern hemisphere. We might add that Pluto is visible only with the most powerful telescopes and its planetary movements can be detected only by successive photographs, all proof that our ancestors could not have known about the existence of this planet. *Yet it seems that they did know.*

The sidereal year of Pluto has been estimated by American astronomers to be 90,465 solar days. But sometimes, as in the case of the comet Kohoutek, in 1975, astronomers too make some mistakes. Since its discovery, Pluto has made only about one fifth of its voyage around the Sun, so a slight mistake in observations is possible. A negligible error in the calculated long year of Pluto would be perfectly excusable. So let's suppose that the true year of Pluto is, in reality, 90,720 solar days. Now the constant of Nineveh represents exactly 25,000 revolutions of Pluto and this can be no more of a coincidence than the fact that it also represents exactly 240 cycles of precession of the equinoxes. Without a doubt, our ancestors knew about the existence of Pluto and used its sidereal year together with the Great Year as the base of the great constant of the solar system, the constant of Nineveh.

We will have to wait until 2178, when Pluto will conclude its first revolution around the Sun since this planet was discovered, to know the precise length of its sidereal year. If it is 90,720 days and not 90,465 as preliminary observations indicate, we will have more proof concerning the Nineveh constant. Strangely enough, the number 90,720 days can be found in the Sumerian mathematical series of the constant.

What we still do not know is who the astronauts were who brought knowledge about Pluto to our ancestors. But whoever they were, these astronauts also instructed our forefathers about the existence of Proserpine, a planet much larger than our Earth at a distance of almost ten billion kilometres from the Sun, with a revolution period of 512 terrestrial years.

Nobody on Earth can say for sure that he has seen Proserpine and I doubt very much that it ever will be visible from a terrestrial vantage point. Yet our ancestors had knowledge of its existence. Some people might be surprised about my assurance that our ancestors knew the planets Uranus and Neptune as well as the precession of the equinoxes. This assurance is shared today by many authors trying to explain our ancestors' astonishing knowledge of astronomy.

A good example is the planet Uranus, which is usually not visible with the naked eye, but sometimes shows up for a few weeks with an apparent diameter larger than Mars at its greatest distance from Earth. Uranus was well known long before its official discovery by Sir William Herschel in 1781, but it took some time to make sure that it was a planet and not a star.

The ancient astrologers also could have noticed the acceleration and slowing down of a known planet when it passed another unknown planet. At the last conjunction of Uranus and Saturn on 4 May, 1942, the acceleration of Saturn was 2 minutes a day in February, 4 minutes in March, 6 in April, 8 in May, then 7 in June, 6 in July, 4 in August, and 2 in September when the conjunction of these two planets was over. By this same method Neptune was discovered in 1846 by Urbain Leverrier in France and by J. C. Adams in England.

There is some talk at this time about the big conjunction of planets that will take place on 10 May 2,000. Seven planets will be lined up with the sun. Some people have expressed fear that that combined force of attraction could cause tidal waves and earthquakes on our planet. Some even predict that California will break off along the San Andreas fault and drift away into the Pacific.

For me, a resident of San Diego, such thought is not very reassuring; but neither does it upset me much, since I have decided to retire to Tahiti anyway. However, for sheer fun, I have made some calculations to see how much influence the combined gravitational forces of the various planets could exert on our Earth.

As everyone knows, the gravitational force is directly proportionate to the product of the masses of the objects and inversely proportional to the square of the distance between them. The planet that exerts the strongest attraction on Earth is Venus, but this force is no more than 1/180 of the gravitational pull of the Moon. Jupiter has about 1/4 of the pull of Venus; Mars is about one hundred times weaker; Saturn is the same as Mars; and finally, Pluto has but one two-millionth part of the gravity that the Moon exerts on the Earth.

Some might ask if the orbits and revolution periods of comets also agree with the Nineveh constant. The comets that frequently return to our Sun do not prove the validity of the constant, but the revolution periods of the rare ones fit perfectly into the cycle of the constant. Whiston's comet, for example, makes 10,800 revolutions around the Sun in 2,268 million days, while Crigg's comet makes 37,800 revolutions during that same period of time. As for Halley's comet, which passed its closest point to the Sun in February, 1986, it makes exactly 81,000 revolutions in 2,268 days!

I could not close this chapter without a word or two about the possible existence of some more planets out beyond Pluto. At this moment there are to the best of my knowledge at least three candidates. First there is the planet which Brady named Proserpine - the same name that our ancestors gave to this body. According to him, the planet is sixty-four times farther away from the Sun than we are and needs 512 years for one revolution around the Sun. The constant of Nineveh indicates a revolution period of 187,005 days.

Next is the planet of William Pickering that, according to the constant, should have a year of 238,536 days corresponding to 653 terrestrial years. Third and lastly, there is the planet of Schuette and, as the constant of Nineveh shows, it should have a sidereal revolution period of 246,951 days or about 676 years. It could very well be that all three of these planets are one and the same -- the famous Proserpine that has been seen by three different astronomers on three different occasions in three different positions, and at three different distances.

All that, however, does not explain how our ancestors knew about the existence of Proserpine any more than it explains who told them that Mars has two satellites, Jupiter four, Saturn seven, and Uranus two. And how did the Dogons, a primitive tribe of Mali, know that an enormous planet circles around the star Sirius, with a revolution period of fifty years? I certainly do not want to give the impression that I am entirely devoted to extraterrestrial civilizations and flying saucers; but in all honesty, one has to wonder how our distant ancestors of the Stone Age could possibly have had all of this knowledge of astronomy and mathematics? *They could not have found it all by themselves. Somebody had to have helped them, a god or an astronaut.*

45

THE MAYAN CALENDAR

The mystery of the Mayan calendar has always been a hotly disputed subject among archaeologists. Everyone had his own theory and defended it firmly. But most of the time this dispute went on between the French and the German archaeologists and that is probably one of the reasons why I became interested. The situation was complicated by the fact that there were two Mayan calendars - one that was quite well known and another that no one had yet deciphered.

To measure short time spans, the Mayas used a cycle of 104 years and this cycle was well known and accepted so that everybody could agree on it. This cycle of 104 years or 37,960 days represented for the Mayan astronomers 1,285 cycles of the Moon, 327 cycles of Mercury, 219 cycles of eclipses, 146 sacred years, 104 profane years, 65 cycles of Venus, and 48 2/3 cycles of Mars.

The Mayas celebrated in a very original way, the meeting of 73 sacred years with 52 profane years. They extinguished all the fires in the household, smashed all the pots and pans in the kitchen, and sat up all night long in fear and trepidation that the end of the world might be there and that they might never see the Sun again. When nevertheless the Sun rose again in the morning and the Mayas had to acknowledge that the world was still there, they relit their fires and sacrificed a few virgins and prisoners and went back happily to enjoy life for another 52 years. Evidently, every 104 years, when the planets Mercury and Venus were in conjunction with the Sun, and especially every 312 years, when Mars joined the group, the celebration was even bigger and the number of virgins and prisoners sacrificed was substantially increased.

To compute long periods of time and to make astronomical calculations, the Mayas used a calendar that was based on the Great Cycle - a period of time that was not precisely known to our scientists. It was vaguely thought that the last cycle had started about 3,000 years before Christ. It was also thought that this cycle had to run out soon. Finally, it was assumed that this long span was divided in cycles a little shorter than twenty years each. For this very scant knowledge we have to thank the bishop of Yucatan, Diego de Landa, who in 1549 ordered all the ancient Mayan documents and manuscripts to be publicly burned because he could not understand these treasures. To him they were the work of Satan.

Any one who wants to tackle the mystery of the Mayan calendar today has to solve three different problems: the starting date of this calendar, the length of the time span this calendar covered, and the duration of its short cycles. Opinions on all three questions differ widely. Originally, the dates proposed for the start of this long calendar were as much as 520 years apart. Recently this discrepancy has been reduced to 260 years and there are only two groups of American archaeologists who dispute each other. The team led by Herbert Spinden maintains that the long Mayan calendar started in 3373 BC. The team led by Edward Thompson thinks it began in 3113 BC. As the Mayas counted time, this 260 year difference represents thirteen periods of 20 years each that are called 'katuns'. Twenty katuns, or 400 years, are equal to one 'baktun'.

The duration of the Mayan long calendar was accepted by the archaeologists with good reason to be 5,200 years, or 260 times 20 years, because the scientists were well aware of the fact that for the Mayas the numbers 13, 26, and 260 were very important. The short cycle, as everbody thought, had to be about 19.75 years, but nobody could explain why it had to be a number that does not correspond to any of the cyclic motions of either the Sun, the Moon, or any known planet or comet.

When the radiocarbon dating method was introduced, the archaeologists were sure that in no time all the mysteries of the Mayan calendar would be solved. Carbon dating seemed tailor-made for this purpose because all Mayan temples had heavy wooden beams made from a tree called 'sapodilla', which has a rich latex content and does not rot. Also insects do not affect this evergreen which is now cultivated to produce chicle, the main ingredient of chewing gum. Furthermore, all inscriptions on Mayan temples mark the exact date according to the Mayan calendar when they were built.

The Mayas used the vigesimal counting by 20, with a dash and dot system. The numbers were represented by an eye that had the value of zero, a dot that counted for 1, and a dash that counted for 5. As the carbon-dating system was thought to be at that time very reliable, all that supposedly had to be done to bring our calendar and the unknown Mayan calendar into accord was to take a sliver of

48

sapodilla wood from the beam of the temple, find out by its radioactive carbon content how old it was, and then compare its age with the inscribed Mayan date on the lintel of the temple.

In the middle of the tropical jungle of Guatemala stands the magnificent Mayan temple of Tikal built in a year indicated thus: one dash four dots three dashes two dashes one eye and one more eye - which in our numbers would mean 9 15 10 0 0 or the Mayan year nine baktuns, fifteen katuns, ten tuns, zero months, zero days, or about 3,900 of our years since the last start of the Mayan long calendar.

The Spinden team estimated this date to be AD 481, but the Thompson team insisted that it was the year AD 741. Carbon dating was to resolve the dispute and everybody went down to Tikal to obtain fresh samples of the old temple lintel for the laboratory where it was to be tested by the newest, most precise methods of radiocarbon dating.

The first results obtained from burning the Tikal sapodilla slivers indicated that the Spinden group was right, but later tests with a greater number of samples proved finally that the Thompson group was the winner. All were satisfied because each team had won one set of the match, but the mystery of the Mayan calendar was not solved. As we will see later on, the real winner was the Thompson team that came very close to the right answer - the year 739 or two years less than 741 that they had proposed.

The most amusing aspect was that this astonishingly precise prediction was obtained from a wrong starting date and a wrong short cycle. A similar case in history is the precise calculation by Eratosthenes of Alexandria who 2,200 years ago establisted the circumference of our planet by using two wrong values whose errors cancelled each other and thus yielded the right answer.

I had long been intrigued by the mysteries of the Mayan calendar but never had the time to take a closer look. Then, after a dinner date in Paris with a French specialist in Mayan culture, I decided to try the impossible. I knew that the Mayas, like the Sumerians, were great astronomers and I had long suspected the two cultures had something in common.

The Mayas also knew of the precession of the equinoxes and the existence of Uranus and Neptune. They had calculated the periods of revolution and conjunction of different planets and discovered, as I already mentioned, some equivalent astronomical cycles, such as 65 revolutions of Venus which are equal to 104 solar years, or 327 revolutions of Mercury. They also used the cycle of 33,968 days to predict eclipses, and this cycle was equal to 5 lunar precessioins, 93 solar years, 196 eclipses, and 1,150 lunar months. We will look at these figures later once more. Meanwhile, the Mayas had also discovered a cycle of 1,886,040 days that represented exactly 260 conjunctions of Jupiter and Saturn, 2,310 of Mars and Jupiter, 2,418 of Earth and Mars, and 3,230 of Earth and Venus.

This particular cycle was the key to the mystery of the Mayan calendar. It was based on the conjunctions of Jupiter and Saturn, something nobody had cared to consider. All other periods of sidereal or synodic revolution of all planets had been tried, but somehow nobody had tested the conjunctions between the planets.

Mayan astronomical calendar from 3144 BC to AD 2020

Mayan Great Cycle of 260 katuns or 5163 years

						baktuns						
0	1	2	3	4	5	6	7	8	9	10	11	12
3144	2747	2350	1953	1555	1158	0761	0364	0034	0431	0828	1226	1623
3124	2727	2330	1933	1536	1138	0741	0344	0054	0451	0848	1245	1643
3104	2707	2310	1913	1516	1119	0721	0324	0074	0471	0868	1265	1662
3084	2687	2290	1893	1496	1099	0702	0304	0094	0491	0888	1285	1682
3065	2667	2270	1873	1476	1079	0682	0285	0114	0511	0908	1305	1702
3045	2648	2250	1853	1456	1059	0662	0265	0133	0531	0928	1325	1722
3025	2628	2231	1833	1436	1039	0642	0245	0153	0550	0948	1345	1742
3005	2608	2211	1814	1416	1019	0622	0225	0173	0570	0967	1365	1762
2985	2588	2191	1794	1397	0999	0602	0205	0193	0590	0987	1384	1782
2965	2568	2171	1774	1377	0980	0582	0185	0213	0610	1007	1404	1801
2945	2548	2151	1754	1357	0960	0563	0165	0233	0630	1027	1424	1821
2926	2528	2131	1734	1337	0940	0543	0146	0253	0650	1047	1444	1841
2906	2509	2111	1714	1317	0920	0523	0126	0272	0670	1067	1464	1861
2886	2489	2092	1694	1297	0900	0503	0106	0292	0689	1087	1484	1881
2866	2469	2072	1675	1277	0880	0483	0086	0312	0709	1106	1504	1901
2846	2449	2052	1655	1258	0860	0463	0066	0332	0729	1126	1523	1921
2826	2429	2032	1635	1238	0841	0443	0046	0352	0749	1146	1543	1940
2806	2409	2012	1615	1218	0821	0424	0026	0372	0769	1166	1563	1960
2787	2389	1992	1595	1198	0801	0404	0007	0392	0789	1186	1583	1980
2767	2370	1972	1575	1178	0781	0384	0014	0411	0809	1206	1603	2000
2747	2350	1953	1555	1158	0761	0364	0034	0431	0828	1226	1623	2020

(rows labelled katuns 0–20 at the left margin)

This Mayan calendar of 1,886,040 days was based on 260 conjunctions of Jupiter and Saturn, which occur every 7,254 days. It was divided into 13 baktuns of 20 katuns each, as well as into 7,254 sacred years of 260 days or 5,239 calendar years of 360 days. Each baktun also represented 186 synodic revolutions of Mars or 5,310 sidereal revolutions of the Moon.

The conjunction period of Jupiter and Saturn is actually 7,253.445 days, but the rounded-out Mayan value of 7,254 days is valid because they did not use decimal parts and counted in whole days only. So the Great Cycle of 260 Mayan conjunctions was 1,886,040 days, or 5,163.8 of our years.

I finally discovered that the Mayan chronology was based on several Great Cycles of 5,163 years, or 260 conjunctions each, counted in succession. Once the duration and the rhythm of the Great Cycle was established, it was not difficult to find the starting point of the Mayan calendar. I presumed that at the start of the last Great Cycle some remarkable astronomic phenomenon must have occurred. The joint arrival of four planets in the same corner of the sky, the meeting of Jupiter, Saturn, Uranus, and Neptune, takes place every, 4627 years after each of the planets has finished an exact number of conjunctions and is again lined up with the others. And the last time such a phenomenon took place was the year 1484 of the Christian era.

Stepping now 4,627 years back, I marked the year 3,144 BC and took three more times the same cycle of 5,163 years to arrive at the date 18,633 BC, a date only three years off of the year 18,630 BC mentioned as an important date in a sacred Mayan codex preserved in the Vatican. For me that constitutes proof. Also, if my calculations are reasonably accurate, some other quite rare astronomical occurrence took place in the skies over the Mayan temples in that year - a double eclipse of the Sun and of the Moon during the same year. The exact dates were 23 November for the eclipse of the Sun and 3 June for that of the Moon.

When I also discovered that the count of days in each sacred year was 260, the same number as katuns in the Great Cycle, all of the pieces of the jigsaw puzzle began to fall into place. For the Mayas the katun of 7,254 days was not only a measure of time but also an astronomical unit to express the synodic periods of revolution of planets, or the count of days needed for each planet to be aligned with the Sun and the Earth. For example, 5 katuns were equal to 313 revolutions of Mercury, 13 katuns were equal to 121 revolutions of Mars, or 27 katuns were equal to 7 returns of Halley's comet.

It seems that, like the Sumerians, the Mayas were familiar with the constant of Nineveh - but in another form. Their time was counted in days, not seconds. For years the professional archaeologists searching the ruins of the Mayan temples had found fantastically high numbers engraved in stone. These numbers corresponded to millions of years or billions of days, while the officially recognized age of mankind, according to scientists of that time, was only 6,000 years - one reason why the gigantic numbers meant nothing to those early archaeologists and were simply dismissed. Many years later a courageous author suggested that one of these mysterious numbers represented a cycle of 23,040 millions of days, or 64 millions of Mayan years of 360 days each, called an 'alautun'. But still nobody paid any attention, and the huge Mayan numbers were forgotten once more.

The date of this Mayan Disc of Chinkultic had been estimated as AD 587 but it could be much older. It actually shows, since the origin of the calendar, an elapsed time of 11 days, 14 months, 12 years, 17 katuns, 7 baktuns, and 9 Great Cycles. That seems to indicate the year 14 BC for the disc and the year 49,611 BC for the origin of the Mayan calendar. After all, it is only 1 baktun before the start of the Egyptian calendar in 49,214 BC.

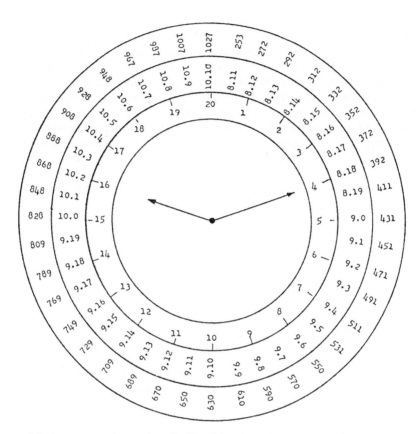

Mayan astronomical clock

Classical period from AD 233–1027. The outer circle indicates
the dates of our present calendar. The middle circle indicates the
Mayan dates in baktuns and katuns. The inner circle indicates the
Mayan dates in tuns

This clock showing the classical Mayan period, AD 233–1027, is
based on the same principle as the calendar, but for only 290,160
days, or 372 Mars cycles. The Mayas also had a shorter calendar of
37,960 days representing 65 Venus cycles of 584 days, or 104 solar
years of 365 days, or 146 sacred years of 260 days.

53

I must admit myself that when I first heard about the gigantic Mayan numbers I saw no importance in them and simply decided the ancient Mayas had been addicted to big numbers as some people are addicted to drugs, religion, or sex. It was only after I had discovered the constant of Nineveh and the secret of the Mayan calendar that my new respect for the achievements of our ancestors made me wonder if there could have been some common knowledge between the Sumerians who counted by sixty and the Mayas who counted by twenty. Most other people of antiquity used the decimal system like the Egyptians or counted by the dozen like the ancient Gauls or Babylonians.

One day as I looked at some notes taken years ago in Paris during a long discussion with my French specialist in Mayan culture, I noticed two especially mysterious numbers that had been found engraved in some Mayan ruins. One was 34,020 millions of days or about 93 millions of years and the other 147,420 millions of days or a little more than 403 millions of years. Expressed in sacred years of 260 days, the second number represented exactly 567 million years.

It is difficult to blame the archaeologists for ignoring these numbers. But since I am not an archaeologist and am used to the huge numbers involved in space exploration, the Mayan numbers did not discourage me. Before long I saw that the 34,020 million days represented fifteen times the Constant of Nineveh, while 147,420 million days represented it 65 times.

I spent a lot of time pondering why the Mayas would have used these huge constants before the answer came to me: they made all their calculations by 26 or 260 conjunctions. They needed a constant of the solar system that would be divisible by 260; and since the Nineveh constant represented for them 312,680 conjunctions, which cannot be divided by either 26 or 260, they invented a new constant of 34,020 millions of days that represented 78,170 great cycles of 260 conjunctions.

It is surely beyond imagination to think that thousands of years ago the Mayas could have, all by themselves, calculated a constant of 147,420 millions of days - a number that had twelve digits. But it is even more surprising to see that the same number, only 65 times smaller and expressed in seconds instead of days, has been used by Sumerians, a nation on the opposite side of the globe. This fact seems to indicate that the Mayas and the Sumerians must have had direct connections with each otber or that they shared a common origin.

I would like to emphasize here that the first constant which the Mayas used equals exactly 3,600 Sumerian cycles of precession of the equinoxes of 9,450,000 days each. The reader can draw his own conclusions. But the number 3,600 certainly seems to be the root of all the astronomical calculations our ancestors made, as it is a basic number in the geometry of our planet. We have exactly 3,600 tenths of one degree in the circumference of the globe; and at the equator, each of these parts is equal to 36,000 Babylonian feet.

Most of the calendars of antiquity, no matter where, have been calculated from the movements of the celestial bodies, and the Mayan calendar is certainly not the only one that had been worked out from the conjunctions of Jupiter and Saturn. It is certainly interesting to observe how many important religious and political events coincide with the alignments of these two planets.

The conjunctions of Jupiter and Saturn behind the Sun take place quite rarely. The last such event happened in 1881 and the one before that in 503 BC. Yet this cycle of 2,383 years was known to the astrologers many thousands of years before our era, as it repeated itself in the years 10,035; 7,652; 5,269; and 2,886 before Christ. The oldest date comes close to the time when the fabled Atlantis disappeared and the most recent seems to indicate the time of the Great Flood described in the Bible.

Among other ancient calendars, some were based on relative motions of the Moon and Sun and the most frequently used cycle was 10,800 years, or 599 Saros common to the Hindus, the Sumerians, and the Babylonians. Forty of these cycles made the great cycle of the Hindus and the great year of Berossus, high priest of Babylon.

The figure 10,800 also repeats itself in many other places. Multiples or fractions of this number can be found in sacred texts from all around the world. The Rig-Veda, the most important sacred book of the Hindus, has 10,800 verses and the altar of the Vedic god Agni has been built of exactly 10,800 bricks. The Greek philosopher

Heraclitus, who 2,500 years ago was the first to propose that matter is transformable, counted time in aeons of 10,800 years each.

Another example of this number is to be found in Cambodia in the temple of Angkor Wat. This place is much older than most people think and it is decorated with 540 statues along five avenues. Each statue represents 20 years of time. They are erected exactly like the stone pillars, or steles of the Mayas which also represent 20 years each; and when you add them all, they represent 10,800 years. Finally, the German legend of the Nibelungen speaks of the 10,800 souls of dead warriors who enter the gates of Valhalla - the abode of the immortal heroes.

Can one really believe that all this is a coincidence or must one assume that all the legends containing the same exact number could have a common source or origin, be it terrestrial, solar, or galactic? These enormous 10,800- or 432,000-year spans prove at least that our ancestors many thousands of years ago had no fear of complicated calculations and that indeed they knew how to predict eclipses and other astronomical events for thousands of years in advance of their own time. But who were the gods or the astronauts who taught them this wisdom and presumably also brought them agriculture, metallurgy, and many other skills leading to civilization?

The answer may well be buried in the ancient Mayan city of Palenque in southern Mexico. It was there that on 15 June, 1952, Alberto Ruiz, a Mexican scientist, made a fantastic archaeological discovery. A few years earlier Ruiz had started to clear the ruins in Palenque and found a stairway leading to the inside of a step pyramid. The passage was clogged by debris. It took several years to clear the stairs and break through several walls. All of the work in Palenque had to be done during a few short months in between the rainy seasons. But when it was done and Ruiz went down into the stairwell, he found a magnificent burial chamber and an enormous bas-relief tombstone.

The stone slab was 1,600 mm wide, 2,200 mm long, and 250 mm thick. It weighed over 2 tons. And not one of these dimensions fitted the measurement systems of the Mayas or other Amerindian civilizations. Neither the Maya foot measuring 300 mm, nor the Tiahuanaco foot of 297 mm, nor the Cuenca foot of 348 mm seemed applicable to measure the Palenque tomb cover. It was clear that the builders of this tomb had used some much older system of measurement, possibly an ancestor of the metric system, like a foot of 360 mm and a hand of 90 mm, which were used for the Dresden Codex.

To top it all, the very well-preserved bas-relief depicted an astronaut sitting at the controls of a space vehicle! And it was unmistakably a spacecraft propelled by a jet exhaust. As a consequence, it is not difficult to imagine the amazement and even the furor of most establishment archaeologists when they heard of this discovery. And as is usual with them, crying 'Fraud!' was their only explanation.

However, the grave itself contained more shocks. When the heavy tombstone was finally lifted, the sarcophagus contained the well-preserved skeleton of a white man who must have been at least 180 cm, or 70 inches tall; but the average height of a Maya rarely exceeded 150 cm, or 60 inches. The bas-relief was engraved with twenty-four hieroglyphs not yet deciphered. The sarcophagus was in the form of a fish - a symbol common to many ancient religions and probably hinting at the aquatic origin of man. Did Ruiz discover the tomb of the great Mayan god Kukulcan who, according to the legend, was tall and blond with a beard and blue eyes and had arrived one day from the land where the Sun rises?

THE SECRET OF THE PYRAMID

So many books have been written about the Great Pyramid of Cheops at Giza, that it seems impossible today to write anything new about the subject. This statement is not quite true, however, since there is always some previously overlooked angle that can bring out new facts.

The majority of men specializing in exploring and mapping of the Great Pyramid agree today that the length of its base was 440 Egyptian cubits, one such cubit being one and a half millionth part of the territorial length of Egypt. Corresponding to a cubic cubit of 0.144 cubic metre, that makes the Egyptian cubit equal to 0.524148 metre and gives the pyramid a base length of 230.625 metres. This is slightly different from certain measurements made in inches, but the values of those inches are not clearly defined and nobody can really say how long the base of the pyramid was because its entire outer layer has been removed and used to build the mosques and palaces of Cairo. Also more than one Earth tremor has shaken the pyramid during its 5,000 years of existence, one of the most severe being an earthquake whose epicentre was the Aegean island of Thera, and which is thought by some to have destroyed the Cretan civilization in 1521 BC.

The main point of disagreement about the Great Pyramid of Cheops is its height. It cannot be measured today any more because the whole top part has been carried away and destroyed by men and nature. Its height must have measured between 279 and 281 cubits; but it is very difficult to compute because three different mathematical concepts were used in building the pyramid and all three of these ways of calculating are slightly at odds with the methods of modern mathematicians working with decimals.

The first concept calls for exact proportions between the pyramid and our planet Earth. The height of the pyramid should be proportional to the radius of the Earth and the perimeter should be proportional to the circumference. The second principle requires that the area of each side be equal to the square of the height. The third demands that the volume of the pyramid be of exactly eighteen millions of cubic cubits.

At first glance these three conditions seem incompatible. But let us try, nevertheless, to reconcile them. To do this, we will have to calculate the triangle formed by a half-base line, the height, and the apothem - the shortest line between the summit of the pyramid and the middle point of one base line. We will have to make all calculations in cubits; and to make us understand the feeling the Egyptian architect must have had 5,000 years ago, we must remember all the time that the proportion between the height and half base of the pyramid has to be a very simple one because hundreds of thousands of stones will have to be cut to these specifications.

The first condition calls for the proportion between the height and the half-base to be 1.273239, or 4 divided by 3.141592. In that case, with a half base of 220, the height is equal to 280.112 cubits and the apothem to 356.178, which gives us the volume of the pyramid as 18,076,605 cubic cubits. Conditions two and three are not fulfilled but the dimensions are proportional to those of our Earth - the height to the radius and the perimeter to the circumference.

The second condition exacts a proportion of 1.272019, the square root of 1.618034 which is the golden section or factor PHI. Then the height is 279.84 cubits, the apothem 355.967 cubits, and the volume l8,059,288 cubic cubits. Conditions one and three are not reached, but the surface of one face is equal to the square of the height.

Condition three requires the proportion between the height and the half base to be l.267843. In such case, the height is equal to 278.925

---

opposite Pyramid of Cheops

Original dimensions in metres and cubits

Edge : 219.392 metres ; base area : 53,188 square metres ; volume : 2,592,000 cubic metres

Originally, the Pyramid of Cheops had a base side of 230.625 metres, or 440 cubits ; a base area of 53,188 square metres, or 193,600 square cubits ; and a volume of 2,592,000 cubic metres, or 18 million cubic cubits. The cubit used in this pyramid had a length of 524.148 millimetres.

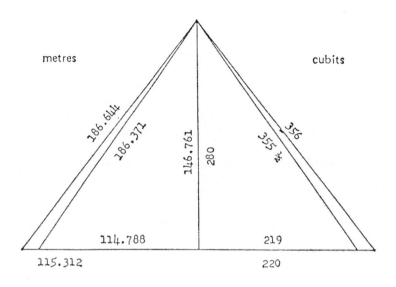

metres   cubits

186.644
186.371
146.761   280
355 ¼   356
114.788
115.312   219
220

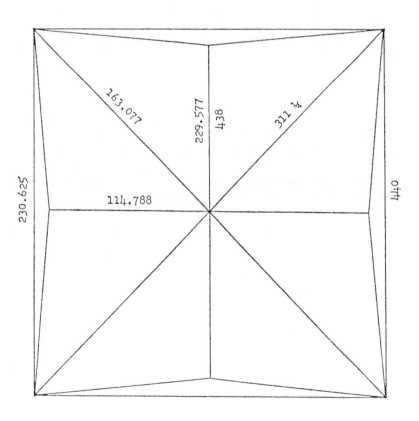

163.077
229.577   438   311 ¼
114.788
230.625   440

cubits and the apothem to 355.245. The volume now is exactly 18 million cubic cubits, but conditions one and two are not satisfied. As one can see from these examples, the three conditions are incompatible with modern mathematics using the decimal system. But the Egyptians did not use such a system; instead of decimal parts they used fractions. And if we use fractions, the problem can be solved.

For the Egyptians, as for all ancient mathematicians, the factor PI was 22 divided by 7, or the fraction 22/7 with a decimal value of 3.142857. The factor PHI was the fraction 196/121, or 1.619834. If expressed as simple fractions, both factors are related because the square root of factor PHI is now equal to 4 divided by PI, 14/11, or 1.272727. Here you have the secret of the Great Pyramid, or at least one of them.

With this factor, 1.272727, and a half-base of 220, the height is exactly 280 cubits and the apothem 356.089. The volume is 18,069,333 cubic cubits. The first two conditions are fulfilled in Egyptian fractions but the third is not. To satisfy it, we will have to discover another secret of the Great Pyramid - that its base, contrary to previous assumptions, is not exactly a square.

One of the strange qualities of the Great Pyramid is the fact that its faces are not entirely flat. They are concave and the apothem recedes by about one cubit. The first to discover this concavity was Edme Francois Jomard, one of the French scientists accompanying Napoleon on his Egyptian expedition in 1798. A sketch of the Great Pyramid done by Napoleon himself is still extant and it clearly shows the receding apothem on the two visible faces.

This anomaly was forgotten for nearly a century until, in 1881, Sir Flinders Petrie rediscovered it and measured it to be 37 inches, or 1.8 cubits, on the north face. This value was too high, but what can you expect from ancient measurements? Besides, there is now an excellent aerial photograph showing the dihedral angle of the sides in superb clarity

As could be expected, each pyramidologist has his own explanation for this angle. The fact is that it renders the outlines more distinct and the shadows more recognizable. This was of great importance for the astronomers because it made their observations much more precise. Also the luminosity of the faces is enhanced greatly by the two semi-faces forming the dihedral, and thus observations of the Sun, Moon, and stars by the line of the apothem are made much easier. This especially applies to observations of the stars Sirius, which was the base for the Sothic year, and Alpha Draconis, the star that was the north polar star in those days. The slight dihedral of the faces also reduced the volume of the pyramid to make it exactly 18 million cubic cubits, which for some unknown, but probably religious or astronomical reason, was of utmost importance to ancient Egyptians.

It is not possible now to measure the exact recession of the apothem because all of the exterior stone plates have been carried away, but the dimension can be calculated with great precision. With a base of 440 cubits and a height of 280 cubits, the surface of the base has to be reduced by 743 square cubits to obtain a volume of 18 million cubic cubits. That results in shortening the apothem by 0.521 cubits and receding its base by 0.844 cubits.

The most astonishing result of this arrangement is that it pushes back the two half bases of the pyramid by a quarter degree so that the two halves form an angle of 1/2 degree. This results in a difference of 2 minutes of solar clock time and could have served the ancient astronomers to set their water clocks or hourglasses to the exact solar time.

Let us have a look now at the angle of inclination of the faces. With the dimensions of 220 cubits and 280 cubits, the angle is 51° , 50' 34", or 52 degrees in round numbers, which leads to another interesting discovery. We know now that in the distant past the poles of our planet have wandered considerably. According to the latest geological data, the poles seem to stand still for a period of about 30,000 years, then move around for 6,000 years and lie still in the new place for another 30,000 years. These cycles are in harmony with the solar constant and the ice ages.

It is now estimated that the present positions of our poles were established about 12,000 years ago and that they will stay put for another 18,000 years. Let's also remember that the inclination of the Earth's axis varies in cycles of about 42,000 years. With that in mind, we can return to the Great Pyramid of Cheops.

We can assume for a moment that the Great Pyramid was constructed at a time when the inclination of the terrestrial axis was 22 $1/2^O$ and the site of construction was at 29 $1/2^O$ N - explaining why the faces of the pyramid had an inclination angle of 52 degrees. Under these conditions the south face of the pyramid would at the time of the winter solstice be perpendicular to the direction of the Sun, while at the summer solstice the angle would be 45 degrees.

Now, it could very well be that the angle of 52° belonged to a smaller and much more ancient pyramid that now is inside the larger Great Pyramid of Cheops, a possibility indicating that the Great Pyramid might be much older than we believe and that Cheops was not the builder but only the enlarger of a smaller pyramid that could be anywhere between 5,000 and 20,000 years old. Nothing has been found so far that would allow us to determine its true age. And that might be one of the reasons why so many people, including Napoleon, were so utterly fascinated by this big heap of stones.

But why was the exact volume of I8 million cubic cubits so important to the Egyptians that the writers of antiquity never forgot to mention it? I might have found an answer to this question, too, even though this may lead some to think I'm so obsessed with the constant of Nineveh that I seem to find it everywhere.

We know that the pyramid was built in successive steps separated by long periods of inactivity. This was done for good reasons. First, the enormous weight of the construction needed time to settle and take its final position before the last corrections or realignments could be made. Then the observation platform at the top was probably used as an observatory during these building intervals to make adjustments so that the inner corridors of the pyramid would be precisely in line with the stars at certain times, especially with Sirius and Alpha Draconis which were the most important for the Egyptian astronomers. It has been found that 3,400 years before Christ, the ascending gallery was aligned with Alpha Centauri and the descending one aimed at Alpha Draconis, the polar star of that time. But the possibility exists that both these galleries could have been used similarly to sight two other stars separated by the same celestial angle several thousand years before.

Sir Gaston Maspero, director of the French archaeological mission in Egypt in the I880's, found a curious hieroglyph in inscriptions around Sakkara. It showed a truncated pyramid with an obelisk on top of it supporting the solar disk. At first Maspero had no explanation for it. Later on, the conclusion was made that it showed the unfinished Great Pyramid of Cheops at the level where the ascending gallery terminates. The Maspero hieroglyph is an indication that the work on the pyramid was interrupted for a long time at its half height.

When the Great Pyramid was at the halfway mark, the surface of the platform was one quarter of the surface of its base and the volume of the pyramid to be finished was one eight of the whole volume. The finished part, therefore, was seven eights of 18 million cubic cubits, or 15.75 million cubic cubits. When you translate this latter volume into our metric system, it equals 2,268 million cubic decimetres and 2,268 million is the exact value of the Nineveh constant. We must add here that the ancient Egyptians were quite familiar with the metric system. In the same region of Sakkara, where the hieroglyph of the truncated pyramid was found, archaeologists have gathered metric standards used by ancient Egyptians.

Once more we find the great constant but expressed in cubic decimetres. Coincidence? A coincidence is possible, of course, but I have seen so many of these coincidences that I do not believe in 'coincidences' any more. And then there was the discovery that the length of the granite coffer, which is not a coffin but a standard of measure placed in the king's chamber inside the Great Pyramid, is exactly 2,268 millimetres and that the total volume of the pyramid in cubic cubits multiplied by the historically sacred number 126, again gives us the number of the great constant: 2,268 million.

It seems that for the Egyptians, too, this number had a sacred meaning, which could mean that in different forms the Nineveh constant was known to the entire ancient world and that it was used for thousands of years until our Sacred Mother the Church systematically destroyed all traces of earlier civilizations. Moreover, this magic number has also been discovered at Teotihuacan in Mexico.

The majority of the scientists and pyramidologists who explored the Cheops pyramid tried to discover in its dimensions all kinds of mathematical and astronomical data. Some among them even invented new units of measure to adjust their measurements to the values they wanted to obtain. It is true that many astronomical data are to be found in the dimensions of the pyramid, but the most surprising aspect is that nobody thought of a much simpler solution that seems obvious to me. Could it really be sheer coincidence that each of the eight principal dimensions of the pyramid are exact multiples of planetary conjunction and revolution periods if we measure them with the Cheops finger of 18.719 mm, or 1/28 of the Cheops cubit?

These eight dimensions are the perimeter of the base, the sum of the two diagonals of the base, the side of the base, the edge, the apothem, the height, and the two perpendiculars drawn from the centre of the base to the edge and to the apothem. When measured in Cheops fingers, these dimensions give us the following numbers: 49,280; 34,850; 12,320; 11,720; 9,970; 7,840; 5,840; 4,840. As anyone can verify, each of these numbers is an exact multiple of some planetary revolution or conjunction period measured in days. For example, 4,840 is equal to 55 sidereal periods or 42 synodic periods of Mercury while 5,840 represents 10 synodic periods of Venus. This can be no coincidence, no more and no less than all the other inexplicable cases where we always find the same numbers and calculation methods.

Much has been written also about the purpose for which the Great Pyramid was built. My opinion is that the basic reason for it was to serve as an astronomical observatory. Because of its enormous dimensions, the shadow of the pyramid moved very rapidly on the ground and made it possible to measure time with great accuracy. Even the year of the star Sirius was measured that way and the Egyptians figured it at 365.250681 solar days. This value was abbreviated to 365 1/4 days that coincided with the civil year of 365 days every 1,460 years.

The Great Pyramid of Cheops was also a space beacon. Today millions of people around the world have become familiar with UFOs and the idea that space vehicles have visited our planet for aeons and continue to do so, so that the possibility of space visitors does not seem so strange any more. From high above, the pyramid is visible at a very great distance to the naked eye, and in space it shows on the radar screen much farther out because of its slanted sides that reflect radar beams perpendicularly if the approach angle is 38° above horizon.

It is easy to calculate that the polished stone surface of nearly 21,600 sq m on each face, is a radar reflector with a directivity factor of over 600 million for a 2 cm wave length, for example. Such a powerful reflector could have served as a beacon for the approach of a space ship and possibly has been serving for this purpose for a long time. We know that the pyramid had been painted in various colours, which could have been metallized to increase the reflectivity to laser or radar beams.

We have not yet talked about the next largest pyramid at Giza, the Pyramid of Kephren which is a true wonder of geometry and mathematics. It is built in proportions of 3:4:5 in strict adherence to the sacred triangle and the theorem of Pythagoras. The cubit which was used to lay out this pyramid's dimensions is seven-sixths of the ordinary cubit because by that time Lower Egypt had been annexed to Upper Egypt and the length of the kingdom had grown to seven-sixths of its previous size.

In reality, the architects who built the Pyramid of Kephren used another simple standard - five-thirds of the royal Egyptian cubit, that is, seven-eights of a modern metre, and this is one of the most direct correlations that I have found between the ancient measurements and the metric system. (Such is also the ancient Mycenaean 18-foot standard, that equals exactly 5 m.). To keep these measures separated, let's call the Kephren unit the 'Kephren yard' as opposed to the 'Cheops cubit' that was the basic measure for the Great Pyramid.

The perimeter of the base for the Kephren Pypramid is then 984 yards, or 861 m; half side of the base itself 123 yards, or 107.625 m; the pyramid height 164 yards, or 143.5 m; and the apothem 205 yards, or 179,375 m. Each of the last three dimensions can be divided by 41 to give us proportions of 3:4:5. The base area and the volume of the Kephren Pyramid are both 87 per cent of those of the Cheops Pyramid, so that pyramid is not so small after all.

The smallest pyramid at Giza is the Pyramid of Mykerinos, the son of Cheops who was the successor of his uncle Kephren. This pyramid is about 72 m high and has a base side length of 108 m. At first glance it seems that it was built with a 30 cm foot, but precise measurements show that the unit used was the foot of 0.301845 m - a unit of length that could be more than 10,000 years old and was

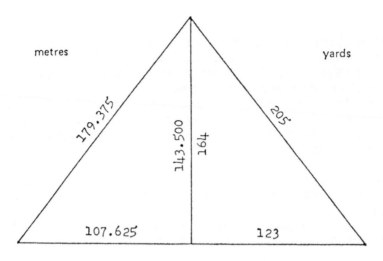

metres   yards

179.375   143.500   164   205

107.625   123

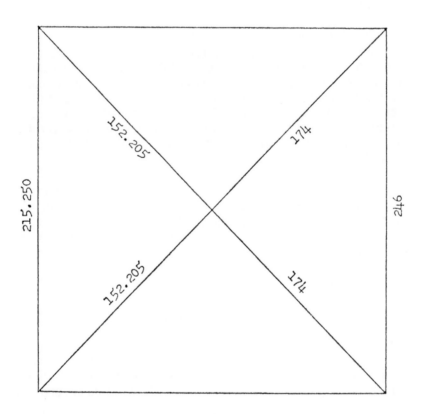

215.250   152.205   174   246

152.205   174

68

used also in the valley of the Indus River in Pakistan. Measured with that foot, the Mykerinos Pyramid also corresponds exactly to the sacred triangle proportions and is about 22 per cent in surface and 11 per cent in volume of the Great Pyramid.

Why did Mykerinos build such a modest pyramid? Legends tell us that he wanted to be the 'king of the people' and was disgusted with the luxury and cruelty of both his father and his uncle. To show the difference, he chose a small foot as standard for his monument instead of the royal cubit and picked a unit of length that was very ancient and half-forgotten. Mykerinos died very young after a reign of only eighteen years and it was probably his son Shepseskaf who finished the pyramid. The lower part is clad in red granite, and since the outer covering of pyramids was always done starting from the top while all the working ramps and scaffoldings were still in place, the bottom was the last part added to the Pyramid of Mykerinos, after his death.

Both the Kephren and Mykerinos pyramids are so perfect in their simple mathematical proportions that nobody seemed to pay much attention to them until one of the world's most prominent nuclear physicists, the 1968 Nobel prize winner Professor Luis W. Alvarez, of Berkeley, California, proposed to use cosmic rays to discover the hidden passages and secret chambers that everybody hoped to find in the Kephren pyramid. His plan looked very promising. Cosmic rays, discovered in 1911 by the Austrian physicist Victor Hess, would show a higher intensity if they encountered hollow passages on their way through the pyramids, and those changes would be registered by the most modern devices and analysed by computer.

Alvarez had the full cooperation of the Egyptian government. He had all the equipment he could dream of, and the archaeological frater-

opposite **Pyramid of Kephren**

Original dimensions in metres and yards

Edge: 209.185 metres; base area: 46,332 square metres; volume: 2,216,240 cubic metres

With the foundation, the volume was rounded to 2,268,000 cubic metres or 7/8 of that of the Pyramid of Cheops.
    The volumes of both pyramids were exact fractions of the volume of the Earth of $108,864 \times 10^{16}$ cubic metres.

nity was positive Alvarez would solve the secrets of the pyramids just as they had been sure carbon dating would unlock the Mayan mysteries.

A cosmic ray detector was installed in the inner chamber of the Kephren pyramid, which Alvarez had chosen because of its simpler structure. The general idea was to find the historical archives and scientific data hidden by the ancient Egyptian priests. Since cosmic rays penetrate even in the deepest mines and go through lead shields, the search was expected to be easy. The detector was turned in different directions to take two million readings of cosmic ray intensity changes throughout the pyramid, and the readings, registered on magnetic tape, were fed into a computer for analysis.

A modern computer installed in Cairo did the analyzing - and out came a lot of garbled nonsense. The cosmic rays were registered all right, but heavy interference from an unknown radiation source in the pyramid covered the cosmic rays with such great density that regular readings and interpretations were impossible. Not even the faces or edges could be distinguished and there was not a chance to find hidden chambers. It was a complete scientific failure.

All the equipment was dismantled and checked out again and again, and it worked fine everywhere except inside the Kephren pyramid, no matter how hard they tried. Nobody could explain it; and finally, after several futile attempts to remedy the situation, Professor Alvarez gave up and returned to California to do something more useful and controllable.

As impossible and improbable as it may seem, apparently the ancient Egyptians must have been capable of predicting the future and set up radiation barriers against us, impenetrable even to electronic scouting. It looks as if some space astronauts thousands of years ago had installed electromagnetic radiation sources in at least one of the pyramids or their vicinity just to prevent the electronic devices of later generations from discovering their hidden secrets.

Another possibility, of course, is that the radiations, which many persons who spent time in pyramids or even near them claim to have felt physically, are from beacons radiating signals for astronauts in space. In any case, if indeed there is radiation, it will be possible sooner or later for us to detect it and to identify its source. For me

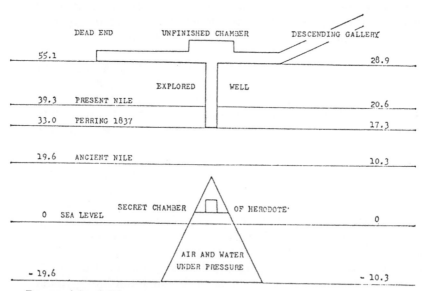

South   North

cubits   metres

PYRAMID

113.7   59.6

NATURAL ROCK

CUBIT OF 524.148 MM

DEAD END   UNFINISHED CHAMBER   DESCENDING GALLERY

55.1   28.9

EXPLORED   WELL

39.3   PRESENT NILE   20.6

33.0   PERRING 1837   17.3

19.6   ANCIENT NILE   10.3

SECRET CHAMBER   OF HERODOTE·

0   SEA LEVEL   0

AIR AND WATER
UNDER PRESSURE

- 19.6   - 10.3

Pyramid of Cheops

Secret chamber of Herodote

The outer water level has to go up 640 metres to reduce the height of the chamber to 1/4 of its original height, with a pressure of 64 atmospheres

This drawing shows the possible location of a secret chamber under the Pyramid of Cheops, according to Herodotus and other ancient writers. If opened from the top, it would be flooded.

71

it seems only a question of time, considering the crowds of archaeologists and other scientists from all around the world exploring the pyramids.

The interest is immense just because these secrets seem to be so well guarded. The more valuable the treasure is, the better hidden it should be. Some believe these treasures will be a fortune in gold and diamonds, but it seems much more probable that what will be found some day will be hieroglyphs inscribed on gold plates containing the whole history of man, including the true secrets of our terrestrial or astral past. And if that is so, the scientific and historical value of the records will far surpass that of the metal they are written on, even if the plates were made out of platinum.

In the museum of Father Crespi in Cuenca, Ecuador, visitors can see a heavy, solid-gold plate covered with hieroglyphs not yet deciphered and this plate could contain some secrets. It seems that similar plates are still hidden in caves around Cuenca, but it is difficult to obtain reliable information about this treasure and may be better not to talk about it before seeing it.

Legends tell us that when the Spaniards invaded their land, the Aztecs hid all their precious artifacts in caves and, as the story goes, the most valuable treasure consisted of fifty-two solid gold tablets engraved with all the history and science of the Aztec culture. It would be surprising if the Egyptians, whose land was invaded so many times by Assyrians, Greeks, Romans, and Arabs, would not have done a good job hiding their most precious treasures. Herodotus, the father of history himself, claimed that the Egyptian priests of Sais, in Lower Egypt, told him of a secret chamber lower than the level of the Nile River that would flood automatically if intruders tried to gain access to it.

In 1837 a British civil engineer, John Perring, dug down deep inside the Great Pyramid into hard rock to find the hidden chamber, but his digging was not deep enough and he found nothing. If a hidden room exists, it could have very interesting contents. Among other items, it could conceivably hide the resting place of the very first pharaoh of celestial origin and also, no doubt, a freeze generator and an electromagnetic radiation source of some kind, all probably powered by changing water levels of the Nile, the cause of which for the Egyptians was the star Sothis, their name for Sirius.

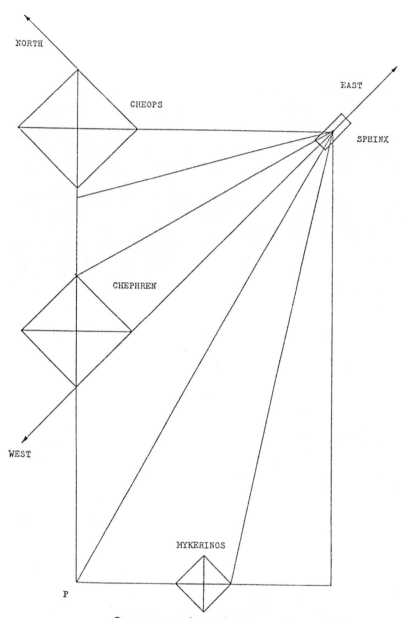

NORTH

CHEOPS

EAST

SPHINX

CHEPHREN

WEST

MYKERINOS

P

Geometry of the Sphinx and pyramids showing the possible position of an underground temple

Point *P* could be the location of an underground temple containing the astronomical and mathematical secrets of the ancient Egyptians or their ancestors.

73

As we saw from the experiences of Alvarez, some radiation source exists under the Pyramid of Kephren and it is very probable that the hidden chamber of the priests is no figment of imagination. An indication in favour of this suspicion is the fact that no historical, scientific, or astrological documents of the ancient Egyptian priests have ever been found, even though the search goes on with the full approval of the Egyptian government, which is eager to have more of the country's glorious past discovered and revealed to the world.

Of course, modern technology plays the most important part in these archaeological explorations. Infrared photography by plane and satellite has revealed hundreds of ancient sites buried for millennia in desert sand. One single infrared photograph taken during one of the first Apollo space missions in the 1960s uncovered more than one thousand towns, villages, canals, and highways under the desert. What can be glimpsed from space is merely the tip of the iceberg, but we can be sure that with our modern technical means much more will be discovered very soon. The methods of search are developing fast and successfully.

Meanwhile we can discover a few things just by contemplation and reflection. When I was in Egypt studying the alignment of different monuments, I was struck by the different angle of each addition to buildings that had been made over long periods of time. Thus the temple at Karnak, adjacent to Luxor, larger than the cathedrals of Milan, Rome, & Paris together, has been elongated on three occasions with new sections. The change in the longitudinal axis between the first and the last added sections is 15°. And it's not hard to determine why.

We know that, unlike many other calendars, the Egyptian calendar was not based on movements of the Sun, the Moon, or even the planets Jupiter and Saturn, but on apparent motions of the star Sirius. This celestial reference point moves by 1° every 72 years, so that 15° correspond to 1,080 years, or 3 times 360. That tells us that the temple at Karnak was realigned with the star Sirius once every 360 years, so that the priests could maintain their line of vision on certain stars or constellations on certain days of the solar year.

One thousand and eighty years is one-tenth of the great year of the Babylonians and the Hindus, and the 108-year cycle of the Rosicrucians is one-hundredth of the 10,800-year Great Cycle. This international fraternity, devoted to the application of religious mysticism to modern life, alternates its secret activities with public action every 108 years. So it was secret from 1807 until 1915 and will close its present public period in 2023.

To come back to the hidden treasures of the pharaohs, let's examine the map of Giza, a western suburb of Cairo, where the three pyramids and the Sphinx are situated. The diagonals of the Cheops and Kephren pyramids both run on the same axis northeast to southwest, and one of the diagonals of the Mykerinos Pyramid cuts the alignment of the other two pyramids at a given point P. When we observe now the geometrical centre of the Sphinx, we find that it can be aligned with the southern face of the Kephren Pyramid, which has its special significance.

More importantly, however, another alignment at an angle of 15° with the central axis of the Sphinx cuts the extensions of the diagonals of all the three pyramids at the same point P that we found above. It could be a coincidence, but if I were looking for the lost treasures of ancient Egypt, P is the spot where I would start digging first.

Inside of the Cheops pyramid, a team of French scientists has recently done some research with gravity-sensitive equipment to find new chambers in the pyramid. Another Japanese team has done the same thing with very high frequency radiations which can penetrate the walls. And strangely enough, both teams have detected the same spots where there could be empty chambers behind the walls, so there is still some hope after all.

THE MALTESE CROSS

Ethnologists consider the Aegean Sea, between Greece, the Island of Crete, and Turkey to be the cradle of our Western civilization that started 4,000 years ago as the Cretan and Mycenaean cultures. Everybody knows that. But few are aware that 5,000 years before Crete and Mycenae prospered, civilized people lived in small villages and towns of Anatolia in Turkey and places like Dorak in the northern part of Anatolia, which were famous before Troy was built. The tools and weapons of these people were made of obsidian, a black volcanic glass that they also polished into mirrors. Cattle were raised and cereals grown there 9,000 years ago.

How could the inhabitants of this region become civilized so early? We can find the answer if we are willing to accept the discovery that these early humans used even more surprising knowledge than animal husbandry and agriculture, namely, astronomy and mathematics.

In the centre of the Aegean Sea exists a small island by the name of Delos. It has always been considered the most sacred place of ancient Greece, even though no one seemed to know why, of all places, Delos should be so sacred. It was simply an accepted belief apparently carried over from a past unknown. To me it seems there can be only one logical explanation for this belief. Delos is the geometric centre of a true design of the gods - the Maltese cross of majestic proportions that extends over hundreds of miles over the Aegean Sea, Greece, and Turkey.

To show that this gigantic geometric figure is not the figment of imagination and no science-fiction invention, please follow me in tracing this cross with a compass and a straight-edge over a good map of the Aegean Sea. Let's put the sharp point of one compass arm in the middle of Delos and measure a radius of 1.500 ancient Egyptian stadia, or 270 km, and run the trace arm of the compass full circle. We will have passed in succession through Cape Matapan and Delphi in Greece; the island of Psathura in the Northern Sporades; Antandrus and Sardis in Anatolia; Camirus on Rhodes; and Akra and Araden on Crete.

Now let's trace a smaller circle with Delos still in the centre. A radius of 1,000 Egyptian stadia, or 180 km, will give a ring that connects Hermione in Greece; a high bank between the islands of Lesbos and Skyros; Didyma in Anatolia; and a point now submerged north of the Dia Island. Thus, if we include Delos, we have *thirteen geographic sites that have always been sacred places marked by temple ruins* constructed over even more ancient ruins from time immemorial. Thirteen has always been a magic number for astrological reasons. All of the places that we have found tracing the circles around Delos are not on firm land; but we must remember that in the past, the Mediterranean had a much lower water level. At any rate, these sites were not chosen by chance, as our next step of tracing on the map will prove.

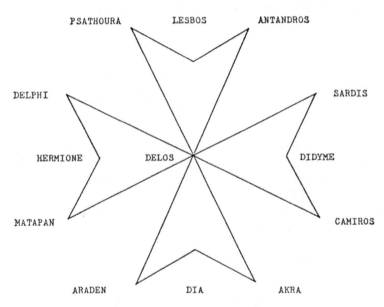

The Maltese cross of the Aegean Sea

0	90	180	270	360	450	540	kilometres
0	500	1000	1500	2000	2500	300	stadia

A beautiful Maltese cross, centred on the island of Delos and 540 kilometres wide, can be obtained by tracing lines between thirteen famous Greek temples around the Aegean Sea, but ancient Greeks did not know it. Was that cross traced by astronauts from outer space several thousand years ago ?

78

When we connect all of the sites with straight lines going from point to point in the following order: Delos, Matapan, Hermione, Delphi, Delos, Psathoura, Lesbos, Antandros, Delos, Sardis, Didyme, Camiros, Delos, Akra, Dia, Araden, and Delos, we have drawn a magnificent geometrical figure known as the 'Maltese cross', a sacred pagan sign since antiquity as well as the sign of the Crusaders who fought to liberate Jerusalem from the Infidels. Indeed, the designs of the Lord are beyond human comprehension!

What interests us now is how and why such a gigantic pattern was marked on the Aegean and surrounding lands. I do not believe that even today's land surveyors could so precisely mark such a gigantic figure *of over 335 miles* jumping from island to island and stretching over sea and mountains. Except from high up in the air, this Maltese cross would not be visible. To measure and mark all of the salient points, two very modern tools of mapping are an absolute necessity. First, a synchronous satellite orbiting at the Delos latitude of 37° 23' with a space velocity of l,328 kmph. Then, to keep that satellite stationary over Delos, one of our newest devices that was perfected only a short time ago - a navigation and distance-measuring airborne radar with metallic reflectors installed at distances of l80 and 270 km around the two circles.

The Maltese cross of the Aegean must have been constructed by just such means or with other much better devices still unknown to mankind. The ancient Greeks did not know about its existence; and they had no knowledge of astronomy or geometry until the Egyptians gave them the basics of these sciences. To find out for what purpose and to whose benefit this geometrical marking was set up, we have to continue our logical deductions and look back many, many thousands of years.

The geometric figures of Nasca in Peru that have been described in dozens of books are not so unique. Straight lines, triangles, and trapezoids have been discovered by aerial photography in many other places around the world. These designs cannot be recognized while your feet are on the ground. Some, like the Maltese cross of the Aegean Sea, can be perceived only on good maps. And all of these baffling markings have one thing in common - they have been measured and laid out in stadia of 600 ft, or l80 m, the same as in Mayan and Egyptian measurements. These stadia and the feet and cubits that were derived from them are the very oldest prehistoric standards of measurement.

The Maltese cross presents a very curious characteristic. When the eight outer points are set on a circle, the eight radii divide it in sections of 3/28 and 4/28 of the circle. That could have been just a whim of the creators of this geometric figure, but a closer look reveals some hidden meaning. In ancient cultures, the circle has been divided into 5, 6, and 7 parts, in 8, l2, and 360 sectors. The Arabs seem to have used 11 and 44 parts, but as far as we know no one in classical antiquity divided a circle into 28 sectors.

However, if we cross the Alantic and go to the Mayas, Incas, or even the Wyoming Indians, we find this division. The Medicine Wheel of Wyoming was divided into 28 equal parts, and the temple of Tiahuanaco in Bolivia was divided into 28 sectors by 29 columns. Also the cubit of Cuenca, in Ecuador, has 7 hands of 4 fingers each, or a total of 28 fingers; because the gods of that time had only 4 fingers on each hand as many sculptures and drawings show it. Twice twenty-eight is 56, and such is the number of hieroglyphs on the solid gold plate of Cuenca. Note also that megalithic Stonehenge, in Wiltshire, England, has 56 Aubrey holes. In the classical antique world only the royal cubit of the Egyptians was divisible into 7 hands of 4 fingers each, and that brings us to the possible conclusion that the Egyptians, as well as the creators of Stonehenge and the Maltese cross, had a connection or a common origin with the civilizations of Cuenca, Tiahuanaco, and Wyoming.

There are ancient Greek temples and cities that have been submerged by the Mediterranean. Today no one has a right to doubt that reality. Aerial photography has rediscovered what old Aegean fishermen found thousands of years ago - sunken temples, villages, and streets. Just outside of the small port of Halieis, between Mycenae and Tiryns, there reposes under many feet of water a former temple of Zeus built in 780 B.C. Just like the Karnak temple near Luxor, it was rebuilt several times, with new additions reoriented at angles up to 40° from the origin, representing a time span of 2,880 years, or l0 times 288 years, the Tiahuanaco number.

That means the oldest part of this temple was constructed 5,600 years ago. The building at Halieis is constructed with the Mycenean foot of 0.277 m, which for all practical purposes equals the Celtic foot of 0.276 m. This same measure was employed in the megalithic sites of England, France, and Spain, which according to the latest estimates date back 10,000 years or more, preceding the ziggurats of Mesopotamia and the Egyptian pyramids.

All of the legends of Mediterranean people mention the cataclysmic variations in the level of the sea and the eruption of a volcano on the island of Thera, in 1521 BC, or 3,500 years ago. The eruption and the following tidal waves destroyed the Minoan civilization. Many islands around Crete disappeared under water and the bottom of the sea caved in. The conquest of the Aegean Islands by Mycenaeans from Greece followed. But before this catastrophe, about 12,000 years ago, there was the really big one - the flooding of the Gibraltar Strait by the Atlantic Ocean, and the sudden rise of the Mediterranean Sea level by at least 200 m, or 600 ft.

Modern calculations have been made to see what would happen to the Mediterranean if the Strait of Gibraltar were dammed up. All of the rivers that bring fresh water to the Mediterranean could not equal the volume of water evaporated by the heat of the Sun. The sea level would descend rather rapidly, reducing the evaporation area and finally settling at a point of equilibrium where the water flowing in from the rivers would equal the amount evaporating. This new level would be about 600 ft. below the present level. The past would return. The islands of the Aegean Sea would be much larger and all thirteen points of the Maltese cross would be visible.

When the isthmus of Gibraltar gave way to the pressure of the Atlantic, because some cosmic event caused the northern polar ice cap to melt and raised the level of the oceans, all of the coastal lines of Greece and its islands were submerged. Whole civilizations disappeared. A few ignorant shepherds high in the mountains survived and carried over to future generations legends of this deluge.

But all was not lost. The arid mountains were now closer to the sea and the climate changed. With more frequent rains, agriculture prospered and domestic animals grew fatter. This may well have been the time of Paradise on Earth, as the Hebrew legends recall it. It may have been the period chosen by the Bible as the starting point for the cultural evolution of man by simply ignoring all previous civilizations. Most certainly what the Bible calls the Garden of Eden is the golden age of Mediterranean legend.

Legends are usually not simple inventions. Most of them are based on historical facts, precisely dated, sometimes in very esoteric terms. The legend of Hercules, the strong and brave Greek hero who won immortality by performing the twelve heroic labours demanded by Hera, is a good example. In this tale of antiquity, we find the lion of Nemea, the hydra of Lerna, the pillars of Hercules, and the bull of Crete. Translating these into the signs of the zodiac, we have Leo, Cancer, Gemini, and Taurus. For the astrologers of the Mediter-ranean basin, the cycle of precession of the equinoxes, a revolution of the Earth's axis around the pole of the ecliptic, was 25,920 years divided into twelve periods of 2,160 years each.

Until our modern astrologers finally agree where we are at the present time on the zodiac, we can assume that the era of the Fishes started on 21 March in the first year after Christ. In that case, the zodiacal era of Leo started in 10,800 BC; that of Cancer in 8,640 BC; that of Gemini in 6,480 BC; that of Taurus in 4,320 BC; and that of Aries (or the Golden Fleece) in 2,160 BC, ending at the start of the present era of Pisces. Consequently, we can assume that the Her-cules legends indicate that the collapse of the land between the promontories at Ceuta in Africa and Gibraltar in Europe happened about 12,000 years ago, and that it took nearly 6,000 years for the floodwaters to settle at the present level.

It is not necessary, however, to go to Greece or South America to find geometric designs and alignments of mysterious origin. In England, surveyors long ago found that nearly all megalithic monu-ments repose on lines of magnetic or telluric flux, or ley lines, as the English call these pathways. These ley lines, when photographed from high altitude, show up quite clearly as they can be detected by lusher vegetation and electromagnetic radiations interfering with radiowaves. Also exposures on photographic film over these ley lines tend to get fogged by some radiation. Like avenues converg-ing in Paris at the Arc de Triomphe, so these magnetic boulevards intersect at important megalithic monuments of great fame and past glory. And flying saucers frequently follow these lines in their flights.

Four of these lines run parallel from east to west through England, France, and Spain at 42°, 45°, 48°, and 51° north latitude and at a distance of 333 km from each other, so that the most southern line is separated from the most northern by exactly 1,000 km. That seems

82

surprising since, according to established science, the metric system was not known to prehistoric man. But on the English ley line at 51°, we find such sites as Glastonbury, Stonehenge, Avebury, and Canterbury. The line in France at 48° intersects Chartres, Domremy, Sainte-Odile, and other sites that are well known for ancient cathedrals and remarkable monuments.

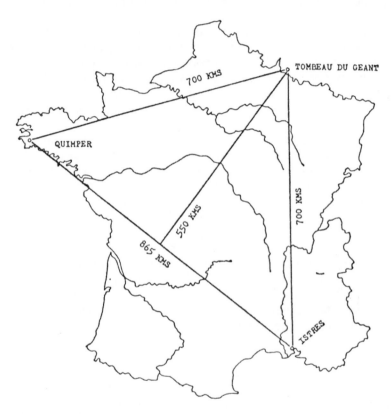

The triangle of France

A huge triangle, proportional to the dimensions of the Great Pyramid of Cheops but 14 million times larger, can be traced within the borders of France. Each side of the triangle is lined up with prehistoric and historic monuments, but the French did not know it. Could it also have been traced by ancient astronauts like the Maltese cross of the Aegean Sea?

83

The 45° line runs through Les Eyzies, Lascaux, and Le Puy - a region that is considered one of the most valuable repositories of prehistoric sites anywhere in the world. The caves of Lascaux and Les Eyzies are well known, but it is possible that still much more will be discovered there in the future. The 42° line in Spain starts near Noya on the Atlantic Ocean, where the refugees of sunken Atlantis probably came to land, and runs through Santiago de Compostela, Burgos, Logrono, and Roncesvalles - all historic sites of ancient fame.

In France, too, several other mysterious lines exist that act just like their counterparts in England and are followed by flying saucers in flight. These lines do not form geometric figures like the Maltese cross in the Aegean, nor do they show up like the designs in Nasca, Peru; but they are most interesting even though no one has discovered exactly what they represent, since they form a huge triangle.

About 15 km north of Sedan, there stands a megalithic monument called the Giant's Grave. When a line is traced on a map from this monument straight south for 700 km until it reaches Istres in Provence, it goes through an unbelievable number of historical sites, from dolmens and menhirs of prehistoric times to cloisters and castles of the Middle Ages. Another such line dotted with megaliths drawn 76° of the Giant's Grave-Istres line about 700 km stops in Quimper, on the coast of Brittany. When the two lines are connected by a third to form a triangle, that line goes through the most concentrated assembly of dolmens, menhirs, and cromlechs in the world - the region of Carnac in Brittany. Is there a connection with Karnak, in Egypt? The names sound alike; but as far as I know, nobody yet has found the common denominator.

Other surprises keep piling up when we continue to analyze this gigantic triangle of France. If a fourth line is drawn from the Giant's Grave to the centre of the base between Provence and Brittany, it is just as rich in ruins of antiquity as the two sides of the triangle. The triangle has now an apex of 76°, two side angles of 52° each, two sides of 700 km, a base of 865 km, and a height of 550 km. Hold on to your hats - *you have the exact same proportions and angles as the Great Pyramid of Cheops!* The 'triangle of France' is exactly 14 million times bigger than the area of the cross section of the Cheops Pyramid. The surface of this triangle is 237,000 sq. km, and the area of the circle into which the Aegean Maltese cross could be placed is 237,000 sq. km, which is the same. Can you believe that we have here again a simple *coincidence*?

The triangle of France is not the only example having dimensions that are proportional to those of the Great Pyramid. The tiny pyramid of Falicon on a mountain above Nice, built in I260 by Crusaders who had returned from Jerusalem, is exactly l/288 the scale of Cheops. This number, 288, is known to us from the Temple of Kalasasaya in Tiahuanaco and its calendar year of 288 days. Why the Crusaders who built the pyramid in Falicon chose this scale of l/288 is not known, but the precise proportions with the Great Pyramid are surprising because the Crusaders on their way and back from Jerusalem never passed the original one.

Much more surprising is the study made of some of the great cathedrals in France and their mathematical structure, where again astounding similarities with this Great Pyramid of Cheops crop up. The monumental cathedral of Chartres shows the same constants and proportions as the pyramid and, above all, seems to be of much older age in its original foundations taken over from a previous pagan temple on the same site.

The standard foot of Chartres that was used to construct the cathedral was 0.3684 m. The length of a longitude degree at Chartres is 73,680 m, exactly 200,000 of these feet. The most surprising derivative of this dimension is the cubic foot of Chartres. It equals 50 litres or 50 kg of water - when there was no metric system!

The cathedral of Reims is farther north than Chartres and there the dimension of the basic foot is 0.3557 m, also proportional to the longitude degree, and the cubic foot equals 45 litres or kg of water; but this is the Russian standard unit of weight called *pood,* which so far has not been explained.

The cathedrals of France have another mystery in the pattern of their locations. If you paste over the map of France little gold stars in Abbeville, Amiens, Bayeux, Chartres, Evreux, Laon, Le Mans, Paris, Reims, and Rouen, where the most famous cathedrals stand in the middle of the cities, you have the same configuration as the stars in the constellation of Virgo. The main star in Virgo is Spica; this brilliant star has always been venerated as the goddess of fertility and

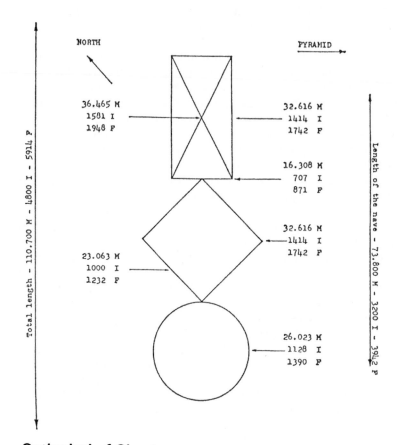

Cathedral of Chartres

Dimensions of the three tables in metres, Chartres inches, and Cheops fingers

Area of each table

5,318,789	square centimetres	or	531.8789	square metres
1,000,000	square inches	or	3906	square feet
1,517,824	square fingers	or	1936	square cubits

or 1/100 of the base area of the Pyramid of Cheops

The floor plan of the Chartres cathedral is based on three tables, a round one, a square one, and a rectangular one. Each of these tables has exactly the same area, which is one hundredth of that of the Great Pyramid of Cheops. The area of each table is 531.88 square metres while that of the Great Pyramid is 53,188 square metres. A maternity. In the group of cathedrals, Spica is Reims. Again, I have difficulty dismissing this symbolism as an accident or *coincidence*, since religion has always been the twin sister of astrology.

But I would like to come back once more to the giant triangles. The map of Egypt shows two of them so far never noticed. The vertical axis of Lower Egypt is the line drawn from Bedet to Kubra to Giza while the horizontal axis goes through Sais to Kubra and Mendes. If we now construct the northern triangle Sais to Bedet to Mendes, we have exact distances of 400, 300, and 300 stadia of 180 m. The southern triangle Sais to Giza to Mendes measures 400, 650, and 650 stadia.

Now let's jump to the American continents and measure the distances between three religious centres of the ancient Mayas - Copan, La Venta, and Chichen Itza. Each of the sides of this triangle is 3,600 Mayan stadia of 180 m each. *Yes, the same 180 m as that of the Egyptian stadia!* This cannot be a coincidence. The distances on another Mayan pattern - a trapeze between four religious centres, Teotihuacan, Chichen Itza, La Muralla, and Monte Alban - are 2,000, 4,000, 6,000 stadia of 180 m each. But the biggest of the figures, the South American triangle between Nasca, Tiahuanaco, and the caves of Cuenca, measures 3,750, 7,500, and 10,000 Tiahuanaco stadia of 178 m adjusted to the local latitude and therefore shorter than the previous by less than two metres.

The most logical explanation for these triangles is that they were navigational patterns for spaceship landings, very similar to the re-entry corridors we calculate today for our space missions. For me, who has seen many such patterns drawn theoretically in the Pacific for our Apollo missions, the analogy is striking.

---

special Chartres inch of 23.0625 millimetres, representing one ten-thousandth of the side of the pyramid, was used for the construction but the Church did not know it. Who did actually design the Chartres cathedral in 1194 and build it in twenty-six years according to the size of the Great Pyramid?

And there are other reasons why such speculation is not at all impossible. *First, we have all the legends in folklore and religious records from around the world attesting to the theory. Then we have paintings, engravings, and sculptures showing the celestial visitors descending in flaming chariots that look just like retro-rockets firing; there are even bronze figurines of astronauts.*

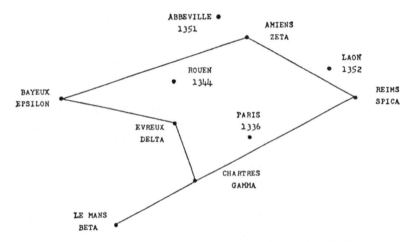

The Virgo constellation and French cathedrals

The relative positions of the stars are the same as those of the cathedrals

The relative positions of the ten major cathedrals in France are the same as those of ten stars in the Virgo constellation, over a distance of 300 kilometres, although there were no maps in France 800 years ago. Did ancient astronauts determine the locations of these sites long before the construction of the cathedrals? Again, the Church did not know that.

Now, some legends indicate that space visitors came from the planet Venus. That too, is not impossible. Much of the information we have today points in that direction. First Venus is unique among planets in that it spins clockwise. Mercury, Earth, Mars, Jupiter, Saturn, and the rest spin counter-clockwise, which makes scientists think of Venus as an alien who drifted from outer space into our solar system and was captured by the gravitational field of our Sun. On its way to solar orbit it nearly brushed our Earth; and in doing so, both Venus and Earth synchronized their rotation and revolution periods.

The Mayas had discovered that 2,920 days represents 5 synodic periods and 13 sidereal periods of Venus, as well as 8 sidereal periods of the Earth. Venus has the same face turned to Earth every time they line up after 584 days. In my opinion, that could be a proof that Venus almost got captured by our planet, but its velocity and mass were too great, so that eventually it settled into a closer and faster orbit around the Sun.

There was, however, a moment when the Venusians could have landed on Earth as easily as we landed on the Moon. And that may have been when the first missions established markers and glide patterns in suitable locations like the plains of Nasca, the highlands of Tiahuanaco, and the Mexican jungle. When, after a while, the new arrivals got accustomed to our air and water, they showed themselves to the local inhabitants, who promptly promoted them to the rank of gods under many different names like Kukulcan, Viracocha, Orejona, Taaroa, Maui, and even Elohim, the Hebrew name of the messengers of God in our Bible.

The question is *when did this happen?* Two dates are possible - the first great flood of 12,000 years ago and the last inundation of our Earth about 6,000 years ago. As far as I know, there are no records about the existence of Venus in our skies that would be older than 6,000 years. However, I am skeptical about this date, because there are still enormous quantities of manuscripts and books of very old age that have not been read or translated or even discovered; and any day now we could find a proof that 12,000 years ago Venus entered our skies like a gigantic comet and created cataclysms of a fantastic scale all over the world.

What conclusions are possible from the facts presented in this chapter? First, the biblical idea that our culture started only 6,000 years ago in the Middle East is false. Very intelligent and capable humans lived in Tiahuanaco, in Bolivia, where the ruins are 30,000 years old. The caves of Cuenca (Ecuador), Lascaux (France), and Altamira (Spain) must have at least 20,000 years to look back on. The Maltese cross with its temples is probably 12,000 years old, older than the agricultural centres of Dorak and Hacilar in Anatolia. The lost continent of Atlantis sank into the deep in the year 9564 BC if we want to believe the Tibetans, or it happened 11,500 years ago according to the Egyptian priests who told it to Solon, one of whose descendants told it to Plato.

For very good reasons, ethnologists have concluded that the earthlings of 30,000 years ago were not highly developed. But we have seen that around that time, *astounding knowledge was demonstrated on several continents, always in the same basic style.* This can make sense only if we are willing to accept the theory of visiting space gods, that it was astronauts who caused the great change by insemination and selective mutation, thus creating a new hybrid human race adapted to the climate and living conditions on Earth while retaining at least some of the high intelligence and knowledge of the original visitors.

THE RHODES
CALCULATOR

Most sensational discoveries happen by chance, perhaps because of what we may call the *benevolent intervention of the gods*, as long as there is no better explanation for it. One such haphazard revelation, which simultaneously revolutionized archaeology and the history of science and technology, occurred in October 1900, without anyone noticing it.

It was the finding by Aegean sponge divers of the Rhodes calculator, or the computer of Antikythera, in an ancient sunken Roman ship. It changed all of our ideas about the history of science. It also started a new science - underwater archaeology. Since I was one of the very first addicts of the aqualung and deep-sea diving from the times when all equipment was handmade by the dedicated few themselves, let me tell you about this discovery in a little more detail.

On that day in October of 1900 a Greek tartan, a large, single-masted Mediterranean ship with a large lateen sail, returning from a diving expedition along the African coast where it had been gathering sponges, ran into a stiff southwester and had to look for a harbour to let the gale blow over. It was a typical Greek sponge divers' rig. Captain Demetrios Condos, a seasoned veteran of sponge diving, knew that the straits between the islands of Crete and Antikythera was one of the worst places to be in a storm. So he pulled fast into the port of Potamos at the nothern tip of Antikythera island. There, guarded by the enormous bulk of the Glyphalda Cape he found calm water.

The Greeks are charming people whom I love very much; but when they have nothing else to do, they can't stop drinking, gambling, and fighting. The trouble is that they seem to have very little to do, far too often. That is exactly what happened to Condos and his crew of twelve. The storm lasted for days; and to keep both his tartan and his diving boat where the air pump and the diving suits were kept from being turned into shambles by his wine-loving crew, Condos sent all of them on a wild goose chase - to look for sponges along

91

the shelf of Cape Glyphalda. He could not care less whether they found sponges or not. He had to keep them occupied.

In the grey of the early morning, while the gale was still blowing in the open sea, the diving boat left the tartan in the port of Potamos and was rowed to Pinakakia, where the water was calm and clear and good for diving. Captain Condos looked through his glass-bottom pail set in the water and could see down about thirty fathoms to a protruding ledge. Thirty fathoms is about 180 feet, which is the outer limit for a diver in an air-pump suit, but Condos' divers were probably among the world's best at that time and he thought he would try his luck and keep his men busy by sending them down one after another at five-minute intervals. Six divers could explore the bottom for half an hour while the other six would man the oars and the air pump.

Diving is very dangerous business and Condos' men knew it. The six divers stood assembled in the bow of the diving boat, smoking one cigarette after another to calm down hunger pains. Nobody had eaten breakfast because food in the stomach increases the chance of contracting cramps, the terror of all divers. One after another they flipped their cigarettes into the water, soaped their wrists with black soap so that the diving-suit cuffs would close airtight. With the help of the youngest boy on the boat, an apprentice seaman, they put on their cumbersome diving equipment. When the deck boy had rinsed out each helmet with sea water and cleansed the visor glass with a special sponge to prevent fogging, the casque was screwed on to the diver's suit, and after some weights were added to his breastplate and the soles of his boots, the diver at the end of the air tube was on his way to the deep.

The lead weights which pulled them down were good old historic metal, mostly from Roman foundries. All Roman ships used wooden anchors, some as many as six, with lead crossbars, and the standard Roman galley had as much as two or three tons of lead. Mediterranean fisherman and divers had divested the sunken wrecks long ago of every scrap of metal to build their own boats and anchors, and the Condos vessel was no exception.

The historic moment started when the second in command on the boat, Mercurio, gave order to one of the oldest divers, Elias Stadiatis, to descend into the water. The deck boy called out loud the air-pump manometer readings; and when the needle indicated 15 fathoms, a sand hourglass was turned over to time the descent for another full minute. When sand ran out, the depth of the shelf was reached and the pump pressure indicated a depth of 30 fathoms - the limit at which a diver can work for five minutes. But Stadiatis did not stay down his allocated time. A few moments after reaching the bottom, he yanked the descent cord in panic and started his ascent.

Condos and Mercurio both ran to help get him out because no old, experienced diver would do such a thing unless there was real danger or emergency. When Stadiatis' face appeared through the visor of the helmet he looked like a corpse, pale and with bulging eyes. The metal casque came off and Stadiatis could barely speak. He stammered something about naked women and horses but was otherwise incoherent. He mentioned the Holy Virgin in the same breath and made no sense.

Finally Condos got angry and ordered him to calm down and tell exactly what had happened. Stadiatis did his best, but that wasn't much. He insisted that many horses, naked women, and women in flowing robes were on the bottom and that most of the pretty faces were pockmarked. Captain Condos was a calm and practical man and would not buy this fool's story. So he put on his own diving suit and went down himself. Mercurio was holding the descent line, and after a minute of descent he felt one strong pull - the signal to slacken the cable and that everything was all right.

The captain stayed down for only a few minutes, not using up all of his time. When his helmet was unscrewed he looked very satisfied, even smug, but did not say a word to anybody. He simply ordered his cable basket pulled up. In it the astonished crew saw a green metallic human hand, hollow and full of sand. Then Condos let loose his best salty sea language and called all of his crew, and Stadiatis especially, the dumbest idiots who ever sailed the Mediterranean. He told them that down under there was a whole ship full of stone and bronze statues! A sunken treasure.

Up to this point the history of this event is clear and simple, but not so, further on. The official version of the authorities and the stories of the crew are quite different. To understand this discrepancy, we have to talk a little about the Greek sponge divers, particularly from the Aegean. First of all, they are great divers, who can stand and

93

survive water pressure down to 180 feet for several minutes. Anything of value that could be retrieved from such depth is their prey. Flooded houses and sunken galleys have been mines of gold, silver, copper, bronze, and lead. As I mentioned before, a Roman galley usually had as many as six big wooden anchors with crossbars of lead; and one single shipwreck could yield two or three tons of this valuable metal. Condos and his crew would not let their prize of naked women and horses drift away - not if these statues were made of precious metal that could be sold with no questions asked.

Condos became a rich man, for a while at least. He ordered a new, bigger ship built for himself and started smuggling arms across the Mediterranean - mostly French army rifles. He wanted to be a big businessman and went broke. His ship was sold for debts, and he had to return to the sea and dive for sponges until the cramps got him, and he became half paralyzed. He died in 1926 in the home of his daughter, who had given him his last shelter in Suez, Egypt. The gods had abandoned the man who once was so lucky.

But to return to that time in October 1900, off Antikythera: after Condos had cleared the wreck of anything valuable that he could lift out and sold it, he informed the owners of his tartan, the Lyndiakos brothers, about the wreck off Atrikythera. He also suggested that the Greek government should be informed and put in charge of the salvage operation of this historic sunken art, which was to be presented as his patriotic gift to Greece. It was done, and Condos felt great. His own home was on the Dodecanese island of Syme, at that time ruled by Turks, whom Condos hated. As you see, history does not change. The problem of the Greeks and the Turks is the same today as it was eighty years ago.

The Greek government ordered its navy to carry out the salvage of the statues in the sunken ship. It was done the military way: get things done fast no matter how. Big crane ships arrived, and the crews pushed over the coastal shelf on which the treasure ship rested, all of the big stone blocks from the deck of the galley that hindered the divers from getting at the bronze statues. Nobody noticed that the big stone blocks were huge statues turned upside down; so that the square sockets alone were visible to the officer in charge of the operation. When this mistake was finally noticed, orders were given to retrieve, without fail, everything that was on or inside the sunken ship.

94

The museum of Athens received the whole lot - the stone sculptures, the bronze figures, a heap of broken bronze heads and arms, and some lumps of indefinite shape that would be sorted out later. By the end of summer in 1901, the sunken galley was nothing but an empty hulk, 100 feet long and 40 feet wide, the standard measurements for a Roman galley of 83 BC. This wreck remained there totally abandoned for another fifty-two years, until 1953 when Captain Jacques Cousteau and his divers visited it.

Meanwhile, back in 1902, a young Greek student by the name of Valerio Stais had been sorting the broken pieces of bronze at the National Museum in Athens. His task was to find and match missing heads and arms so that the sculptures could be restored; but he noticed a calcified lump of bronze that did not fit anywhere and was not a part of a statue. While drying, the calcified mass had split in half, and what was visible looked like the insides of a big watch - gears and pinions and dials with inscriptions in ancient Greek characters and signs of the zodiac.

Valerio Stais guessed that it must be an astronomical clock of some sort or an instrument of navigation; he wrote a paper to announce this finding to the scientific world, with the result that he was declared to be a fool. The date of the sunken galley was indicated by artifacts in several places on the ship. It was without any doubt, determined to be the year 83 BC, and everybody knew that at that time there were no clocks - or any other device - made with gears. Neither were mechanical calculators constructed in ancient Greece.

To tell time, both Greeks and Romans of the last century before Christ used sun dials, water-dripping *clepsydras*, or handy sand hourglasses. Never before had anybody found or read of gear and dial mechanisms for that purpose. Besides, nobody seemed much concerned about keeping the exact time. Night and day were divided into twelve parts each and only at the spring and the autumnal equinoxes were the divisions of equal length.

Thus the conclusion of the scholars was that the mechanism found in the galley of Antrikythera simply could not have been made 2,000 years ago. It had to be a clock perhaps 200 or 300 years old, tossed overboard by the captain of a ship passing over the wreck of the ancient galley. That was an explanation acceptable to the twentieth-century scientific establishment, and for the next fifty-six years nobody had the nerve to speak about it again. To avoid controversy, the find was registered in the museum catalogue as an astrolabe. That's where things rested more or less until 1958, when a young English mathematician, Dr Derek J. de Solla Price, working at the Princeton Institute of Advanced Study, obtained a grant to study the Antikythera mechanism and later published his findings in the scientific magazines *Natural History* and *Scientific American*.

Luckily, the museum technicians had taken good care of the clock remnants. There were four main pieces, each composed of many layers of bronze gears and some smaller lumps. Some parts were missing and are probably still on the bottom of the Aegean. As he studied what was there, Price had the good idea to use radiation with different intensities and frequencies to photograph separate layers of the mechanism that could not be taken apart.

These layers were minuscule, about two millimetres thick each, and all together there were as many as thirty different gears. This method of selective photography also proved that the clock contained a differential gear - a sensational discovery indicating a very high technological achievement; since differential gears have been invented only in very recent times, to make it possible to obtain the sum or difference of two angular velocities with gears.

The differential mechanism of the Antikythera clock is of the flat type. It consists of one big crown gear, a pinion in the centre, and satellite gears between the pinion and the crown. These satellites are mounted on a rotating support that moves with an angular speed representing the difference between those of the big crown and pinion. For somebody who lived 2,000 years ago to have built this mechanism, would reallly have been a superb achievement. The size of the whole calculator must have been equal to that of a portable typewriter of today, with two dials in the back and one in the front. This front dial had two concentric bands - one with the signs of the zodiac, and the other, a moveable one, with names of each month in Greek. A pointer that was moved by the mechanism indicated the position of the Sun in the zodiac for each day of the year.

The two dials in the back seemed to indicate the phases of the Moon and the movements of the five planets known at that time - Mercury, Venus, Mars, Jupiter, and Saturn. The mechanism was set in motion by a worm gear that had to be rotated by one turn every day, probably at noon. The last information available about this calculator is that it may have had five dials - two in the front and three in the back - and that all of them were adjustable.

This discovery was revolutionary in every sense of the word. Many called the Antikythera clock a computer because the purpose of the gadget was probably to avoid tedious astronomical computations. Price himself said in a scientific meeting in Washington, that finding a thing like this computer in a Roman galley was like finding a jet plane in King Tutankhamen's tomb.

The probable builder of this astronomical calculator must have been the Greek astronomer, mathematician, and philosopher Geminus, who was the apprentice of Posidonius. The birth and death dates of Geminus are not exactly known; but his teacher, Posidonius, a philosopher of the Stoic school founded by Zeno, lived from 135 to 51 BC, and taught on the island of Rhodes.

Geminus was a near contemporary of his master in philosophy and became famous through his manuals of astronomy and mathematics. He also invented most of all known combinations of gears, the worm gear, the differential gear, the bevel gear and probably also the crank and connecting rod that transforms uniform circular motion into alternating linear movement. If there was anyone in Greece at that time who would have been able to build the calculator of Rhodes, it was Geminus. Only he could have had the idea to put together differential gears with bevel gears and astronomical dials in a single box to make a navigational computer. The complicated mechanism of more than thirty separate gears was probably put together by his pupils, since all Greek masters of that time had apprentices.

The date for which this calculator was set for the last time is the year 86 BC, as can be seen by the relative positions of the dials and pointers. The Roman galley which was transporting the statues from Rhodes to Rome probably sank near Antikythera three years later, in 83 BC.

The year 86 BC was a remarkable date. There were five conjunctions of planets in four zodiacal signs that year, an ideal time to set an astronomical calculator precisely if it was already built, or to start constructing one. So here we have another trail-blazing achievement

97

of the famous Greeks, permitting the Graecophils once more to claim that all science came from Greece.

Unfortunately not all people agree on that, and I am one who disagrees. In recent years one discovery after another has shown that all the scientific knowledge of Greeks was inherited and borrowed from the high priests of Egypt, who had obtained it thousands of years earlier from an unknown source. The calculator of Rhodes can give us some indication where this mysterious unknown source of all science was located, or at least it can indicate the direction in which we will have to look for the beginning of our civilization.

If somebody wants to construct an astronomical calculator by using intermeshing gears, the first condition is to find the number of cycles necessary to obtain an exact number of whole days. Some of these cycles are easily found but many are nearly impossible. A good example is the tropical year - also called the 'solar year' or the 'calendar year' of 365.2422 mean solar days. To fit a number of full days, we need 5,000 solar years, or 1,826,211 days! Anything less won't do.

And the sidereal year of 365.2564 days is not much better. It takes 2,500 of these years representing 913,141 days. The gears of the computer would have to be too big to be practical. But the Sothic year of the ancient Egyptians fits like a glove for a small mechanical computer. It has 365.25 days, so we need only a gear ratio of 4:1 to obtain whole numbers of days and years. Every four years of this Sirius, or Sothic, calendar will give an exact number of days. The gears are small and manageable.

This simple and practical year of the Egyptian priests makes many complicated astronomical cycles equally simple, an advantage which modern astronomers, with their ingrained traditions have so far ignored. Use of the Sothic-year cycle makes it easy to calculate all periods of revolution or conjunction, of all planets, as well as all phases of the Moon.

The second important condition for a successful construction of an astronomical calculator with gears is to find a simple relationship between the cycles in full, whole days. The Mayan calendar almost made it. So did the Sumerian calendar, which was based on the Saros cycle of eighteen tropical years. The Greeks used a calendar based on the Metonic cycle of nineteen tropical years. This system has no practical value for a gear computer either, which proves that the Greeks were not such great mathematicians after all. Whoever constructed the marvel of Antikythera was a real genius.

We are left with the ancient Egyptian calendar. It is the only one that fulfills all of the requirements, and it is the basis for the Rhodes calculator. The seemingly complicated Egyptian calendar, based on Sirius, the Sun, and also the Moon, actually works like a charm. Every four years represents exactly 1,461 days which in turn represent 49.474 synodical moon months. This last number has to be multiplied only 19 times to give a number of whole days - 27,759 - equal to 940 months, or 76 Sothic years, which is the cycle of the Rhodes calculator!

It seems to me that the mechanism found in the Roman galley was a small, reduced model of a much more complicated and refined machine that the Egyptian priests used to calculate all of the planetary movements in the solar system and more. But the calculator has not yet been found.

When men decide to make a really serious effort to explore the ground under and around the pyramids near Cairo, we will probably find it. We know that, as a rule, all the other pyramids stand on top of underground systems of passages and temples, sometimes whole subterranean villages; and it would be very surprising if the Great Pyramid of Cheops didn't follow the rule. We are bound to find those hidden chambers some day; and once we find them, we will have evidence that it was astronauts from space who elevated us to our present pedestal.

Most of the ancient civilizations used the Sothic year to calculate the ages of mankind and of the world in fantastically high numbers. The Hindus estimated man was 4.32 million years old and the Earth 4.32 billion. The Mayas arrived at far greater numbers. But the Sothic year is the basis of all great cycles known by either Mayas, Hindus, Sumerians, Egyptians, Greeks, or others that we know of. Aside from the cyclic relationships that were built in the Rhodes calculator, the Egyptians also used others, all based on Sothis-Sirius, who for them was the 'good god who makes all things green grow'.

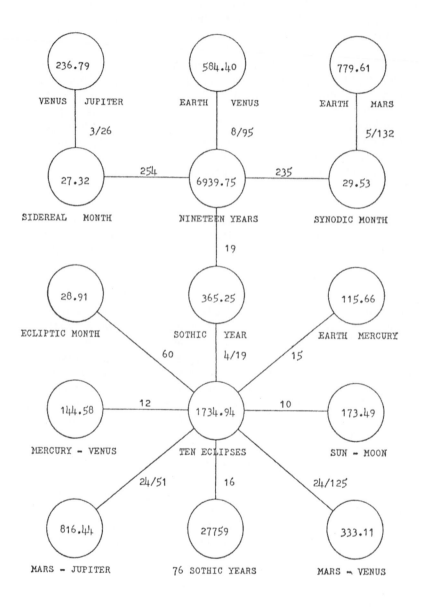

One of these regular repetitions came every 1,460 Sothic years, or 1,461 civil years of 365 days each. Then both of these years coincide with each other on 19 July, the day when the Nile starts to rise, as the Egyptians believed, by the command of the Sothis, the Dog Star. These long Sothic cycles were documented by Egyptian astronomers as having occurred on 19 July in the years 1320 BC, 2780 BC, 4240 BC, and 5700 BC. The Sothic cycles are bringing us far into the past indeed.

The Rhodes calculator and the recently popular Piri Reis maps that show the ancients knew the Antarctic continent are both copies of much older originals. Since neither bronze nor parchment are very durable materials, the survival as well as the rediscovery of these items do make one wonder if there wasn't some of what I describe as *benevolent intervention of the gods* involved in the findings. The fact is that only stone does not change over aeons. Under favourable conditions, in places like the Dead Sea region, some documents can survive a few thousand years, but not ten or twelve thousand. This is why we will never find the originals of the maps that the Turkish admiral and cartographer Reis copied in the fifteenth century and we may never see the original model of the Rhodes calculator.

Opposite: THE RHODES CALCULATOR

With Fifteen Astronomical Cycles

Egyptian lunisolar cycle of 27,759 days or 76 Sothic years.

This astronomical calculator, discovered in 1900 at the bottom of the Aegean Sea west of Crete and probably built more than 2,000 years ago, was based on a long-forgotten Egyptian cycle of 27,759 days, or 76 Sothic years of 365 1/4 days each. By means of gear trains, this cycle was divided into fifteen different astronomical cycles. The cycles indicated here are the most accurate that could be obtained with a minimum of gear trains.

However, the existence of the copies is enough to make us understand that some of man's highest achievements date back to the dawn of time and that the Rhodes calculator is a link in a chain that leads back to great civilizations of an unknown past. There is a message for humanity in this ancient machine that I cannot decipher and even makes me suspect that we are still not sufficiently developed to grasp its true meaning. This is a fact that annoys and disquiets me, and yet there are in this world some even more disturbing findings.

I am talking about recent findings in all parts of the world of perfectly machined metal parts that were buried in strata of coal or rock hundreds of feet under ground and millions of years old. Cubes, spheres, and cylinders of perfect geometrical form have been dug

up from such strata and nobody yet has been able to explain these findings without admitting the possibility that indeed our most ancient forefathers were capable of making precision gears out of thin sheets of bronze and to assemble them into clocks useful for astronomers, mankind's oldest scientists.

It is very difficult for me to respect those scientists whose minds seem permanently closed. After all, most of today's scientific equipment and techniques just did not exist a short one hundred years ago, when Paris and London academies of science thought they knew everything already and wanted to ignore every discovery that disturbed their theories. If in the last century we have achieved as much progress as we actually have, it had happened only thanks to independent, unprejudiced minds outside the academic establishment.
We were told that machines heavier than air would never fly, that the sound barrier and air friction would kill pilots and melt the planes, and that rockets would never be able to overcome Earth's gravity. Man will never walk on the Moon, said most scientists not so long ago.

Well, man did, and I was part of the team that made it possible. To tell you the truth, before the landing module from Apollo 11 landed on the Moon we were not so sure either. The monumental project needed constant changes and inventions that were not even conceived of at the start. We went along improvising and improving and making impossible things possible. Apollo was designed and built in a few short years by several thousand capable engineers. There were real geniuses among them, and they came from all nations.

We all recognized one fact - that in our native countries, be it England, France, Germany, Japan, or China, we would never have had a chance to prove our true potential. It was the free and untrammelled state of mind that made the Moon shot possible; and, naturally, the unlimited access to means and material to make every new concept or idea work. All that was attainable only in the United States and nowhere else. The gods themselves know that I am not always a proud American, as I am not every day proud of my French origin. But I am proud to have been born and educated in France and proud to be an American by adoption and profession.

I want to say in conclusion to this chapter that the freedom of the unbiased mind has to be applied also to the recognition that probably everything we invent now has been invented already, and reinvented, thousands upon thousands of years ago. Civilizations come and go, often without leaving a trace. Sometimes a remnant of the past is left behind to make us at least suspect that man was more intelligent and advanced in an earlier civilization that disappeared. The Rhodes calculator is such a remnant of the unrecognized past that miraculously escaped the destruction of a very ancient civilization.

THE KINGS OF THE SEA

Until a few years ago everyone believed that it was impossible to navigate oceans without compass, sextant, chronometer, or the sighting of land. The question of how our ancestors then managed to reach distant lands across open seas was unanswered. We know primitive compasses and sextants existed, but there were no chronometers deemed necessary to determine the longitude. The first such transportable clock movement was fabricated in France around 1525, but the first ship chronometer dates back only to 1736 when, after after eight years of hard work, John Harrison of England completed his masterpiece.

The official scientific answer to the riddle of how men could navigate was simple. We were told our forefathers never let land out of sight and navigated along the coast only. This we were taught in school and this we were supposed to believe even though it was only one of the many blunders that our learned academicians were guilty of. Another fallacy in the same category was the tale that the American continent was populated by migrants who came from Asia over the frozen Bering Strait, even though archaeological and ethnological discoveries demonstrate conclusively that men did know how to navigate tens of thousands of years ago and had no need to wait from one ice age to the next to make the crossing to Alaska. In fact, they didn't hesitate to cross the ocean on rafts or on ships.

Still, how exactly did they do it? By what means were they able to determine in open sea the two coordinates of longitude and latitude in order to know where they were and where to go? The theory that all ancient ocean crossing were accidents caused by wind or current could not be true. Too many legends report of planned voyages and of heroes who visited distant lands and returned to tell about their adventures.

When ancient Roman coins were found in Venezuela, Sumerian mining colonies discovered in Peru and Bolivia, and Hindu cotton and jute plantations traced in Mexico, I began wondering and searching again for the answer to the riddle of ancient navigation, and now I believe that I have found the answer. Instead of chronometers, they used sunset and moonrise tables that were skillfully calculated for every day of the year, in the case of long voyages, and for many years to come. Thus at anytime a navigator of a ship on open sea could determine his location by comparing the actual intervals of sunset and moonrise to those charted for the same day for his home port.

Since latitude is easily determined by an strolabe or primitive sextant, the difficult part was the determination of the exact time span between the moments when the Sun disappeared and the Moon showed up. It was done by a battery of hourglasses set to measure a fraction of a minute. Let me explain with an example from our recent past what the sunset-moonrise timing has to do with the geographic longitude that has to be found.

Astronomical phenomena of short duration, like an eclipse, are never seen at the same time at different points of the globe. So, for instance, during the solar eclipse of 30 June, 1973, that lasted 7 minutes 3 seconds, the shadow of the Moon was running eastward over our Earth in a narrow band 240 km wide at a speed of 2,150 km per hour.

In order to observe the eclipse a little longer, seven astronomers from England, France, Scotland, and the United States used a supersonic Concorde equipped with all necessary instruments to fly east at an altitude of 17,000 m (56,000 ft.) so they could watch the eclipse for 84 minutes. To enable them to do this, the plane naturally had to move with the same speed as the shadow of the eclipse - 2,150 kmph - which it did easily. This eclipse came exactly nineteen years after the mysterious one of 30 June, 1954, that we will discuss later on in this book.

The time of totality of the June 1973 eclipse varied one full minute for every 36 km at the same latitude. If the eclipse took place over point A at noon, seeing it in point B a full hour later would mean that the distance east from A to B, if both of these points are on the same latitude, was exactly 2,160, or 60 times 36 kilometres. Now, eclipses are not a daily occurrence, so our ancestors had to find some other phenomenon of short duration that could be timed by simple means every day. Sunset and moonrise made possible for them to use the principle just explained and find more or less precisely how far away they had moved since they had left home port or had passed some

106

marker that was calculated for sunset and moonrise in their tables. Such astronomical tabulations written in cuneiform script have been found by the thousands on clay tablets in archaeological excavations in Mesopotamia.

With the help of these timetables, ancient navigators could easily determine their longitude by using every 2 minutes of sunset-moonrise difference for 15 longitude degrees of travel since the start of the voyage. If, for instance, the trip had started in Alexandria going west and the local sunset-moonrise difference in the open sea was 54 minutes instead of 48 minutes for the same day in Alexandria, the ship had to be as far west as the Canary Islands, 45° west of Alexandria. When at the same time the astrolabe reading indicated a latitude of 28°, the captain would order the lookout on top of the mast and the helmsman to take extra precautions because these readings told him that his ship was in between the Canary Islands.

If all of this sounds complicated to the uninitiated, believe me, it is not. Such checks and comparisons were entirely within the capabilities of our ancestors who figured even much more complicated movements of celestial bodies, like the cycles of conjunction of Jupiter and Saturn and the precession of the equinoxes.

The Sun and the Moon are exactly in line with Earth every 28.885 days. This period is called the ecliptic lunar month, because it is the minimum interval between two solar eclipses, sometimes followed by a lunar eclipse two weeks later when our planet, passing between the Sun and the Moon, throws its shadow on the latter. The average interval between two solar eclipses is 173.310 days. Whether or not these events will occur at all or whether there will be total or partial eclipses depends on complicated movements within the celestial vault that are well understood and present no problems to astronomers. I will skip the procedure of these calculations here because this book has too many numbers already.

Astronomers who specialize in calculating eclipses have made up tables for thousands of years in the past and the future, showing the dates, hours, and zones of visibility for all eclipses around the world. These modern tables are very useful to archaeologists and historians for checking the dates of certain past events described as having occurred during eclipses. For instance, it is one way to confirm that King Herod died on 13 March, in the year 4 BC, since historical documents mention a lunar eclipse on the day when he passed away.

Some eclipses have a history of their own. Such is the oldest recorded darkening of the Sun, in China, about 4,000 years ago on 26 April, 2137 BC. Two official astrologers of Emperor Chung Kang, who were paid mainly to predict eclipses so that the population could be told in advance not to panic, got stone drunk on rice wine on this day and forgot to give the warning. Neither could they, as the custom required, stand up to shoot arrows at the monster devouring the Sun. So the two culprits, Ho and Hsi, were decapitated on the spot, and since that time Chinese astrologers drink nothing but water on days when eclipses are expected.

Another famous solar eclipse took place on a battlefield in Lydia where, on 9 October, 583 BC, the Medes and the Lydians, after five years of war had lined up for the final attack at sunrise. The Sun rose in a blue sky and disappeared in a black shadow. The combatants laid their swords aside and promised each other never to fight again. To make sure that the promise would be kept, each king married the other's daughter. Peace was kept for several generations, as long as this historic eclipse was remembered.

The knowledge of precise dates for eclipses of the past has advantages for scientists who study the biblical events and try to rectify obvious errors. For example, we read in Amos VIII: "I will make the Sun disappear at noon and I will cover the earth with shadows on a clear day." This is the perfect description of a solar eclipse, but most Bibles note 787 BC as the year when this event took place. Our tables show that this date is an error because the only solar eclipse around that time that was visible in Samaria, then the capital of Israel, happened on June, 763 BC, or twenty-four years later than the Bible annotators tell us. Besides, when this time adjustment is applied to other dates of biblical events, these dates coincide perfectly with the dates given by Egyptians in their chronicles.

But let's return to navigation. We know now for certain that even before the chronometer was invented, the ancient mariners using luni solar tables and hourglasses could, whenever the moon was visible, determine their longitude within one degree, or sixty nautical miles. This is remarkable accuracy considering the errors later navigators report making *even long after the chronometer had come into common usage.*

In l703 French mariner Rene' Duguay-Trouin was leading his ships for nine days through thick fog along the Dutch coast and tried desperately to keep track of his longitude with hourglasses and pocket watches. When Sun was sighted on the tenth day and readings of precise solar time made, the error of the sand hourglass timing was eleven hours and the difference that the pocket watches had accumulated was even greater.

The Solomon Islands were discovered by Spaniards in 1567 and carefully charted by solar sightings, but for two hundred years after nobody could find them, although this chain of islands stretches for over 1,500 miles in the Pacific. When by accident the Solomon Islands were rediscovered in 1767, all maps of the Pacific had to be changed because the first entry had been false. The same thing happened to Pitcairn Island. Fletcher Christian, the chief of the mutinous crew of the British ship *Bounty*, arrived there in 1789 and found that his refuge was off by several hundred miles from the spot where it was shown on the nautical maps. This was the reason why he decided to stay there. He was proven right in his assumption that the British Admiralty, using its own erroneous maps, would not find him.

All these examples show that during the Christian era the great skill of navigation which was demonstrated by our distant ancestors, slowly deteriorated. In the last couple of centuries, all kinds of silly proposals were made on how to improve navigation over wide oceans. None of them was so simple and efficient as the ancient moonrise tables. Some scientists proposed to measure the apparent angle between the Moon and certain stars that is different at different points of the globe; but the precision needed for such measuring makes it impractical for small instruments aboard a ship. It was even proposed that a satellite of Jupiter be observed for calculation of longitude at sea, an operation that I certainly would not like to be in charge of, especially when Jupiter is above us only in daytime and no pair of binoculars usable aboard a ship will show its moons.

Another fanciful proposal without any practical merit was to anchor ships on each meridian and let them shoot coloured flares every hour on the hour to indicated longitude to vessels passing by. But how do you measure exact distance over open water with the techniques that were at the disposal of seamen in the nineteenth century? And how do you anchor a ship in mid-Pacific? The well-known American writer of the last century, Edward Everett Hale, wrote a science-fiction story called 'The Brick Moon', in which he came up with a brilliant idea, and established himself as the inventor of the navigation satellite, the backbone of modern navigation today.

In Hale's book, a manmade moon constructed of bricks was orbiting our globe with the precision of a pendulum, every ninety minutes. The time of passage of this satellite through the local meridian, gave the exact longitude, much as a passenger on a train that is exactly on time, could tell where the train is just by looking at his watch and timetable, not out the window.

Today, the navigator of any ship lost in the thickest fog can easily determine his positon within a few hundred feet, an achievement made possible by the three Transit satellites which the US Navy in 1961 placed 120° apart on the same polar orbit and circling the Earth every ninety minutes. Each parallel is crossed every thirty minutes, and because of the rotation of our globe, each following passage is 7 1/2° further west than the preceding one.

After three passages of the satellites, the ship's navigator can trace a very small triangle on his chart and knows that he is within these limits. The principle is very simple and only an hour is needed to do the job. A robot calculator using the Doppler-Fizeau effect usually does all the work. When the satellite passes, it emits a crystal-controlled frequency, a stable tone that changes as the whistle of a train changes when it passes by. The frequency of the tone received gets higher as the source moves towards you and drops as it moves away.

I know the Transit satellites very well indeed, because the first three that were put into orbit were equipped with spherical spiral antennas that I invented and described in detail in *Aviation Week* on 25 August, 1958. I also applied for a US patent; but it was never issued to me for this invention, because then the Navy would have been forced to pay me a compensation for the unauthorized use of this improvement in electronics. NASA also tried to use the same tactics with most inventors. They had to change this course rapidly, however, because NASA did not have quite the pull of the Navy; and everyone who came up with a good invention kept it under wraps until a patent was issued to him, which normally takes at least two full years. NASA could not wait that long; and therefore decided to recognize the rights of the inventors.

Aside from the debatable methods that were used to obtain the elements of Transit satellite, this system is of great simplicity and unsurpassed precision. The calculator keeps working all the time and tells your position with an error margin of less than 100 feet. The only drawback is the price of this computer. Only the Navy, cruise ships, and the big oil tankers can afford it. The Air Force has long been peeved that it has to use the Navy system and satellites; and announcements have been made recently that a new and better system, using more satellites and more precise receivers, will be soon put into operation by the Air Force. When that day arrives, every electronics engineer will be able to construct less expensive equipment and make navigation even more precise and easier than it is already.

Now that we have seen how difficult it was to develop good navigation on Earth, you can imagine how much more complicated it is in space. In fact, it is so difficult that up until now, not a single space vehicle has been steered by its own navigational system. All depended on ground guidance. Tracking radars measure the distance and the angular coordinates of the spacecraft from widely based stations. Ground computers establish the navigational data and corrections of trajectory, which are transmitted by radio. Even the astronauts in Apollo spacecraft who had a sextant and a telescope linked to an onboard computer did not make the slightest move without previous approval from the Houston Space Center. The crew was advised of all necessary maneuvers; and the astronauts carried these orders out without questioning them.

But the day is not far away when interplanetary spacecraft will roam so far in space that they will be impossible to guide by radio or check by radar from Earth. What then? Again, the same principle discovered by Austrian scientist Christian Doppler in 1842, and used for the first time by French physicist Armand Fizeau to measure the relative velocity of stars, will come to our aid. We will use the powerful radio signals transmitted by some stars to guide our spaceships. These invisible radio stars are very powerful transmitters in space. Some keep sending continually in the 21 cm band, on the frequency of atomic hydrogen, l,420 MHz. Three of these sources that have been chosen to guide our future spaceships are situated in the constellations of Cassiopeia, Sagittarius, and Taurus respectively.

The distribution of these sources on the celestial vault is very favorable to the navigation of interplanetary spacecraft, which are always launched in a plane close to that of the ecliptic. Negative or positive Doppler frequencies obtained with the aid of a computer will guide our vehicles with great precision automatically, being compared all of the time with the real course of the spaceship and checked against the radio space markers of the stars. The radio source of Cassiopeia, which is the strongest one and always 'visible' to radio telescopes at 40° N, is subject right now to intensive studies.

It is true that our ancestors had discovered electricity. Very old electrical batteries have actually been found around Baghdad, Iraq, and a design for an electrostatic generator was disccovered in Dendera, in Upper Egypt. But they did not use electronic gear to navigate around the world. Much simpler means were available. They used currents and winds that year after year flowed and blew in the same directions at the same time of the year. Just like the travellers of not so long ago who had to change from one steamship line to another to go to faraway places, so did our ancestors manage to cross the oceans by using the winds to pass from one current to another when the first one turned in a direction different from that where they wanted to go.

The global map of sea currents shows six main ocean currents, all of circular form, caused by the rotation of the Earth. This is the Coriolis effect, and it is also what makes the water in your bathtub drain rotate clockwise in the northern hemisphere and anticlockwise in the southern.

With the help of the circular currents, it was always possible to come back home. The chance of a safe return was so good that regular transport lines probably were strung across the Atlantic and Pacific oceans.

The great North Atlantic current flows south along the coasts of Portugal· and Mauretania to the Cape Verde Islands, where it turns westward to the Antilles, northwest between Puerto Rico and the

Bahamas, then north to Newfoundland, across the North Atlantic and back to Portugal after skirting the shores of Brittany.

This current has a curious feature - it forms at its westernmost tip a smaller separate current of a circular form that encloses the Bermuda Triangle, where ships and planes disappear without a trace, and the Sargasso Sea where migrating birds fly in circles for hours as if searching for an island that is there no more. This is the only place where the eels come for spawning, as if there were a river estuary there for them to ascend. The genetic memories of a distant past are demonstrating here most visibly the possibility that 12,000 years ago this part of the Atlantic could have been the sunken continent of Atlantis.

The South Atlantic current starts at the Cape of Good Hope, flows up along the West African coast as far north as Gabon, then crosses the Atlantic at its narrowest from east to west until it reaches Natal in Brazil. It then descends in southerly direction to Buenos Aires, where it turns back east to the Cape of Good Hope.

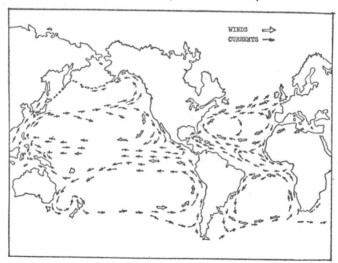

Circular navigation routes using winds and currents

This map shows how our ancestors could have crossed wide oceans without sextant, compass, or chronometer, using only winds and currents that would bring them back home a few years later. They could determine their latitude from the height of the polar star and their longitude from the relative motions of the Sun and Moon.

113

Both of these currents played very important roles in the past. After circumnavigating Africa, Hindu and Sumerian sailors used the South Atlantic current to go to the estuary of the Amazon, the Antilles, or the Gulf of Mexico. If the search for traces they left behind continues successfully, we will eventually have a map of all their incredible voyages.

The current of the North Pacific moves south along the coasts of California and Mexico, turns west at Acapulco, crosses the Pacific at its widest, passing south of Hawaii, and arrives at the Philippines, where it starts flowing north until it reaches Japan, turns east, and comes back to California. This current must have played an important role in the migration of the Asiatic races who came to America between ice ages, when the passage over Bering Strait was not frozen solid.

The South Pacific current moves north along the coast of Chile up to the northern part of Peru, then turns west and traverses the Pacific north of Tahiti and south of New Caledonia and the New Hebrides. It skirts the east coast of Australia, hooks to the north and then twists south to evade New Zealand before returning to Chile by way of Easter Island and the Juan Fernandez Island group off Chile. This current played a decisive part in the migration of Polynesian people to South America or vice versa. The only thing that we have to find out is who brought civilization to whom. In my opinion, the Polynesians are much more civilized than the Indians of South America, but that does not prove a thing, because I have been off the mark in my judgment many times.

The north current of the Indian Ocean starts from the east coast of Africa at the latitude of Zanzibar and flows north up to the estuary of the Indus River in Pakistan, then turns southeast to Ceylon, reverts in a northerly direction up to the River Ganges in the Bay of Bengal, flows south to Sumatra, in Indonesia, where it takes a western direction and flows back to Zanzibar by way of Diego Garcia. It carried Egyptians from the Gulf of Aden, and Sumerians or Hindus from the Gulf of Oman; and, after a cruise along the Sunda Isles, it brought them back to Africa, the Mozambique Channel and the current of Agulhas that led them to the South Atlantic current for a passage to the Amazon, the Antilles or Mexico.

114

The southern current of the Indian Ocean has not been sufficiently explored. We know that it runs south along the coast of Madagascar, turns east at the latitude of Cape of Good Hope and crosses the most desolate ocean of the world, passing the islands of New Amsterdam and St Paul, to arrive at the West Australian coast, where it changes direction and returns to Madagscar, flowing north of the islands of Reunion and Mauritius. We do not know the history or prehistory of this current, which probably also had importance in the very distant past when the continent of Antarctica was not ice covered and could have been the cradle of an advanced civilization.

In all three oceans there is an equatorial countercurrent between the big northerly and southerly circular currents. These countercurrents are linear and they flow from west to east making it easier for navigators to change directions and pass from one hemisphere to the other. It was these countercurrents that enabled the Phoenicians, who, once through the Pillars of Hercules, or Strait of Gibraltar, sailed south to reach the Antilles or, going a little farther south, the mouth of the Amazon River. Then, by sailing up the river, they could get close to the mines of Peru and Bolivia.

Access routes to South American metals from Atlantic to Amazon

This map of northern South America shows how ancient navigators from the Mediterranean, after crossing the Atlantic with winds and currents, could navigate up the Amazon, cross the Andes, and reach the continent's gold, silver, copper, and tin mines. Moreover, the whole Amazon basin could have been a huge inland sea many thousand years ago, making navigation much easier.

115

A map of these worldwide ocean currents looks very much like a big city's subway map. You have your different lines and the transfer stations from one line to another. One of the busiest changing stations must have been the Canary Islands where all of the traffic from and to the Mediterranean flowed by.

Once we understood how the ocean currents helped men to migrate, we can also understand why the monuments of Easter Island look so much like the ancient buildings of Tiahuanaco and the submerged ruins in the Bahamas; we can explain how Roman coins could be found in an old amphora on a beach in Venezuela and the remnants of Hindu plantation colonies, where cotton and jute were grown, on the east coast of Mexico. Sumerians and Phoenicians established mining towns in Peru and Bolivia to obtain copper and tin. To get there, these intrepid sailors had to navigate the Amazon for thousands of miles, and that is why mysterious inscriptions resembling the Phoenician alphabet have been found all along the banks of the world's biggest river.

In short, the use of the sea currents for navigation explains why all ancient civilizations seem to have so many things in common; so that it looks as if all of them developed from one much older and much more advanced central civilization. The men of this central civilization were the 'kings of the sea'; and their art of masterful navigation and knowledge of astronomy and mathematics could very well have been gifts of astronauts who came from another world to educate and civilize them. Unfortunately, we may never know who these astronauts were or where they came from.

THE SIGNS OF THE ZODIAC

Today astrology has grown into such an important social phenomenon that it takes courage to try to unravel its secrets and mysteries. But we must attempt to determine once and for all whether astrology is an exact science like astronomy and mathematics or just an enormous imposter.

Quite a few people before me have already tried to do it. But they could not come to clear conclusions because they started with the intention to demonstrate the validity of their preconceived theories. Some even went as far as to fabricate their own evidence.

As for myself, astrology, like most other things in my life, came to my serious attention by accident. I am supposed to be a man of science; but I love many other activities, like diving for old gold doubloons off the Florida Keys or exploring the history of science. The latter activity focused my attention on astrology which, maybe, is not a science at all, but without which we never would have had astronomy. *After all it was the ancient astrologers who, during many thousands of years, accumulated their observations about the positions and movements of the heavenly bodies and tried to relate them to human or terrestrial events.* Considering the very primitive means at their disposal, these men left behind incredibly precise records that can be easily matched with the best modern astronomical tables.

If astrology is a science, it must be a very complicated one. It interwines the objective information about the movements of the celestial bodies with the subjective projections of supposed influences that these configurations of stars may have in the lives of men and human destinies of Earth. But the foundations for such speculations are very shaky.

First of all, astrologers have not, up until this day, calculated which is the most important moment when the stars cast their spell - is it the moment of birth or the moment of conception? Similarly, they have no final and clear definition of what is meant by an astrological conjunction of two planets. Is it the moment when they are at the same point in longitude as calculated by their cycles, which we will call the 'theoretical conjunction', or is it the geocentric conjunction when we see it from the Earth? Or, finally, is it the heliocentric conjunction, the instant when these planets are in line with the Sun?

In addition, the second case of astrological planet conjunctions, the geocentric one, is totally confusing, because over a period of six months the variable angular velocities of Jupiter, Saturn, and Earth can create as many as three such conjunctions and nobody can decide which is the right one.

The most famous of these triple conjunctions happened in 7 BC, the year when Christ was born, in the sign of Pisces. If we can believe the latest tables of planetary conjunctions established by our best computers in 1962 - and who else can we trust? - three different alignments in the same area of the skies took place that year between Jupiter and Saturn: first on 14 May, lasting to 3 June, with a maximum on 24 May; the second on 1 October, lasting to 21 October, with a maximum on 11 October; and the third on 5 December, lasting to 15 December, with a maximum on 10 December.

This triple conjunction between the two planets so excited the astrologers of that time that the legend about the star of Bethlehem was born and with it the beginning of a new era in human history.

Triple conjunctions are very rare and seem to come only once every 973 years. The first one of our era arrived in AD 967 in the sign of Aries, on 5 June, 13 October, and 12 December. Again in 1940, in the sign of Taurus, we had triple conjunctions on 24 July, 6 November, and 26 December. There must have been others, but so far I have not had the time to find them. At any rate, these three examples should be enough to show that astrology, be it a science or an art, is not easy to master and requires a certain intelligence. Before even trying to decide if astrology is an exact science or a sham, which in itself is a delicate question, we should study a little the very basis of our modern astrology as transferred to us by the Chaldean Magi: the zodiac with its twelve mysterious signs.

Since the dawn of time, men must have noticed that certain stars hanging in the vault of the sky seemed to disappear behind the Sun and that each return of the yearly seasons brought these stars back. Too, they must have soon realized that the stars were immobile and the Sun was travelling around, and that the same path, only slower, was followed by the planets. In such a way, certain characteristic groups of stars were chosen to indicate every season of the year. The whole ring of constellations was given the name 'zodiac' - or circle of animals - because of all the animals our ancestors seemed to recognize in these star groups.

Depending on the region and the way they counted their sheep, goats, or cattle, our ancestors divided the band of the zodiac into eight, ten, twelve, or thirteen parts. One division was as good as the other because the constellations are not evenly distributed at equal intervals. The Chaldeans, like the Sumerians before them, had divided the band of stars into twelve parts because they counted everything by 12 or by 60. Actually, it is better to divide the zodiac into thirteen parts, since it is easier then to give each segment one characteristic constellation without gaps or overlap.

It is quite easy to design, with groups of the brightest stars in the zodiac, thirteen different triangles that have dissimilar forms and orientations and whose centres are evenly spaced about $28°$ from each other all around the great highway of the celestial vault. Again, we have here the same magic number, 28, or 4 times 7, that we find all over the world, as in the 28 parts of the Maltese cross of the Aegean, the 28 sectors of the Medicine Wheel of Wyoming, or the 28 inches of the cubit of Giza, Tiahuanaco, and Cuenca.

Thirteen was a sacred number for the Mayas. I believe they divided the zodiac into thirteen parts, even though I have not been able to prove it. The Mayan calendar consisted of 13 baktuns of 20 katuns each, representing 260 conjunctions of Jupiter and Saturn.

Some modern astrologers have already begun to use thirteen signs of the zodiac. Generally they place a new sign between Scorpio and Sagittarius, but it seems more logical to me to insert a new sign between Leo and Virgo. More available space is found there than after Scorpio, and so a new sign called 'Triangle' could very conveniently be created by taking the bright star Denebola from the very tip of the lion's tail in Leo.

119

When I started to write this book I had no intention of devoting a whole chapter to astrology. It seemed to be outside the subject matter for this account of my discoveries. If at all, only ancient astrology interested me. But my effort to discover as much as possible about the knowledge of our ancestors in all things astronomical, forced me to become an expert in astrology. Doing all of this research in a factual and precise manner, I could not help but notice the pitfalls and empty gaps of the old astrology. This, in turn, made me seriously question the validity of the whole understanding of our modern astrologers and their esoteric merchandise. Either the astrologers did not have the faintest idea themselves what it was that they were doing, or they did not care what kind of product they were producing, as long as it sold.

This map of the Sumerian civilization shows the twelve countries around Sumer as well as the corresponding zodiac signs and constellations in 9700 BC. Apparently, the zodiac originally served as a road map as well as a sky map.

120

However, to make the public believe that high-grade value was offered, today's astrologers have given the old hoax a new twist. The ancient book of the Chaldean Magi is transferred to magnetic tape and from this data a computer can produce a nearly infinite number of different combinations. As a result, every client who pushes the buttons in a modern astrology computer promptly receives a printout of his horoscope. He goes home proudly convinced that for his good money he has received a tailor-made guide for his life based on all of the mysterious secrets of the ancient wisdom and guaranteed to be true because a computer produced it. In reality, all he has received is an absolutely worthless piece of paper. But what he does not know does not hurt him.

I had to ask myself what I could do if I had to reform astrology. Where would I start, considering my knowledge of mathematics, physics, astronomy, and electronics and, above all, my firm belief that the stars do influence humanity. The answer was simple and there was only one - I would have to start from ground zero, from the very beginning, as was the case with the Apollo spacecraft and its communication system that fell into my hands and was my responsibility.

For me, the universe with its billions of stars is a stage where comic and tragic plays are staged that represent each and every life here on Earth. The actors are the Sun, the Moon, and the planets in perpetual motion. Depending on the relative positions of these actors, the life of humans on Earth can be paradise or hell. So I came to the conclusion that a new astrology should be created on a basis that would be fully valid for the next ten, twenty, or even more millennia to come. To do this, we would first have to make an inventory of all visible stars within the zodiacal band, excluding the circumpolar stars, which are different in the two hemispheres. In such a way we would create the permanent background, the stage setting for the main actors, and this background would remain the same for thousands of years.

Next, we should concentrate on the 7 or 8° of latitude on both sides of the ecliptic, which is the superhighway of the sky where the Sun, the Moon, and the planets move majestically and permanently. We should forget about the circumpolar stars for now, even though these will serve other purposes. After that, the stars in the band of the zodiac should be divided into small groups at equal intervals like the spokes of a wheel so that they would be easy to recognize and could

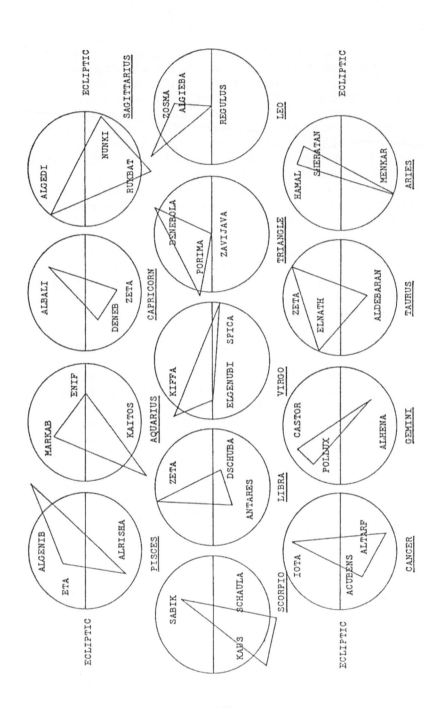

be used as milestones to determine the exact positions of the Sun, Moon and planets at all times.

This concept of a new astrology first came to my mind in 1965 in Tahiti, where everything is so much simpler than anywhere else in this world. The western part of the island is ringed by a good road. It's about 120 km long and it takes about three unhurried hours to drive its whole length before arriving back at the point where one started, like a planet in the zodiac. On Tahiti, except in Papeete, where the solid middle class lives, there are no streets and houses have no numbers. One lives at 'kilometre 13' or 'kilometre 17' and these indications are enough to find everyone. It was at the beach of Moorea, an island twelve miles west of Tahiti, while I was contemplating the incredibly beautiful display of stars at night that I got the idea to reconstruct astrology. I would make the zodiac the dial of the big celestial clock using the Moon, the Sun, and the planets as the hands for seconds, minutes, and hours.

The stars would have their permanent home, say, at 264° or 288° longitude, where anyone could find them at any time when he wants to. This is not quite possible today with even the astronomical zodiac, which moves every year by 50 seconds of arc, and not possible at all with the astrological zodiac, which got stuck at the time of Babylon and has not moved since.

After I had decided to use the stars as mileposts, all that was left to be done was to make small groups of them at equal distances with easily recognizable configurations. Like any astrologer worth his salt, I used a computer and in no time at all I had the results. The best geometrical figure for grouping nearby stars is the triangle; and the best solution to have them divided evenly is to use thirteen irregular triangles. At the same time, the computer, which never does things halfway, gave me all of the celestial coordinates for each of the thirty-nine stars chosen to form these thirteen groups.

---

opposite **The thirteen zodiac signs**

This illustration shows a new zodiac made of thirteen equally spaced triangles and thirty-nine corresponding stars. This is much more logical than our present Babylonian zodiac with twelve unevenly spaced constellations, some above and some below the ecliptic, which does not seem to make sense.

123

The only thing I have not been able to find are the ancient names for all the stars in the thirteen new signs of the zodiac, but I managed to establish a sort of road map showing the triangles, their names, addresses, and the month when the Sun rises in them in the morning.

I think that the new zodiac that I propose was used by the Mayas, who counted by 13 and 26. In this new system each sign would change after every 28 days, 2 hours, 17 minutes, and 3 seconds, and these changes would take place on 21 March, 18 April, 16 May, 13 June, 11 July, 8 August, 6 September, 4 October, 1 November, 29 November, 27 December, 24 January, and 21 February. The spring equinox would come as it does now - between the signs of Pisces and Aquarius; but the autumnal equinox would occur in the middle of a new sign - the Triangle.

This custom of considering the zodiac as a sort of a road map of the skies is well established, and it may indeed be true that the zodiac was first invented because of its usefulness as a road map. Do not laugh - such a thought is less ridiculous than it may seem at first blush. In our times the spring equinox occurs on 21 March, on the line between Pisces and Aries, while the autumnal equinox occurs on the line between Virgo and Libra.

But 9,700 years ago these equinoxes occurred 135° to the east, which means that spring arrived in the middle of the sign of Leo and autumn in the middle of Aquarius, due to the precession of the equinoxes. We have excellent reasons to assume that the signs of the zodiac were invented at that time in Mesopotamia by the old Sumerians, who probably were refugees from some cataclysmic event, though we do not know who they were, where they came from, or when exactly they came to the valley of the Euphrates.

Now let us for a moment put ourselves into the shoes of the Sumerians who lived in their great city of Ur 9,700 years ago. We know that they were great merchants, eager to sell their products to other people living in other highly developed centres of civilization like the valleys of the Nile or the Indus. Since the Sumerians counted by 12 and by 60, they probably divided the horizon around the city of Ur into twelve equal parts corresponding to the twelve regions of active commerce and exchange of materials that they wanted to cultivate with people living there.

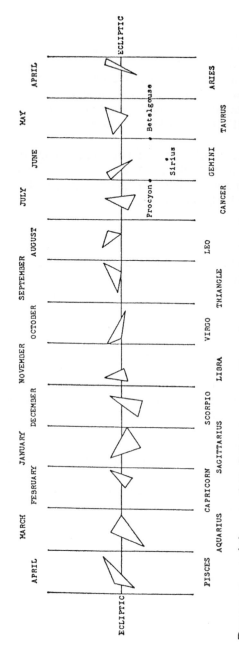

Present positions of the thirteen zodiac signs on the ecliptic and in the solar year

Each of them represents 28.09 days or 27.69 degrees. It also shows the relative positions of three major stars. Such a zodiac seems to have been used a long time ago by the Mayas who divided everything into thirteen and twenty.

125

Just as the Fuller Brush Man and the Avon Lady cover the whole United States door to door and carry along their sample cases, so did the old Sumerians send their travelling salesmen in all directions. If you want to start north of Ur and go clockwise, Caucasus was north, Azerbaijan north-northeast, Turkestan east-northeast, Persia east, India east-southeast, Yemen south-southeast, Hadramaut south, Ethiopia south-southwest, Nubia west-southwest, Egypt west, Palestine west-northwest, and Armenia north-northwest.

Now we have to remember that these travelling salesmen were most certainly illiterate. But they could count and were very good at memorizing their travel orders, which were given to them in the form of small tablets engraved with the signs of the zodiac. Gemini, the Twins, was the sign for Ethiopia; Virgo, the Virgin, for India; Pisces, the Fishes, for Palestine; Leo, the Lion, for Yemen; and so on. The stars of the constellations not only gave them the direction in which to lead their caravans of mules or camels, but also indicated the right time for arriving at their destinations. The best time to arrive for business was when the Sun rose in the morning within the given sign.

This system, however, had a flaw. The precession of the equinoxes changed the direction in which the salesmen were to travel. The spring equinox, which coincided with the sign of Cancer for Hadramaut 9,700 years ago was in the sign of Gemini for Ethiopia 7,500 years ago, and became the Taurus for Nubia 5,300 years ago. Either the signs or the destinations had to be changed to keep things in order; but we do not know whether one or the other correction was made.

This question has never been answered, but we do know that today's astrologers use signs that do not correspond to the actual positions of the constellations in the zodiac. They do coincide approximately with the positions the stars held 2,500 years ago when the Chaldean astrologers did their fine work in Babylon. On the contrary, our modern astronomers use a zodiac where the spring equinox is determined once and for all to fall on 2I March, when the sign of Pisces gives way to Aries, while the constellations where the Sun rises at this date have slowly changed their places and have nothing to do anymore with their positions of 9,700 years ago when the zodiac was probably invented.

126

This is the weakest of all points in our present-day astrology. It does not represent the actual astronomical positions of the stars today. It does not correspond to the signs when the zodiac was invented, but it approximately reflects the state of 2,500 years ago when the Jews were captives in Babylon. The zodiac of our present-day astrologers is the zodiac of the Bible, and this is why astrology is more religion than science. In a religion one is supposed to believe, not to ask questions or search for the truth; and modern astrology is not based, as it should be, on data derived from the stars or the planets, but on ingrained conventions that are interpreted differently by different astrologers at different moments.

The ancient Egyptians, who were great astronomers and in their day constructed the world's largest observatory, noticed that our Sun moves slowly but surely among the stars by one degree every seventy-two years. It therefore could not be trusted as a stable point of reference. This is why they chose the star Sirius instead and calculated their calendar year and all their astronomical or astrological cycles by the apparent motions of the Sun, Moon, and planets in relation to the fixed position of Sirius. This is the most efficient and logical system ever devised and superior to any system used today.

But these arguments alone do not prove that astrology is just a hoax, as the majority of the scientific world assumes. It is nevertheless most probable that modern astrology is based on false assumptions, even though it is true that the Sun, the Moon, and the planets do have a part in everything that happens on our planet. This has been proven in hundreds of scientific experiments. This reminds us once more that our ancestors, who grasped this tens of thousands of years ago, were not quite as dumb as is generally thought. Indeed this knowledge, too, was given to them long ago by the same astronauts who brought about the sudden leap forward in our evolution.

Since it is evident that stars influence mankind, it is not only quite possible but very probable that they also influence each individual. Astrology could be made into an *exact science* if all of the correlations of cause and effect could be determined scientifically, precisely, and correctly. Considering the fantastic possibilities that have been given us by the electronic brain and the magnetic memory, a rational reorganization of astrology would not require too much time.

127

All of us have our good and bad periods. Sometimes we can work twelve hours a day and not feel tired while on other days we have no wish to work at all. Also, we all know how intelligent we can be when feeling good and what stupid mistakes we make when we're not in our best form. There are periods when nothing works out no matter how hard we try. Most certainly this is so in my own life. The trouble is, I never know if at any given moment I am in a good or bad period.

By way of observation, I have found out that these changing periods are cyclic and regular but I have not yet found the governing pattern. It is very likely that these fluctuations follow some astronomical cycle like the conjunction of planets. Besides, we have already proven scientifically the influence that planets, like Jupiter and Saturn, have on space communications. This is why I would not dare to say that astrology is all one big hoax. Maybe all it needs is a new reconstruction of its basic concepts.

I sincerely believe that stars can influence my life, even though I still do not understand the mysterious rules that govern these influences. That, however, does not mean that I can believe in astrology as it is practiced today.

Recently published books about astrology have brought to my attention many interesting astronomical cycles. The works of Louis Mac-Neice and Serge Hutin contain numbers that correspond to calculations I have made with the Nineveh constant, and the results are precise to the fourth decimal point. In my opinion, there is also a correlation that could be explained by influence of the stars between the Russian and American space programs. Both started suddenly, at the same time, when the world was flooded with books and publications all pointing in the same directions, namely that we are not the first astronauts and that there have been visitors from space long before we first heard of Sputnik or Apollo.

One could believe that our fathers in heaven knew long ago that this day of liberation from the Earth's gravity would come, and that our exploration of space would start. If, as this Arab adage says, all is written down that has to come, it is not surprising that we are now offered the insight to understand *our true nature as the sons and daughters of our ancestors who came from outer space.*

128

THE POLAR MYSTERIES

The units our ancestors used for measurements never had any particular fascination for me, but I have always been attracted by ancient coins - the pieces of gold, silver, and electrum that were in circulation thousands of years ago. However, since all coins are also units of weight, and weight is derived from units of volume, which in turn is derived from units of length, I got curious enough one day to find out why some particular coins were made of a certain weight of gold while others represented a different weight in silver. While working on these problems, I did not realize what I was actually trying to discover, but I continued on.

To do my work right, I had first to make a list of all the coins that had been in circulation since the time of King Croesus, who is considered to be the inventor of metallic coins. He ruled in Lydia, an ancient Aegean country of Asia Minor, from 560 to 546 BC and was defeated and killed by the Persians under Cyrus who wanted his riches. Croesus minted the first coins from nuggets of electrum, natural alloy of gold and silver that could be found in the Pactolus River flowing by Sardis, the capital city of Lydia. These electrum coins are now almost 2,600 years old.

There might have been some more ancient coins, but so far none have been found. Legends tell us that 12,000 years ago in Atlantis coins were made of orichalcum, a metal lighter in colour and weight than gold, probably some alloy of copper and aluminum like the aluminum-bronze coins of small denominations that are used in France today. These aluminum-bronze coins oxidize easily, and this is probably why none of the Atlantis lightweight money has ever been found. It must have disintegrated long ago without leaving a trace. However, we still have a few electrum coins from King Croesus.

After I had compiled my list of most ancient coins known to numismatists and archaeologists, I had to make up another one for all measurement units of antiquity, translating these various units into feet and cubic feet. It took some time to get all this done, but it was time well spent. Then I started to compare the two lists and try to find the feet whose cubes represented the weight of a round number of coins.

In most cases, quite naturally, the weight of the coin divided neatly into the local unit of weight for the corresponding country and the time in history when this money was in use; but there were quite a few surprising exceptions. In some instances, relationships showed up between vastly separated geographical locations and even greater differences in time. *Coins of exactly the same weight had been found in geographical locations thousands of miles apart and in different cultures separated by thousands of years.*

This is where my interest became really aroused and my work became exciting. Once more I was certain I had struck upon a mystery of the past worthy of exploration. But to make this more clear, let me first explain how our ancestors arrived at their basic units of measurement, now known as the inch, the hand, the foot, the cubit, and the yard.

All units of measure in the distant past of our civilization had the same basic system in their foundations - *all were determined from the exact dimensions of our planet Earth.* Incredible as this may sound to the uninitiated, our ancestors derived their feet and inches from the length of one degree of latitude or longitude. Quite naturally they used the longitude and latitude at which they lived and that explains why there were so many different feet and other units of measurement derived from the local degrees.

The length of 1° of latitude varies from 110,567 m at the equator to 111,700 m at the pole, while one degree of longitude varies from zero at the pole to 111,321 m at the equator. These two basic units of longitude or latitude were divided by an appropriate round number to obtain a measurement of length that approximated the average natural dimension of a human foot, finger, hand, or forearm. The Semites expressed their units in their usual system of counting by 10, while the Sumerians registered theirs by counting by 12 or by 60, and the Olmecs and the Mayas by counting by 20. But the basis for all these different calculations was the same - the true dimensions of Earth.

The recognition of this fact does not, however, explain where our remote ancestors obtained such advanced scientific knowledge.

Even the Greeks did not have it. Eratosthenes of Alexandria, the philosopher and mathematician, calculated the circumference of the Earth 2,200 years ago and obtained a very passable value for it; but we know now that this happened by sheer luck. He made wrong calculations with wrong data, but these mistakes were opposite in values and compensated each other. Even Pierre Mechain and Jean Delambre, the careful French surveyors who from 1792 to 1799 measured the distance from Barcelona in Spain to Dunkerque in France to obtain the base for the French metric system erred by a full 5 km over the length of 40,000 km of the meridian.

How come then that our forefathers back in the Stone Age had values so exact, which we ourselves were only able to obtain after 4 October, 1957, when the Soviet satellite Sputnik started to trace and measure the first orbits around the globe? We then obtained the exact measurements by observing the irregularities in the orbits of the first artificial satellites in order to calculate the true shape and dimensions of our globe. There is no better or easier way to do it. Yet our Stone Age ancestors had the same data. And this is why the measurement units of our ancestors became so utterly important for the scientific unravelling of the mysteries of our origin.

The numerous ancient drawings and sculptures found all over the globe showing astronaut-like figures in helmets and space suits are *pictorial testimonies from the farthest past that indeed visitors from outer space left their footprints here.* But these paintings in caves and on cliffs are not scientific proofs of extraterrestrial visitations. However, the precise knowledge of our forefathers of the length of 1° of longitude or latitude at any given point on the globe surely is proof; *and so is the constant of Nineveh, the cold undeniable calculation in exact numbers that was used for thousands of years on both sides of the Atlantic by people who could never have obtained such information by themselves.*

Our ancestors who came from outer space circled our globe and calculated the size of our Earth from the time that it took them to orbit it at a given altitude, as they also measured the irregularities of the sphere by the changes in their orbital velocity. This information was later - probably 64,800 years ago - given to the new generation of man. The weight of the ancient coins and the Nineveh constant of the solar system are today two of our best scientific proofs that

ANCIENT GOLD AND SILVER COINS

NAME	COUNTRY	WEIGHT/ GRAMS	NUMBER UNIT	WEIGHT/ GRAMS
Scruple	England	1.296	24,000	31,104
Denarius	Germany	1.428	15,000	21,333
Penny	England	1.555	20,000	31,104
Denarius	France	1.692	20,250	34,265
Ducat	Venice	2.179	12,000	26,148
Dirham	Arabia	2.917	9,600	28,000
Real	Spain	3.400	8,100	27,542
Ecu	France	3.525	9,720	34,265
Florin	Firenza	3.533	7,400	26,148
Ducat	Venice	3,606	7,250	26,148
Tael	China	3.780	9,600	36,288
Dram	England	3.888	8,000	31,104
Denarius	Roma	3.898	6,650	25,920
Tournoi	France	4.230	8,100	36,265
Dinar	Arabia	4,242	6,600	28,000
Drachma	Greece	4.250	6,000	25,500
Kite	Egypt	4.500	6,000	27,000
Solidus	Roma	4.547	5,700	25,920
Dobra	Portugal	4.918	5,600	27,542
Groat	England	6.221	5,000	31,104
Louis	France	6.345	5,400	34,265
Doubloon	Spain	6.800	4,050	27,542
Hexa	Byzantium	6.821	3,800	25,920
Shekel	Palestine	7.294	3,600	26,260
Sovereign	England	7.776	4,000	31,104
Aureus	Roma	7.795	3,325	25,920
Shekel	Chaldea	8.333	3,600	30,000
Stater	Greece	8.440	2,500	21,100
Philip	Macedonia	8.573	2,500	21,433
Kedet	Egypt	9.000	3,000	27,000
Rupee	India	10.769	3,900	42,000
Tola	India	11.666	3,600	42,000

astronauts from space gave us their knowledge. But there are many others.

It is not difficult to understand how our ancestors calculated their coin weight in gold and silver from the local dimensions of their longitude and latitude degrees. Here follow four of the most striking examples.

At the average latitude of Egypt, the length of 1° of longitude is 96,000 m. If we divide this number by 320,000, we obtain a foot of 30 cm, the unit used to build the Pyramid of Kephren. One cubic foot of this basic unit has a volume of 27,000 cu cm, or 27,000 g of water. This is the weight of one Egyptian talent - 27 kg. But the Egyptian way to write it is 60 sep of 450 g each, or 600 deben of 45 g, or again 6,000 kite of 4.5 g. Besides, this is one of the oldest examples of use of the decimal system, if not the very oldest known today.

The median latitude in the region of the megalithic temples in England gives to 1° of longitude the average value of about 66,325 m. When that is divided by 240,000, we obtain l ft. of 0.2764 m that was used to construct Stonehenge, and I cu. ft. of Stonehenge has the weight of 21,l00 g, or cu cm, of water. This weight divided by 2,500 gives a unit of 8.44 g. No old coins of 8.44 g each have been found in England, but the Mycenaean gold stater weighed exactly 8.44 g.

Now, Mycenae in Greece is thousands of kilometres away from Stonehenge, yet archaeologists have long been wondering if there was any direct relation between this old Celtic site in England and ancient Greece. This is because the outline of a Mycenaean dagger has been found engraved on a stone slab in Stonehenge. Now that we know that the Mycenaean stater has been derived from the Celtic foot of Stonehenge, which is much older than Mycenae, we may believe that perhaps it was the Celts who built Mycenae.

In Tiahuanaco, Bolivia, 1° of longitude is about l07,000 m. Divided by 360,000, this geodesic measure gives us a foot of 0.2972 m, which, with the cubit of 0.4458 m. is the construction unit of the Temple of Kalasasaya in Tiahuanaco. The Tiahuanaco cubic foot weighs 26,260 g, the exact weight of the gold talent in Greece, which was also used all over the Eastern Mediterranean region, divided into 60 minas of 437.66 g each or into 3,600 shekels of 7.29 g each.

ANCIENT MEASURING SYSTEMS

Name or Origin of the System	Length in Millimeters		Water Weight in Gramsi of Cubic		
	Foot	Cubit	Foot	Cubit	Yard.....
Hindu	275.892	413.838	21,000	70,875	567,000*
Celtic	276.352	414.528	21,105	71,230	569,840*
Mycenae	277.777	416.666	21,433	72,338	578,702*
Danube	280.000	420.000	21,952	74,088	592,700*
Indus	292.402	438.603	25,000	84,375	675,000*
Greece	295.490	443.235	25,800	87,077	696,610*
Rome	295.945	443.918	25,920	87,480	699,840*
Sumer	297.000	445.500	26,198	88,418	707,350
Tiahuanaco	297.234	445.851	26,260	88,628	709,020*
Inca	298.760	448.140	26,666	90,000	720,000*
Egypt	300.000	450.000	27,000	91,125	729,000*
Indus	301.845	452.768	27,500	92,813	742,500*
Spain	302.643	453.965	27,720	93,555	748,440*
Bagdad	303.659	455.489	28,000	94,500	756,000*
Avoirdupois	304.919	457.379	28,350	95,680	765,450*
Babylon	305.257	457.885	28,444	96,000	768,000*
Florence	306.168	459.252	28,700	96,863	774,900*
Persia	307.796	461.694	29,160	98,415	787,320*
Venice	307.936	461.904	29,200	98,550	788,400
Greece	308.276	462.414	29,296	98,875	791,000
Babylon	308.642	462.963	29,400	99,225	793,800*
Troy	314.489	471.734	31,104	104,976	839,808*
France	321.085	481.627	33,102	111,720	893,754
France	324.639	486.959	34,214	115,472	923,778*
Pied Du Roi	324.800	487.200	34,265	115,644	925,155
China	331.071	496.606	36,288	122,472	979,776*
Baalbek	333.333	500.000	37,037	125,000	1,000,000*
Cuenca	347.603	521.405	42,000	141,750	1,134,000*
Cheops	349.432	524.148	42,666	144,000	1,152,000*
Chephren	350.000	525.000	42,875	144,703	1,157.625
Coffers	350.882	526.323	43,200	145,800	1,166,400*
Reims	355.690	533.535	45,000	151,875	1,215,000*
China	358.140	537.210	45,936	155,036	1,240,290
Chartres	368.403	552.605	50,000	168,750	1,350,000*

* Derived from the ancient Earth volume of $108,864 \times 10^{16}$ cubic meters.

But what is the connection between South America and the Mediterranean?

A degree of longitude at the latitude of the caves of Cuenca, in Ecuador, is nearly lll,230 m. Divided by 320,000, this gives a foot of 0.3476 m and I cu. ft. equals 42,000 g of water. This weight could have been the base for several coins of our ancestors, but it is certainly the foundation of the gold tola in India, weighing ll.66 g and still in use today in the Persian Gulf, where the Arab oil sheiks are paid for their oil in gold tolas freshly minted just for them. The Cuenca foot in my opinion could also be the ancestor of the Hindu foot of 0.2759 m whose cubic foot weighs 2l,000 g. This mystery is even more intriguing when we see it in the light of recent discoveries that the Hindus navigated all the way around Africa, across the Atlantic Ocean, and up the Amazon River to bring home copper and tin from mines in Peru and Bolivia.

No less surprising is the as-yet-unverified information from the Arabian Desert where very ancient pre-Islamic ruins have been found that seem to be built with a foot of 0.3037 m, a dimension that is new to us. Let's call it the foot of Baghdad. Some other sources recently indicate that a very old Arab map has been found, where the equator is divided not in the usual twenty-four or thirty-six parts but in forty-four equal arcs of 8.l8 degrees each.

As archaeological findings go, the two discoveries would hardly seem to have anything in common. Yet if one uses a little bit of imagination and calculation, this first impression changes. The two bits of information could very well be pointing to a system of measurement used by ancient Arabs so very long ago that the Arabs themselves have forgotten it and that no archaeologist ever knew about it.

Thousands of years ago before the decimal system became generally known, they didn't use the Pi factor of 3.141593 to calculate the circumference of a circle. Instead, the much more convenient division 22/7 was employed because it was simpler. If the radius of a circle was 7 units, then the circumference was 44 same units. It was quite logical to use this same system to divide the equator into 44 units of 910,980 m each and to estimate the radius of our planet as 7 times 910,980 m, or 6,376,860 m, which is how the ancestors of the Arabs calculated the equatorial the circumference of the globe

135

at 40,083 km, instead of 40,075 km as we now measure it. Not bad at all, especially when one considers that instead of our precise figure of 6,378 km, they figured that the radius of our globe was 6,377 km.

When we divide 910,980 m by 3 million, we obtain a foot of 0.3037 m, nearly the same as the foot of the Indus valley of 0.3018 m or the feet of the Egyptians or the Mayas that measured exactly 0.3 metres.

This new foot of Baghdad could very well have been the base for at least three monetary systems. One cubic foot of Baghdad would contain 28,000 cc of water and weigh 28 kg. Such a weight would equal 6.600 gold dinars of 4.24 g each as used in Arab lands, or 9.600 silver dirhams of 2.92 g each in circulation all over North Africa, or even 2,600 gold or silver rupees of 10.77 g each in India today.

It is not too difficult to believe that our ancestors knew the approximate dimensions of our planet and used this information, clad in religious rites and rules, to create measures that corresponded to the human limbs. We can even accept the fact that the rotation of the Earth's surface had been estimated at 1,000 Babylonian cubits of 0.4629 m per second or 100,000 Mycenaean feet of 0.2777 m per minute, fantastic as it may be. But when we have to recognize now that our forefathers knew the circumference of the globe better than we knew it up to twenty years ago and that they used this exact knowledge in exactly the same way from continent to continent, such admission becomes very difficult unless we allow our skeptical minds to accept the theory of extraterrestrial visitors participating in the development of our civilization.

It seems certain now that further studies of weights and coins of the distant past will lead to the discovery of a central culture common to all mankind and stemming from the unknown place on our planet where the astronauts from outer space first landed about 65,000 years ago in order to foster a new race of earthlings.

One thing that can be said with certainty now is that all the measuremnent systems ever used, no matter when or where, shared a common relation to the dimensions of our planet and therefore to the metric system. In its modern form, that system was established only some 200 years ago in France. But, of course, the metric system was not invented by the French. Nor was it invented by the

Egyptians who used it 5,000 years ago or by the Mayas who built their terraced pyramids in metric dimensions.

The system must be even older than the Sumerian sexagesimal way of counting or the Mayan vigesimal numeration. It must have been developed by a civilization familiar with decimal counting, positional calculation, and the use of zero, a civilization which we have not yet found and probably never will find on the continents or islands known to us, because it must be more than 100,000 years old and has probably been hidden in the depths of some ocean for tens of thousands of years.

According to the most recent theories, there were four original civilizations that appeared simultaneously at four equidistant points on Earth in the Arctic, Indian, Atlantic, and Pacific oceans. All of these points are now under water, but hundreds of thousands of years ago these were continents; and they will rise again when our present continents in turn sink.

This theory is based on a very simple observation that everyone can make with an orange kept in a dry place. After a month or so, the juice will have partially evaporated and the soft core will have shrunk more than the hard rind. The orange will have changed form from a sphere to a tetrahedron which has a higher surface-to-volume ration than a sphere. Our Earth has shrunk like an orange while its core cooled off and has formed four continents and four big oceans that keep moving all of the time. They travel from one geographical location to another, very, very slowly in relation to the rotational axis of our planet. These global movements could be called the polar rounds and they make it difficult to calculate the correlations between different measurement systems in different countries of the world if these systems are many thousands of years old. It is necessary to know the displacements of the poles to come up with the right results, because each local standard of measurement varies with time. This is why I am convinced that only a system of measurement that does not change with the polar rounds could survive the time, and this system could only be based upon the unchanging circumference of our globe, not the changing longitudes and latitudes. The metric system is like that, and it must be as old as humanity itself.

Not too long ago the geologists discovered that the hard outer crust of our Earth floats on a molten mantle and that continents rest on

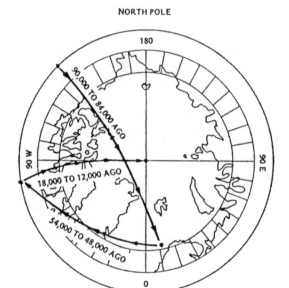

NORTH POLE

180

90 W

90 E

90,000 TO 84,000 AGO

18,000 TO 12,000 AGO

54,000 TO 48,000 AGO

0

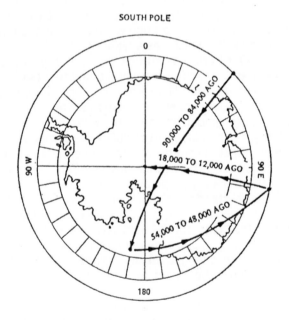

SOUTH POLE

0

90 W

90 E

90,000 TO 84,000 AGO

18,000 TO 12,000 AGO

54,000 TO 48,000 AGO

180

138

separate tectonic plates. There are direct relations between the sliding of the plates and the changing of the polar ice caps. What interests us here are the dates when these changes took place and their influence upon the lives of our ancestors. It appears that, in round figures, the poles remain stationary for periods of about 30,000 years, then move around for 6,000 years, then again stay put for 30,000 years, and so on.

Scientists have established that the last four rounds of the poles started 120,000 years ago when the North Pole installed itself in the territory of Yukon in Canada at 63° N and 135° W; then it went to the Greenland Sea at 72° N and 10° E about 84,000 years ago, moved from 54,000 until 48,000 years ago and settled in the middle of Hudson Bay at 60° N and 83° W; it rested there for 30,000 years; then wandered again from about 18000 to about 12,000 years ago when it came to its present location.

Simultaneously the South Pole went through similar gyrations but in the opposite direction. We have to note that its three previous locations were in their turn in the southern part of the Indian Ocean between Australia and the Antarctic but never on Antarctica itself. Only the last movement 12,000 years ago brought the South Pole to the middle of the great continent of Antarctica.

At least half of Antarctica towards South America and the South Atlantic was ice free for 100,000 years, while Palmer Peninsula and Cape Horn, that may not have then been separated from each other, enjoyed a fairly warm climate. There is no valid reason to doubt that during these periods of the last three polar rounds, a very advanced civilization could have existed in this region and might have been the origin of all civilization and knowledge in astronomy, mathematics, metallurgy, and a variety of arts.

---

opposite   The last three displacements of the poles from 90,000 to 12,000 years ago

This illustration shows the positions and motions of the North Pole and South Pole at different times in the past. It shows in particular that, until 12,000 years ago, Antarctica had a much warmer climate and could have been the site of a long-forgotten advanced civilization.

Much has been written about the polar rounds, but very little has been said about the corresponding shift of the equator. The displacement of the tropical zones around the globe had certainly much more influence upon humans than the shift of the ice caps. Certainly climatic changes in the temperate and tropical zones have caused many more migrations and led to the destruction of many more civilizations than any changes in polar regions.

The polar rounds and the shift of the equator also explain why we have found traces of civilizations in regions of the Earth that today seem unfit for human habitation. The jungles of Guatemala and Cambodia, the high plateaus of Tibet, or the deserts of Arabia were all quite different at different times of the polar rounds; and this simple explanation solves many archaeological, ethnological, and geological mysteries.

If we consider where the equator was 90,000 years ago, we discover that this line was very close to many famous archaeological sites like Hoggar in Algeria; Tibesti in Chad; the southern part of Egypt; Bahrein and Dilmun in the Persian Gulf; Sumer and Akkad in Mesopotamia; the southern part of Persia; the Indus valley; Angkor, in Cambodia; Malekula, in the New Hebrides; Rapa, in Polynesia; Easter Island, in the South Pacific; Pisco Bay and the Nasca plateau in Peru; Tiahuanaco, in Bolivia; and the Amazon delta.

Tracing the equator line of 54,000 years ago and starting again from Africa around the world, we find that it touched the ruins of Zimbabwe, in Rhodesia; the anthropological sites of Java; the Nan Madol ruins of the island of Temuen in the Carolines; the Hawaiian Islands; the Galapagos Islands, in the Pacific; the caves of Cuenca, in Ecuador; and again the mouth of the Amazon.

On the equator of l8,000 years ago we find the kingdom of the Queen of Sheba, in southwest Arabia; the Indus valley; Lhasa, in Tibet; Changsha in China where a 2000 year old mummifed princess was found; French Polynesia; and Easter Island. Naturally, not all ancient cultural sites are on these lines of the equator of the last l00,000 years. But it is significant that we find there the most mysterious ones like Angkor, Nan Madol, Tiahuanaco, Nasca, Cuenca, Machu Picchu, and Easter Island.

There must have been a good reason why all of these impressive civilizations established themselves around the equatorial zones of their period. Three reasons can be seen right away. First, there was the flight from ice ages that most probably in the distant past destroyed great parts of humanity more than once. The second reason is astronomical and nautical. If you stand on the equator, all stars are visible - Polaris, the polar star, and the Southern Cross too. It is the best place to study the movements of planets, also the best place for navigation. All you do is observe the polar star for your latitude, and figure out the longitude by observing the time difference beween the sunset in the west and moonrise in the east. The third reason is extraterrestrial. It is preferable to land a spaceship near the equator than in a polar region, just as it was with our landings on the Moon.

No matter what the reasons were, the zone between the tropics of Cancer and Capricorn, the borders of the tropical belt around our planet, has played the most important part in the development of civilization. During the ice ages the climate there was very pleasant, the sea levels in the oceans were much lower and all distances between islands and continents substantially shorter than now. Navigation was simpler because all centers of culture and commerce were on the same line, and one could simply go with the Sun to find them all. There can be no doubt anymore that human civilization has lasted much longer than was previously thought. For instance, the latest radioactive carbon data collected from megalithic temples in Brittany, Spain, and Wales show that these European remnants of ancient cultures are at least 2,000 years older than the pyramids of Egypt or the ziggurats of Mesopotamia.

But we still have to find out where it all began. What was the beginning of civilization? Was it the time when humans first started to communicate by sounds or gestures? Was it when humans made their first attempts to write or count? Or was it when they began tool-making? Just recently the discovery was made that ancient iron ore mines in South Africa are 43,000 years old. Yet ancient records contain even older indications of culture. Egyptian priests once claimed that their ancestors had seen the Sun rise twice where it sets now, which represented 40,000 years. Mayan documents in the archives of the Vatican state that their time counting started four long periods ago to give us a date almost 21,000 years ago. Unless I made a mistake in my calculations, the Nineveh constant came into human possession 64,800 years ago, and we probably can't go wrong if we assume that indeed civilization began with the Cro-Magnon period 65,000 years ago.

The understanding of the polar rounds and of the wobbling equator will allow us some day to make the ultimate discovery in Antarctica, the most mysterious of all the continents. Antarctica wasn't discovered until 1820, yet there are several very old maps that show Antarctica *without a trace of ice, with rivers and mountains where today one finds nothing but glaciers.* The two Piri Reis maps, dated 1513 and 1528, are copies of much older ones going back thousands of years; and as studies sponsored by the US Navy Hydrographic Office have shown, these maps are utterly precise and in true scale. Even more interesting, they show many details that could only be found by aerial survey, and yet these cartographic achievements must have been made at least 20,000 years ago, when Antarctica was ice free.

This reminds me of the French writer, Rene Barjavel, who wrote a novel about an ancient civilization that was discovered under the mile-thick ice of the Antarctic continent. Why not? As far as I am concerned, I will not be surprised when some day we will discover the Antarctic cultural sites just as we have found, one after another, the cities of Troy, Mycenae, Knossos, and Dilmun. *There is no reason why some day in the maybe not so distant future we could not find the sunken continent of Atlantis and the mysterious Land of Mu under thick sheets of ice or under the waves of an ocean.*

THE UNIVERSAL CALENDAR

The search for a universal calendar that would enable people all over the world to chart the past and map the future exactly and precisely, has been going on since the most ancient times. Our ancestors did try repeatedly to find a time-counting system that would be independent of human events and happenings on Earth, a calendar that would correlate simultaneous moments of time in one common system all over the globe.

It is hard to believe that still no such calendar exists. One of the most backward features of our modern age is our time-counting system, which was introduced during the Middle Ages by a pope who still believed that the Sun circled the Earth and began the counting of time from an event of uncertain date, the birth of a Messiah who may or may not have existed. That we use such a system when we have computers and travel in space, seems beyond belief; but the worst fact is that this outdated calendar has three ways of counting time. There is our Christian Gregorian calendar of Pope Gregory XIII. There is the astronomical calendar known mostly to astronomers. Then there is the calendar of mathematicians, who are the only ones to use it.

As an example, lets take the Gregorian date of 21 March, seven years before the Christian era. For one using the astronomical calendar, this would be 21 March of the year -6. The mathematician needing an expression that can be fed into a computer would in his turn translate that 21 March into the 286th day before the end of the year, the equivalent of 0.783 of one year, and write our date down as -6.783.

Such an expression can be fed into a computer. It can be compared to any other positive or negative dates in Gregorian, Hebrew, or Moslem calendars, and it can indicate the time with a fantastic precision of a few seconds, minutes, or hours, depending on the number of decimals used.

But such a system is neither easy nor simple to use for most people. It would be much simpler to count in whole days and in positive dates only, starting from an event very far in the past, preferably some exceptional astronomical event that took place at least 100,000 years ago, such as the alignment of all planets at the same point on the ecliptic that must have taken place at least once in the history of our solar system.

By pinpointing such a moment, we would establish a zero point for counting time and also a zero point in longitude, a starting line for all planetary movements. The whole world would then have a common chronological system enabling us to make all time computations simple and precise.

I have tried to establish such a starting point in time and longitude for my own use, but encountered some obstacles that seem to be, at the present time, impossible to overcome. The trouble is that the French astronomers on one side, and the Russian and American astronomers on the other, use different values for the same planetary revolutions and conjunctions, with considerable differences for Uranus, Neptune, and Pluto. The French data comes closest to the values obtained from the constant of Nineveh for planetary revolutions, but any attempt to calculate the zero point in time and longitude from French data would be rejected automatically by the Russian and American astronomers. So I have given it up for the present, hoping that the time might come when uniform astronomical tables will be introduced globally.

The main problem is the impossibility to calculate precisely the past conjunctions of Mars, Jupiter, Saturn, Uranus, and Neptune. Here the Russian and American numbers are closer to those of the Nineveh Constant than the French data. The difference shows up in the third and fourth place after the decimal point only, but for calculations over very long periods of time, the accrued error would be far too great for a precise calendar. Over a period of only 5,000 years the difference between the French and the American data would amount to as many as three years, and the same happens when we try we try to calculate the positions of these planets at that time. If I ask a French astronomer what the positions of the five exterior planets were in the year 3144 BC, for example, and if a conjunction took place during that year, the answer will be, "No, there was no

144

conjunction at this date according to the calculations of Leverrier and Gaillot." But an American astronomer will confirm a conjunction of Jupiter and Saturn in that year and another one of Uranus and Neptune thirty degrees further on the ecliptic. I would like to know who is right.

Still, establishment of a universal calendar would be possible if we used only the six planets closest to the Sun, whose revolutions and times of conjunctions have been recorded and are known precisely. These movements have been calculated recently for the past 4,500 years by two American astronomers, William Stahlman and Owen Gingerich, using a modern computer. Their book gives the longitudes of these planets for every ten days throughout this period, and it is easy to find the exact dates of all conjunctions of Jupiter and Saturn, the most regular among our planets. With this regularity in mind, it is not surprising for us to discover that several calendars before the Christian era were apparently based on these regular conjunctions of Jupiter and Saturn.

The Byzantine calendar starts on l4 September, 5509 BC. The Hebrew time reckoning begins on 9 September, 376l BC. Both these years had a conjunction of Jupiter and Saturn. The same characteristic can be shown for the start year of the ancient Hindu time-counting, which was the year 3l04 BC.

I have not checked all other calendars for this characteristic; but if we add to the above three, the Julian, Scandinavian, and Mayan calendars, we already have six that seem to have started in a year when there was a conjunction of Jupiter and Saturn. The Julian and Scandinavian calendars started in 47l3 BC and the last cycle of the Mayan calendar began in 3l44 BC. This looks like more than a simple coincidence.

The only calendar that escapes this rule of Jupiter and Saturn is the Egyptian calendar previously mentioned in this book as being based on the star Sirius, or Sothis. The Sothic year of 365 l/4 days was used in ancient Egypt, as well as a year of 365 days, in cycles of l,460 consecutive years. But even there it seems that the conjunctions of Jupiter and Saturn played a role. After an interval of 56 Sothic cycles, or 8l,760 years, the start of the ancient Egyptian calendar coincides with a conjunction of the two planets. Again, we find the number 56 which has been mentioned several times before.

145

Besides the Sothic cycle, our ancestors had two methods at their disposal for calculating time, the solar-lunar system and the Jupiter-Saturn conjunctions. The first method was used for time periods rarely extending beyond 100 years. Ancient astrologers had noticed that the lunar month coincided with the solar year every 19 years, or after 235 lunar months, a period of time they called a Metonic cycle. They also knew that the lunar month coincided with a solar eclipse every 18.03 years, or eighteen years eleven days, after nineteen lunar years or 223 lunar months, a period they named the Saros.

Using these two periods, the Metonic cycle and the Saros, our ancestors formed longer time periods, like the Celtic Triangle used in Stonehenge that consisted of 2 Metonic cycles and 1 Saros, equal to 56 years. The Mayas combined 2 Saroses and 3 Metonic cycles to make a period of 93 solar years. In my opinion, there must have been many other such combinations of lunisolar cycles that have not been explored so far. Our ancestors also had noticed that after every 521 years, an eclipse of the sun took place on the same day of the year and in the same place on the zodiac. Also, that the Saros and the Metonic cycle coincided every 4,237 years, after 235 Saroses or 223 Metonic cycles, and that 599 Saroses represented exactly 10,800 years. This particular number 10,800 was a sacred one for all ancient cultures.

There can be little doubt that it took thousands of years of careful observations and notations to assemble this knowledge. Such important information had to be transmitted to future generations and not forgotten. This is why our ancestors built their calendars in stone. The most famous one is perhaps the megalithic temple of Stonehenge.

Its age is estimated to be about 4,000 years and its location is in the Salisbury Plain of southern Wiltshire, England. The geographic coordinates are 51.17^o north latitude and 1.83^o west longitude, giving a Celtic foot of 0.2764 m, which is the measurement used in the construction, as well as the corresponding cubit of 0.4146 m. All circles were traced with the ancient Pi factor of 22/7 - the three concentric rings formed by the ring of limestone menhirs called the sarsen circle, the ring of Aubrey holes that probably held wooden posts, and the partially destroyed outer ditch.

The first ring has a diameter of 112 Celtic ft. and a circumference of 352 Celtic ft, the second a diameter of 315 Celtic ft. and a circumference of 990, while the third circle has a diameter of 385 Celtic ft. and a circumference of 1,210 Celtic ft, equal to 334.40 m. These rings are in relatively good condition and can be measured precisely; while three other circles, one made of bluestones and two of post holes, are more difficult to measure because of erosion but can be guessed as having had diameters of 84, 140, and 189 Celtic ft. across and circumferences of 264, 440, and 594 ft., respectively. Inside the sarsen circle five arches indicated the setting and rising of the Sun and the Moon at different times of the year.

These five points of observation are placed like a horseshoe, with the open end facing the northeast and another horseshoe inside, marked by bluestone menhirs. All these stones, the intervals between them, and the wooden posts set in the holes, gave a high number of possible alignments that could be measured with great precision. When all of this data will be collected and fed into a computer to be compared with the positions of the most prominent stars in the past, we will be able to determine with precision the date when Stonehenge was built.

It should be noted that the circumferences of all circles measured in Celtic feet are exactly divisible by 22 and all diameters are divisible by 7 - a proof of sound mathematics 4,000 years ago. Another testimony of the arithmetical ability of our Celtic ancestors is the interesting discrepancy that arises when one degree of the local longitude of Stonehenge is divided by 240,000. The result is a foot of longer length than the foot used to construct the temple.

This difference disappears when the latitude is increased by 2.35°, which could mean, no doubt, that at the time Stonehenge was constructed, the North Pole was 2.35° nearer than now. Here again we have a good way to establish the true age of this megalithic temple. It could also mean that Stonehenge was part of a Celtic empire whose centre was at the latitude of present-day Manchester and that the standard Celtic foot was calculated from the local longitude of the capital city of that time.

When was this time? Computer analysis of twenty alignments of Stonehenge have resulted in the positions of ten most prominent stars l2,000 years ago, giving the exact rising and setting points for

147

CELTIC TRIANGLE

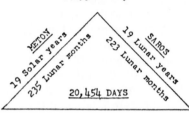

LUNAR MONTH
29.5306 Days

METON
19 Solar years
235 Lunar months

SAROS
19 Lunar years
223 Lunar months

20,454 DAYS

SOLAR YEAR
365.2322 Days

LUNAR YEAR
346.6200 Days

56 Solar years – 59 Lunar years
Difference – 2.976 Days – 72 Hours

CELTIC CYCLE

MAYAN SQUARE

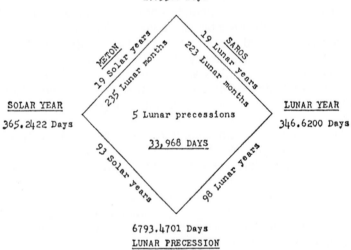

LUNAR MONTH
29.5306 Days

METON
19 Solar years
235 Lunar months

SAROS
19 Lunar years
223 Lunar months

5 Lunar precessions

33,968 DAYS

SOLAR YEAR
365.2422 Days

LUNAR YEAR
346.6200 Days

93 Solar years

98 Lunar years

6793.4701 Days
LUNAR PRECESSION
Difference – 1.247 Day – 30 Hours

MAYAN CYCLE

the stars Vega, Castor, Alcyone, Aldebaran, Altair, Betelgeuse, Rigel, Sirius, Antares, and Fomalhaut. All these stars describe in twenty-four hours a full circle around the North Pole, but only a part of these star circles are visible from Stonehenge, each marking two precise points at which the path of each star cuts the horizon. These twenty points are clearly marked in Stonehenge, earning very high marks in both mathematics and astronomy for our Celtic ancestors.

The solar and lunar alignments of Stonehenge are neither very interesting nor impressive, since identical alignments can be found all over the world. The temple itself is precisely built on the line of the summer solstice in the northern hemisphere - 2l June. Other markers show the vernal and the autumnal equinoxes - 2l March and 22 September. There are also divisions of the circles showing the maximal, north and south points of the lunar rising and setting. All of these marks can be found with sufficient precision by any one who wants to do it in a few years' time.

What really impresses me about the mathematical and astronomical skill of these ancient priests of Stonehenge is the way they predicted lunar and solar eclipses. I would like to call it a program of advanced

---

Opposite: CELTIC TRIANGLE AND MAYAN SQUARE

56 solar years or 59 lunar years
difference = 2.976 days = 72 hours

Celtic Triangle
lunar precession
6793.5l08 days
93 solar years or 98 lunar years
difference = l.247 day = 30 hours
Mayan Square

The Celtic cycle of 20,454 days and the Mayan cycle of 33,968 days were also based on the lunar standstill cycle of 6,798.398 days, the cycle of maximum oscillation of moonrise to the north or to the south. That cycle was often rounded to 6.800 days and computed with circles of 34 stones, like the Q and R circles in Stonehenge.

149

mathematical studies of the Stone Age, done with a few wooden poles and fifty-six holes. We all have long known that the Sumerians, the Egyptians, the Babylonians, and the Mayas were fantastic astronomers and mathematicians. But who expected such prowess from the Celts, the Hyperboreans of the far north, rugged and unpolished ruffians? Yet since the recent discoveries that civilization invaded the Mediterranean basin from the north, and after I studied the wonders of Stonehenge, I must admit that I am very proud of having Celtic ancestors, the star-gazers and time-calculators of the deep dark past.

The scientific skill and astronomical knowledge of Stonehenge is rooted in the fifty-six Aubrey holes, in which were placed wooden poles, giving an astounding variety of precise alignments with the celestial bodies. It also made Stonehenge a huge, cleverly and skillfully executed calculator. The time-counting cycle of these astronomers 4,000 years ago was the span of 20,454 days which, with a minimal error of only seventy-two hours, represented 56 solar years, 59 lunar years, or 118 eclipses. This cycle of one Saros and two Metonic cycles has been called the Celtic triangle.

There is a relationship here to the Mayan solar-lunar cycle, even though that was longer and more precise than the Celtic triangle. The Mayan cycle, that could be called the Mayan square, comprised 33,968 days giving, with an error of only 30 hours, 93 solar years or 98 lunar years, that is, two Saros and three Metonic cycles. Since the Celts lived much farther north than the Mayas and had much less favorable atmospheric conditions for astronomical observations than the people near the equator where the moon is nearly always overhead, I personally (my prejudice granted) give the higher mark to the Celts.

Also, I expect that much more will be discovered at Stonehenge than we have seen so far. No one yet has taken pains to try the markers for the five nearest planets, which must have been well known to the astronomers of Stonehenge. Uranus and Neptune were probably familiar to them too. It could very well be that in the patterns of Stonehenge some alignments are set to indicate the conjunctions of Jupiter and Saturn at the time this megalithic temple was built. Such a finding could help us considerably in estimating its true age.

Stonehenge is so famous mainly because it is so easily accessible and so perfectly preserved. The megalithic temple of Avebury, about twenty miles north, must originally have been much bigger than Stonehenge, as it was formed by 650 gigantic menhirs encircling Silbury Hill. Yet the largest of all is the site of Glastonbury, in Somerset, about forty miles west of Stonehenge. This circle probably had a diameter of some thirty miles, but it is so eroded and leveled with the ground that its exact size and configuration can no longer be readily established.

Some of these prehistoric temples of the Celts are not circular, but are formed by combinations of curves of different radii. Woodhenge, situated next to Stonehenge, has the shape of an egg, also constructed in Celtic feet and with the Pi factor of 22/7. It has an ovoid perimeter of 480 ft, or 132.67 m. In reality, Woodhenge temple is formed by six ovoid curves in perfect concentricity and mathematical relationship. Whoever constructed it was a master mathematician.

The British archaeologists and astronomers have adopted the megalithic yard as their unit of measurement to explore the prehistoric temples in England. This yard, of 0.829 m, equal also to 3 Celtic feet or 2 Celtic cubits, makes it difficult to analyze the true relationship of the Celtic civilization to other cultures of the past. Divided into megalithic yards, the diameters and circumferences of the circles do not comprise whole units and the prehistoric formula 22:7 is not apparent. But the relationship 22:7 is the base of nearly all prehistoric monuments - the Pyramid of Cheops, the temples of Teotihuacan, and others.

There also exists an American Woodhenge, but the resemblance is in the proportion 22:7 only. The American site, at Cahokia Mounds, is constructed with the Tiahuanaco foot of 0.2972 m, which is quite surprising in itself. This prehistoric circle is in Illinois, near East St. Louis, on the east bank of the Mississippi River, and is only a part of an extensive maze of prehistoric temples, habitats, and truncated pyramids. The diameter of Woodhenge Circle is 420 Tiahuanaco ft.; and its circumference is 1,320 ft, divided into 48 equal parts of 27 1/2 ft. each, separated by 48 equidistant poles.

The observation point inside this circle is 5 ft. off centre in an easterly direction, from which point the vernal and the autumnal equinoxes could be observed over the top of a pole at sunrise. Looking east, the fourth pole to the left indicated sunrise at the summer solstice and the fourth pole to the right, sunrise at the winter solstice. There certainly must be many other alignments built into this set-up; but as far as I know, no one has begun a serious exploration.

Prehistoric sites in the United States are not very popular. The Medicine Wheel of Wyoming is known because of its unique division into 28 parts similar to the 28 equal sectors of the Maltese cross, but generally the exploration in the United States has barely started. Most of these prehistoric sites are located in the so-called 'Bible belt', where there is very little interest in pagan temples of the past. However, this situation has recently begun to change rapidly since even the farmers of the fertile Middle West are coming to realize the value of their megalithic monuments and archaeological sites.

Before I close this chapter on Celtic temples I have to mention a kind of configuration that is neither a circle, nor an ellipse, nor an ovoid. It is formed by a combination of a half-circle and a half-ellipse. The very little known and perfect example of this form is a temple called 'Long Meg and Her Daughters', which is situated in the north of England along an ancient Roman wall in Little Salkeld, Cumberland. This temple can also be measured by the Celtic foot and the ancient formula 22:7 of the circle.

The northern part of the monument is a half-ellipse with a long axis of 294 Celtic ft. and a half short axis of l05 Celtic ft. The southern part of the temple is a half-circle, with a l47 Celtic ft. radius. The north-south axis of the site is 30° off the meridian, which could be a consequence of the displacement of the terrestrial poles since the temple was built. The perimeter of the Long Meg must have been originally 858 ft, or 396 Celtic ft. for the northern part, and 462 Celtic ft. for the southern. Translated into our present metric system, the surface of this site is exactly 4,500 sq. m, perhaps another of the recurring mysteries of the metric system. The temple is in such poor state that it is difficult to make out which stones make what alignments. Too many are missing. It seems quite clear, however, that this too was an astronomical site built to measure time. But why the odd shape?

Some think that these configurations are the first signs of prehistoric geometry and that the different dimensions of this temple had the proportions of the sacred triangle of Sumer with sides in the ratio of 3:4:5. This is not impossible, but it would be very difficult to prove it. There could be another simpler explanation, easier to demonstrate conclusively, that will be discussed in a later chapter of this book. The fact is that the apparent diameters of the Sun and the Moon vary appreciably during the years.

These variations of the apparent magnitude can be determined by sighting the object between two poles placed at different intervals in a circle and observed from the centre at a constant distance. It can also be done at a variable distance from one of the centres of an ellipse, using poles spaced evenly on the ellipse. It is further possible that the elliptical orbits of the planets and the Sun and the Moon suggested some religious laws to our ancestors and that they found mystical meaning in the reproduction of such lines on the ground. It is even possible that they had been told to do this long, long ago when our ancestors coming from outer space transmitted their wisdom to earthlings.

All the prehistoric temples, whatever their form and whether built in stone, wood, or heaps of dirt, had but one purpose - to measure time, long periods of time, extending over many generations. Oral transmittance was too vague to be trusted over millennia. For a very long time, science ignored these temples and the Church destroyed many of them. Now these megalithic sites have become very popular, mostly because of the work done by Colin Renfrew, a young English archaeologist, who proved that many of them are much older than any other known relic of human civilization, older than the pyramids of Egypt or the Tower of Babel.

It seems that quite a few among the megalithic sites could be as old as 12,000 years, the time when Atlantis allegedly disappeared into the ocean. It will take some time to prove it, but I do not doubt that it will be done. Right now, official science is beginning to recognize that some dolmens and menhirs in France, Ireland, England, Spain, Portugal, and Morocco are 9,000 or 10,000 years old. And all of these sites are clearly grouped around the eastern coasts of the Atlantic Ocean, like landing sites for an invading army of refugees. The hypothesis of the survivors of the sunken Atlantis becomes more believable with every day spent in exploration. First there is the phenomenon of the Gaelic, Basque, Breton, or Portuguese dialects, that all resemble the dialect spoken in the Azores and Canary Is-

153

lands by the Guanche people, which may be directly derived from the language spoken in Atlantis. Then there is the discovery of the strange blood groups. The Basques, people of unknown origin inhabiting the Pyrenees regions of both France and Spain, have a rare blood group pattern that is found only among other people speaking strange dialects and living near ancient menhirs and dolmens. *Could this be the blood of the Atlanteans or even the divine blood transmitted by the astronauts?*

Above all there are the traditions that mark these people as groups of fearless seafarers inured to gales and tidal waves during a fabulous past. In order to navigate the oceans, this Atlantic race naturally needed the precise calculations of sunset and moonrise and the tables that showed them where they were during their voyages. To establish these tables, they needed observatories and they built them at Stonehenge in England, at Carnac in France, and elsewhere.

The possibility that survivors of the sunken Atlantis found refuge on the east Atlantic coasts and islands 12,000 years ago may also explain why the oldest among the world's sacred texts and legends mention dates much further in the past than the oldest Mediterranean civilizations or even the Egyptian pyramids. We could here examine some of the most distant dates and try to find if there is some correlation or even a similar method of reckoning among them.

Diogenes Laertius, the Greek historian, mentions the year 49,214 before our era as the beginning of the astronomical archives of the Egyptians. This is the oldest recorded date that I know of after the Mayan starting date of 49,611 BC shown on the ceramic disc of Chinkultic. Next to it are the dates of the cave paintings in Lascaux and Altamira going back at least 27,000 years. The age of Tiahuanaco seems to be the same, but we have no precise data. But in 839 BC Babylonian priests recorded the start of the first Babylonian dynasty after the first deluge at the very early date of 24,989 BC, which also was the date of a Mayan baktun. Next in line of recorded documents is the indication in the Vatican codex that the first Mayan calendar started in 18,633 BC. The last cycle, begun in 3144 BC, is to end in the year 2020 of our era.

The Aztecs counted their time in the same way as the Mayas, by the conjunctions of Jupiter and Saturn, but their cycles and the departure dates of these cycles were different. If the translations of the Vatican codex are correct, we live now in the fifth cycle since the creation of the world. The first Aztec cycle, according to the same Vatican source, lasted 202 conjunctions of Jupiter and Saturn, or 4,012 years and ended in a fantastic deluge that drowned everything and everybody.

The second cycle of equal duration ended again in a catastrophe of violent cyclones that brought total destruction. The third period of the Aztec calendar lasted 242 conjunctions of the two planets, or 4,805 years and was finished by volcanic eruptions that burned everything to a crisp. The fourth cycle of 253 conjunctions or 5,024 years ended in general famine and starvation.

We live now in the fifth Aztec cycle which began in 781 BC and should end in our year 2020, significantly the same date as given by the Mayan calendar, though not telling us what to expect at that time. If we take the starting date of 781 BC and go back 17,852 years, the sum of the first four Aztec periods, we arrive at the same first year of the Mayan calendar - 18,633 BC.

Further, we have a date that is common in two different and widely separated cultures, the Mayan and the Hindu. It is the year 11,654 BC. The Hindus counted time in periods of 2,850 years or 150 Metonic cycles of nineteen solar years each. According to my calculations their calendar started in 3104 BC. If we go back three Hindu time-counting periods of 2,850 years each, we arrive at the year 11,654 BC. The Mayas counted time by several different methods, one of them being cycles of 2,760 1/3 years that started in the year 3373 BC. Three such cycles bring us back to exactly the date of the Hindu time-counting, the famous year 11,654 BC.

Then there is the date of 11,540 BC that is common to the Egyptians and the Assyrians. The Egyptians counted by periods of 1,460 years and started one of their cycles in the year 5,700 BC. Four of these Egyptian cycles bring us back to 11,540 BC. The Assyrians counted in periods of 95 Metonic cycles of nineteen solar years each, or cycles of 1,805 years starting in 710 BC. Six of these periods result in the same date - the year 11,540 BC, with the end of the last cycle in 710 BC.

The date for the creation of the world, the year 9657 BC according to Zoroaster, is very close to the year 9564 BC, the year when Atlantis was destroyed, according to the Tibetans.

After that we arrive at more recent dates like the Mayan date of 8,307 BC, and the start of the Mahabharata, the great epic of ancient India, in 7,116 BC. Then there are the calendars of the Byzantines, Scandinavians, and Hebrews, which started in 5508, 4713, and 3761 BC, respectively. Most of these ancient dates have been known for centuries; but no one dared to use or publish them because Irish Archbishop Ussher of Armagh, who proposed a biblical chronology in the seventeenth century, had established that the world was created in the year 4004 BC at nine o'clock in the morning of 26 October. For centuries it was imprudent to doubt such biblical wisdom.

Now the times have changed and the oldest known dates are used by quite a few people. Different authors publish them, and sometimes their dates differ slightly because they use varying methods of calculation. Nevertheless, when all the data is sorted out by computer, only three systems of counting time emerge: the Sun-Moon-Venus method, the method using the Sun and Sirius, and the reckoning by the conjunctions of Jupiter and Saturn.

We can see now that the universal calendar did exist many thousands of years ago. *We have only rediscovered it.* It was based on the conjunctions of Jupiter and Saturn, and the Mayas could start their calendar with the year 49,611 BC by using the same system that started the time-counting of the Egyptians 49,214 years before our era - always in whole numbers of conjunctions of the two planets.

Out of sheer curiosity, I wanted to calculate intermediary dates by intervals of ten Jupiter-Saturn conjunctions of 198.6 years each. Since I am convinced that we will continue to discover older documented dates as we progress in our research and probably reach the date of the Nineveh constant 64,800 years ago, I made up a calendar of thirteen great Mayan cycles counting back from the end of the present one which will end in the year 2020. The thirteen cycles of 5,163 years each brought me to 65,100 years BC.

156

THE FOUR MOONS

There is one absolutely fantastic astronomical theory proposed quite a while ago by Hoerbiger and confirmed recently by Hans Bellamy and Peter Allen, stating that during its lifetime of several billion years, our Earth captured four moons one after another. Three of them exploded as they crashed onto Earth creating the three biggest oceans - the Atlantic, the Pacific, and the Indian - and destroying all living things. The fourth moon is the present one which still hangs in the skies.

This theory, seen as science fiction by most scientists, would not have been discussed in this book if I had not myself discovered some surprising new facts that seem to confirm it. When I first heard of Hoerbiger's theory, I did think that the poor man had lost his marbles. But then I remembered that once everyone regarded the German physicist Alfred Wegener's theory of the drifting continents as pure fiction, until much later discoveries proved his concept to be true. As a result, I reconsidered the possibility that our planet might have had more than one moon in the past and that Bellamy and Allen might be proven right, if we simply keep in mind that nothing in our universe is stable and that everything is in constant motion.

It is evident that our present Moon has not always been there, at the same distance from Earth as it is today. Unfortunately, our science says that this distance must have been greater in the past than now, because all satellites descend in a very slow spiral towards the planet around which they revolve. This is caused by the deceleration due to friction with cosmic dust. The smaller satellites lose their altitude faster than the bigger ones, which have more favorable ratios of mass to cross-section. But there is a contradiction here. While the laws of celestial mechanics tell us that the Moon in the past must have been farther from Earth than today, legends and sacred texts from all corners of the globe tell us the opposite - that the Moon in the past was bigger and closer to us. It even looked much bigger than the Sun. How do we solve this puzzle? Well, let's start by examining the known facts.

In the ranges of the Andes at an altitude of 13,000 feet, geologists have found stretches of marine sediment reaching 640 km all the way from Peru to Bolivia, clear evidence that the level of the ocean, only some tens of thousands of years ago, was 13,000 feet higher than it is today. Similar sediments, dating from the same geological period, have also been found in the Himalayas, in South Asia.

A geologist would be tempted to say right away that it wasn't the sea but the mountains of Peru and Bolivia that rose to this level, because the tectonic plate supporting the Cordillera range was pushed upward. But the sediment line is relatively recent compared to the millions of years since the Andes were created. So it must be the sea that once rose, as it still does around the world twice every day, except that once there was a gigantic pull that made the sea climb 13,000 feet in a huge bulging ring around the equator. Such tide could only have been produced by a big celestial body very close to the Earth. It must have been a closer and larger moon whose gravitational force pulled most of the water from all oceans into that bulging ring, like a gigantic, permanent tidal wave.

Some people think it was the planet Venus that passed very close to Earth in the past. It certainly does seem true that Venus has not always been a part of our solar system. Some think that the phenomenon was caused by a moon, not necessarily the first one that our planet had. Both of these theories may be right and it is even possible that both Venus and our Moon combined forces to raise the highest tides the world has ever experienced. But let's discuss the Moon first.

As I said before, the theory of a very close and very big moon explains the marine sediments at the 13,000 foot elevation most logically. Such a super moon would have enough pull to nearly balance the gravity of the Earth. Together with the spin of the Earth, it would cause immense tides in the tropical zone; and if this moon created four tides during one day, as would be the case with a moon spinning twice faster, there would be no time for the tides to ebb away. The high-water belt on the equator would become a stationary and permanent feature with the resulting accumulation of marine sediment at this high level.

Since it is impossible that our present Moon could have been at any time closer to Earth than it is now and since it is also improbable that it would have been much bigger in the not so distant past, we have to assume that there must have been another moon, bigger and closer to Earth, before we started serenading our present little one. And, if there could have been two moons, why not three or four? The theory of the four moons is not so crazy after all. It seems to be quite sane, because it is in harmony with all of the legends and especially with the mysterious stories about giants who lived at the time of the big moon. Even the Bible tells us about them.

We now have another mystery to solve. What's the relation between the existence of giants on the Earth in the past that no one, including the Church, has ever doubted, and a closer and bigger moon? In my opinion, there is a clear cause-and-effect relationship. While our official science still dismisses the multiple-moon theory, it is not quite so sure that there isn't a direct influence of gravity, among other factors, upon the size of the human body.

The Watusi of East Africa are much taller than the Eskimos, and it could be that this difference is caused by dissimilar gravity, which is lower at the equator than at the poles. But the aborigines of Australia who live close to the equator are very small and so are the people in Borneo and Sumatra, who live right on it. There must be other causes that determine our size, like radioactivity or availability of food. Disregarding these contradictions, we must, however, recognize that there is a direct cause-and-effect relationship between gravity and human size, that seems indeed to be limited by the weight of the body that our limbs can carry.

A powerful, close, and big moon would have reduced the weight of the human body more in the tropical zone and on the equator than in the temperate or polar zones. It so happens that in Tiahuanaco, which is the tropical zone, giant human skulls have been discovered that must have belonged to men nine to ten feet tall. In China, Java, Morocco, Tunisia, and Syria archaeologists have found flint tools and weapons weighing ten to twenty-two pounds which only giants could have made and used.

No one denies the existence of giant animals in the past. We have the bones to prove it. Even if at the present we have only a few skulls and tibias of giant men and not too many of their tools, there is little reason to dismiss the theory of closer moons and giants upon the Earth. It is only natural that first there were giant animals and then

159

huge men. The theory of evolution of the species still has its validity, but with a correcting factor of gravitation.

Until quite recently, the theory of the four moons was supported only by the findings of Bellamy and Allen, whose book *The Calendar of Tiahuanaco* caused much discussion in the scientific world. Some doubted the conclusions of the authors because the hieroglyphs on the Gate of the Sun were only partially deciphered. That is true, but in my opinion the interpretation of Allen and Bellamy, apart from some slight errors, is quite exact and their data from the Gate of the Sun has been confirmed by numbers that I have found from other sources.

The ancient builders of Tiahuanaco, who are still unknown to us, apparently feared that the Gate of the Sun, which carries the hieroglyphs constituting their calendar, might be destroyed in a catastrophe. It was not destroyed although the disaster did come about. By the greatest of miracles, the stone gate was found face down in a dried-out bed of clay about 300 ft. from its foundations. The clay cover saved the mysterious markings on the stone face from erosion; and so to this day, the hieroglyphs are in an excellent state of preservation.

However, to be prepared in case the Gate of the Sun and its engraved calendar might be destroyed, the architects and astronomers of Tiahuanaco built a huge monument that also incorporated their calendar and the relative positions of planets and their satellites known at that time. This superb and unique monument is the Temple of Kalasasaya, inside which the fallen Gate of the Sun was found. No one, so it seems, ever realized that the dimensions of Kalasasaya Temple duplicated the Tiahuanaco calendar.

According to my calculations, which differ only slightly from those made by Bellamy and Allen, the relationships between the Sun, our planet Earth, and the Moon at the time Tiahuanaco was built were the following: the Moon circled the Earth 36 times faster than now. According to the laws of Kepler, the distance from the Earth of the fast orbiting Moon was only 5 1/2 terrestrial radii, or about 35,250 m, l0.903 times closer than our Moon is now.

This proximity of the Moon and the enormous tides it produced slowed the rotation of the Earth down to 288 turns per year, compared to our present 365 turns, so that the year then had only 288 days. However, the time our Earth needed to revolve around the Sun was not affected and remained at 8,766 hours of 3,600 seconds each. All other time periods were, naturally, quite different.

Since we are now living in the era of the electronic pocket calculator and many may find amusement in checking numbers, I will give here the precise astronomical periods that were the cornerstones of the Tiahuanaco calendar. These periods are indicated by three dimensions of the Kalassasaya Temple. Its length of 288 cubits corresponds to the number of days in a solar year. The width of 264 cubits corresponds to the number of days in a lunar year. The distance of l56 cubits from the observation point to the western extremity of the terrace, which will be discussed later in this chapter, gives us the number of eclipses in a solar year and, consequently, indicates the number of synodic revolutions of the Moon, which was 444 at that time.

If we divide 8,766, the number of hours in one solar year, by these numbers, we obtain a solar year of 288 days of 30.4375 hours, and 444 lunar synodic periods of l9.7432 hours each. The lunar year that we obtain from these values is 264 days, or 8,035.5 hours, corresponding to 407 synodic periods of the Moon while it goes through all of its phases. The number of eclipses in one year is l56 cycles for the solar year and l43 cycles for the lunar year.

Exactly as the width of the temple represents ll/l2 of its length, so the lunar year represents ll/l2 of a solar year. This fact alone seems to confirm the interpretation of the Gate of the Sun numbers and the Tiahuanaco calendar; and the theory of the four moons does not seem so improbable any more. In fact, it begins to look very probable.

The Tiahuanaco astronomers worked with a small time cycle of 3,l68 days, representing ll solar years or l2 lunar years. Apparently, they also worked with a great cycle of 9,504 days, which was the time the Sun and the Moon needed to come to the same longitude and the same point on the zodiac after 5,l48 eclipse cycles of l.846 days each.

Some might ask how the Nineveh constant fits in with the theory of the four moons, when the intervals were of different value. So check

161

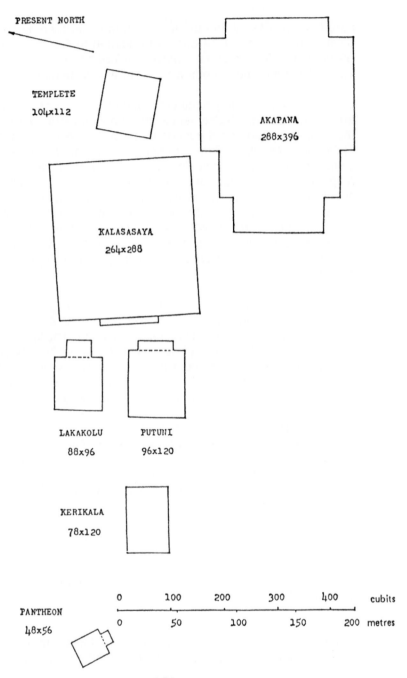

PRESENT NORTH

TEMPLETE
104x112

AKAPANA
288x396

KALASASAYA
264x288

LAKAKOLU
88x96

PUTUNI
96x120

KERIKALA
78x120

PANTHEON
48x56

| 0 | 100 | 200 | 300 | 400 | cubits |
| 0 | 50 | 100 | 150 | 200 | metres |

162

again with your handy calculator - it fits with precision up to the fifth decimal point. Start with the number of hours in the Nineveh constant, which is 54,432 million, or exactly 6,209,445 solar years of 8,766 hours each, or 1,788,320,160 days of 30.4375 hours of that time. Equally precise are the numbers that you will obtain from the division of the Nineveh constant into 564,495 cycles of 11 solar years or 12 lunar years.

Now the Temple of Kalasasaya in Tiahuanaco is built at an altitude of 3,845 m and situated at 16° 27' south latitude and 68° 41' west longitude. One degree of longitude at this latitude is about 106,790 m. Dividing this by 360,000, we obtain a local foot of 0.296639 m, very close to the actual foot of 0.297234 m, which will play an important role in this story.

Kalasasaya is in ruins now. But it was built on a stone masonry terrace that has kept its form and dimensions fairly well. It is oriented lengthwise approximately from west to east as were most ancient monuments, to be in line with the sun, and measures 128.40 by 117.70 m. On its western end the temple has a gallery of eleven stone pillars made of andesite, the hardest locally available stone. This gallery is placed 4.16 m outside the western end of the terrace and the pillars, erected at unequal intervals, are of varying width. The distance between the axes of the first and last pillars is 32.70 m and the outward borders of these two are at 33.30 m from each other. The height of these stone slabs was about four metres. Nine of them are erect, leaning about two degrees westward. The fifth pillar, counting from south, has been displaced by about 200 m westward, while the tenth has been toppled over next to its foundation. The sizes and intervals of these tall stones we will analyze later, determining their astronomical values.

Opposite: TIAHUANACO RUINS
General map in cubits of 445.851 mm

This map shows the orientations and the dimensions of the principal ruins measured in Tiahuanaco cubits of 445.851 millimetres each. The width-to-length ratios of several buildings had astronomical or mathematical meanings. For example, 264 and 288 were the numbers of days in the lunar and solar years at that time, and 288/396 was the tangent of 36 degrees.

163

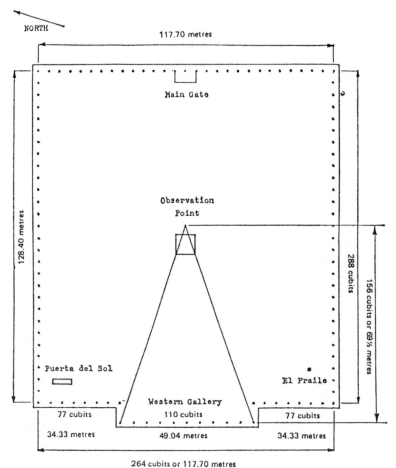

Kalasasaya Temple in Tiahuanaco

Original dimensions in metres

Tiahuanaco cubits of 445.851 millimetres

This map shows the original dimensions of the Temple of Kalasasaya in metres and in Tiahuanaco cubits of 445.851 millimetres each. The Gate of the Sun and the idol called El Fraile are shown in their present locations; nobody knows exactly where they were before the destruction of the temple.

164

The north face of the terrace is in poor shape, but can be reconstructed easily because it is identical to the south side, which is better preserved. This side has twenty-nine pillars of limestone, which are more eroded than the andesite pillars on the west. The length ofthe stonework terrace on which the temple was built is divided by these twenty-nine pillars into twenty-eight equal parts of 4.60 m each. The east end of the terrace was divided into 28 equal parts of 4.20 m each. It is possible that originally, before the western outside gallery was built, the west side of the temple was divided into twenty-four equal intervals of 4.90 m, divided by twenty-five pillars.

All these numbers and divisions sound complicated, but we will see that every dimension had its reason for being and every one was a multiple, sometimes with a slight fraction, of the local foot of 0.297234 m or cubit of 0.445851 m. The cubit was divided into seven hands of 0.063693 m and each hand divided into four fingers measuring 0.015923 m each. As can be seen on the god figure carved in the Puerta del Sol, the gods of Tiahuanaco had only four digits each on their hands and their feet.

Thus the cubit was equal to twenty-eight fingers, just like the twenty-eight intervals between the pillars of the north, east, and south facades of the temple. The only difference shown by the length of the intervals themselves was that the east intervals were of 264 fingers each - the count of days in the lunar year, while the north and south intervals were of 288 fingers each - the number of days in the solar year.

The same numbers are contained in the hieroglyphs of the Tiahuanaco calendar and they are nearly the same as the figures Bellamy and Allen arrived at in their calculations: 264 and 290 instead of 288. This error was caused by the proportion that they used, namely l0:ll, instead of the ll:l2 that I chose because 264 and 288 divided by 24 makes ll and l2. This proportion, by the way, expressed as a trigonometric function of cosine, is very close to that of 23.450^o, the inclination angle of our planet, which could have been 23.556^o at that time.

The Tiahuanaco foot, as calculated from the dimensions of the temple, does not correspond exactly to the local foot as I calculated it from the geographic coordinates. But the difference is only 6/l0 of l mm, and it could be caused by no less than four different reasons.

First, it could be that our ancestors did a poor calculation, which seems to be out of the question, judging by all of the other calculations that they made routinely and exactly. The second reason might be the altitude or the irregularity of the local formation of the Earth's crust, which seems to bulge, giving a longer degree at Tiahuanaco than at sea level. This deformation must have been even greater when the big moon caused the belt around the equator. The third possibility is that Tiahuanaco was part of a large empire, and the local degree was taken from a centre 42 km farther north, from a latitude of 16° 04' south. It would be really curious to find prehistoric ruins at the latter latitude some day. The fourth and most believable explanation is that since Tiahuanaco was built and its calendar calculated, the equator has moved north by 23 minutes of arc.

No matter what the explanation, the foot of Tiahuanaco of 0.297234 m must be the correct value. Bellamy and Allen themselves estimated the Tiahuanaco cubit at 0.4458 m, which gives a foot of 0.2972 m. Another proof that these values are correct is the weight that can be derived from the Tiahuanaco cubic foot - 26,260 g, which is exactly the weight of one talent of gold or silver used for thousands of years throughout the Mediterranean basin. Does that prove that trade existed between these ancient cultures, or is it just proof that both cultures had common roots? Moreover, if we measure with that cubit the dimensions of the different buildings, we always find numbers of cubits that are divisible by 7, 9, 11, 12, and 13, and allow us to calculate important astronomical and mathematical ratios such as 22/7, 14/11, or 12/11, which we have already mentioned.

Now that we know the exact dimensions of the cubit, the foot, and the finger, it is interesting to go back to the andesite pillars of the western gallery and try to find out what the dimensions there tell us. Here are nine dimensions, all in cubits, that can simultaneously explain the irregularity of the spaces between pillars and prove that at the time these pillars were set, there was in the sky a moon much larger and much closer than our present one. Since, of the eleven pillars, the outer two are there only to frame the field of vision, let's look at the nine possible combinations of the nine spaces between the inner pillars and each time add the pillars's own width to the distance. Thus we obtain the following measurements in cubits: 20 1/4, 19, 19, 18, 18 1/4, 17 1/4, 19 1/4, 17 3/4, 19 1/4.

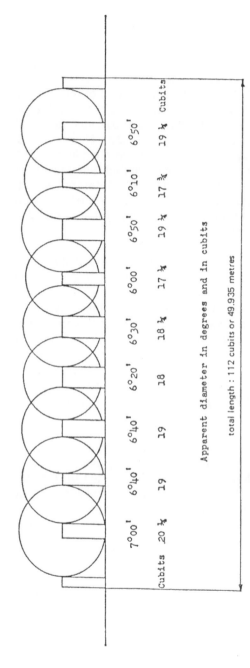

| Cubits | 20 ¾ | 19 | 19 | 18 | 18 ¾ | 17 ¾ | 17 ¾ | 19 ¾ | 17 ¾ | 19 ¾ Cubits |

| 7°00' | 6°40' | 6°40' | 6°20' | 6°30' | 6°00' | 6°50' | 6°10' | 6°50' |

Apparent diameter in degrees and in cubits

total length : 112 cubits or 49.935 metres

Kalasasaya Temple in Tiahuanaco

The nine positions of the Moon 27,000 years ago observed between the pillars of the western gallery

This illustration shows the eleven pillars of the western gallery and the nine positions of the Moon that could be observed between them about 27,000 years ago, when the Moon was much closer to the Earth.

167

We now have seven different intervals, two of them repeated twice, probably to measure something very big, like a moon so close to the Earth that it would vary in its apparent diameter because of the elliptic path it was describing in the sky. But it does not take long to discover that, if an observer places himself 162 cubits from the pillars, the angles from there represented by the above intervals read, starting from the south: 7°, 6° 40', 6° 40', 6° 20', 6° 30', 6°, 6° 50', 6° 10', and 6° 50', giving a total for the observation field of 59°. The average apparent diameter of the moon at that time must have been 6 1/2°, or 11.68 percent bigger than the diameter that we calculated from the laws of celestial mechanics for our present Moon, namely, 5.82^o. We can conclude that the moon of that period was 12 percent larger than the present one.

We have yet to talk about an additional problem tied in with the theory of the four moons, the age of Tiahuanaco. One way to estimate its age would be to use the climatic cycle of 21,000 years that we discussed when we talked about ice ages in *The Constant of Nineveh*. This cycle is the time period needed for the date of the equinox to arrive at the same moment when the Sun is at its perigee - the point closest to Earth. If we want to believe the Tiahuanaco calendar, this timetable was calculated on a date when the spring equinox in the southern hemisphere coincided with the Sun in perigee, a situation that last occurred 6,000 years ago and, before then, 27,000 years ago.

Now, the Tiahuanaco calendar could not possibly have been calculated only 6,000 years ago. The ruins are obviously much older than that, and also, all of the legends from 4,000 BC tell us that our present Moon was already there, shining bright and silvery. So we must believe that the true age of the Tiahuanaco calendar is about 27,000 years, about the same as the cave paintings of Lascaux and Altamira. What is even more surprising is the fact that the numbers 264 and 288 were used by other ancient civilizations in South America, and that the phenomenon of the big moon was known throughout Central America.

In the region of Cuenca, in Ecuador, Juan Moricz found buried caves in 1965 that until then had been known only to the local Indians. His information is scant and inaccessible, but the discoverer reported that the central hall of treasures of these caves has dimensions of 137.7 by 150.2 m, proportional to 264 and 288, numbers that I found and that were not known to anybody until my first book was published. Another surprise is that these two dimensions of the hall of treasures in the Cuenca caves correspond exactly to the local foot of 0.3476 m and the cubit derived from it of 0.5214 m. These dimensions are real and we will find them later. They also give us the precise length of one degree of longitude at 2 1/2° south latitude, which is nearly the latitude of Cuenca.

Father Crespi, who died recently, used to run the local gold museum in Cuenca. He had been a lifelong friend of the local Indians and custodian of the treasures that were brought to him by his Indian friends when they needed something. Most of the objects in the Cuenca museum are pure gold and of extraordinary beauty. The masterpiece is a golden plate 52 cm long, 14 wide, and 4 thick with 56 hieroglyphs. Next to it is a weeping god, also solid gold, 52 cm high, which happens to be the length of the local cubit. *And the god's hands and feet have only four fingers, like the god of Tiahuanaco.*

Strange coincidences? A cubit of longitude, the hall in the caves, the gold tablet, and the gold idol with four fingers; that makes four times the same measurement appears, which we will call the Cuenca cubit of 0.5214 m. When we divide it by 28, we obtain one finger of 18.62 mm. The gold plate of the Cuenca museum keeps surprising me. At first it seemed to be only a standard of length. Then it looked also like a unit of volume of 28 x 2 x 7.5 fingers, or 420 cubic fingers. Finally, with a specific gravity of 19.37 for the very pure Inca gold, it certainly was a unit of weight of 52,520 grams, or two gold talents from the Mediterranean. Now, call *that* a coincidence!

So far none of the fifty-six hieroglyphs has been deciphered. It could be an alphabet of fifty-six letters. It could be a lunar calendar of fifty-six years. It could be anything else. We simply do not know. *But these discoveries have already told us that the civilizations of Tiahuanaco and Cuenca had more than just the four-fingered gods in common.* And we also find the same basic numbers in Monte Alban and Teotihuacan, in Mexico.

The sunken court in Monte Alban measures 78.50 by 85.60 m, or exactly 264 by 288 Tiahuanaco ft, even though the two sites are separated by thousands of kilometres. Even more surprising are the pyramids of Teotihuacan whose dimensions again seem to be based on the two sacred numbers. However, the measurements at

Teotihuacan are a very controversial issue. I have three recent books on the subject all giving different numbers. Only one thing seems almost certain. If we divide 2,400 m, the length of the Grand Avenue, by the Teotihuacan yard of l.0582 m, we obtain the Nineveh constant of 2.268. Is that another coincidence?

In short, we have convincing evidence that four separate American civilizations used the same numbers and the same units of measurement to express the two sacred numbers of astronomy that had the greatest importance for them, the numbers of days in the lunar and in the solar year at that time.

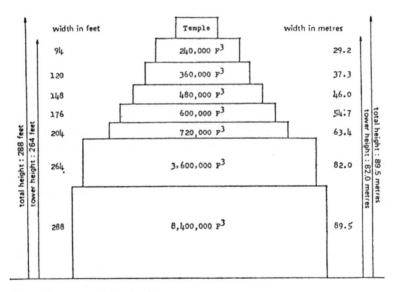

The Tower of Babel

Original dimensions in metres and in Sumerian feet of 310.723 mm

This drawing shows the original dimensions of the Tower of Babel in metres and in Sumerian feet of 0.310723 metres. The tower was built with 57.6 million bricks and its volume of 14,400,000 cubic feet, or 432,000 cubic metres, was ⅓ of the volume of the Great Pyramid of Cheops. In Babylon, 432,000 was also the length in years of the Great Year, and the ratio of 264 :288 was the same as the one used at Kalasasaya in Tiahuanaco.

There is another mysterious example of the use of the same sacred numbers on the other side of the world, namely, at the famed Tower of Babel. It was constructed in units of the Sumerian foot of 0.3l0723 m, out of 57.6 million clay bricks, each with a volume of 0.25 cu. ft. The volume of the whole tower was I4.4 million cu. ft, or 432,000 cu. m, six times smaller than the Cheops pyramid. The tower was 264 ft. tall, and on its top stood the 24 ft. high Temple of Marduk, making the total height of the tower 288 ft. The statue of Marduk was cast in solid gold and weighed 800 Sumerian talents, or 24 metric tons.

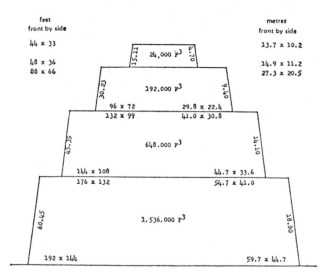

The Ziggurat of Ur

Original dimensions in metres and in Sumerian feet of 0.310723 mm

This drawing shows the original dimensions of the Ziggurat of Ur in metres and in Sumerian feet of 0.310723 metres. It was built with 9.6 million bricks and its volume was 2.4 million cubic feet, or 72,000 cubic metres, which represented $\frac{1}{6}$ of the volume of the Tower of Babel, or $\frac{1}{36}$ of that of the Great Pyramid of Cheops. The first tier has a 132:144 ratio equal to 264:288.

171

It really seems that the Tower of Babel was built with the Tiahuanaco proportion of 264/288 because not only its measurements in height but also the proportion of the two first terraces is such. Its total volume of 432,000 cu m ties it in with the metric system and with the number of 432,000 years, which is used even today by the descendants of the ancient Hindus as an astronomical and religious time cycle. The Babylonians used the same cycle, but divided it by 40, creating the time cycle of 10,800 years, which is found in many cultures. As for the Ziggurat of Ur, its volume was 1/6 of the Tower of It Babel, or 1/36 of the Great Pyramid of Cheops. Also, the surface of its first terrace was 2,268 sq. m!

We must recognize here, whether we like it or not, that widely separated cultures used similar systems for measuring length, volume, weight, and time, standards whose original sources have disappeared without recognizable trace. Yet the common heritage seems incontestable; and if we want to believe the Egyptian, Tibetan, and many other legends, the common source of all culture was a great island in the middle of the Atlantic Ocean that disappeared in the waves 12,000 years ago, the fabled Atlantis, which we will discuss next.

THE MYSTERY OF ATLANTIS

Around 580 BC, when the Athenian statesman Solon had estab-lished the code of law that made him famous, he took a long vaca-tion and went to Sais, then the capital of Lower Egypt. Sais was the centre of culture at that time and people of fame and talent used to congregate there to hone their intellects. It was there that Solon met the high priest of Egypt, Sonchis, who generously showed him a part of the famed Egyptian archives, dating back many thousands of years, and also told him a fascinating story about a terrible disaster that had occurred 9,000 years before. It was the story of the sunken continent of Atlantis.

This legend, which is still considered by many as pure mythology, was retold by Solon to his nephew Dropides, who in turn transmitted it to his descendants, one of whom told it to the philosopher Plato. Two of Plato's most famous works, *Timaeus* and *Critias*, have preserved most of the legend of Atlantis in all its passionate and tragic greatness.

Personally I am convinced that the story of Atlantis, as Solon heard it from Sonchis, and as Plato has given it to us, is true from begin-ning to end; and some day the ruins of Atlantis will be found, just as one after another we found the once legendary Troy, Mycenae, Tiryns, and Knossos. Meanwhile, we can look at the information that has been assembled about Atlantis and the catastrophe that made it diasappear.

According to Sonchis, 9,000 years before his time, there was an im-mense island in the middle of the Atlantic Ocean, due west of the Pil-lars of Hercules, now called the Strait of Gibraltar. This island was bigger that all of North Africa and the Near East put together. Its name was Atlantis and it was inhabited by very advanced people of unknown origin, who were great mathematicians, astronomers, land cultivators, and masters in metallurgy. Their capital city, Poseidonis, was named after the god of the sea, Poseidon, and built in the middle of a vast plain, protected by mountain chains and connected with the ocean by a manmade waterway 600 ft. wide and 100 ft. deep. The canal ringed the entire city and served not only for local transportation but also for ocean-going vessels. The fields around Poseidonis were rich with crops; and horses, cattle, and elephants grazed there. Atlantis was protected both from east and west by a maze of small islands, and navigators had to go through these archipelagoes to come to the fabled place.

Atlantis had lived many thousands of years in peace and prosperity until one day the leadership of the land was taken over by a military clique who decided to conquer all the people who lived around the Mediterranean. The generals of Atlantis raised an army of 750,000 men with many war chariots and easily conquered both sides of the Mediterranean, all of southern Europe except Greece, and all of North Africa except Egypt. Then they decided to push forward and make their victory total by smashing Greece and Egypt.

At that time the highly cultured Egyptians were no match for the invader; but the best warriors of that era, the Greeks, saved the Egyptians by winning decisive victories over the invaders. They even liberated all the conquered Mediterranean land. When the invader fled, the Greeks put together an expeditionary army and sent it to Poseidonis to make sure that there would be no new invasions. It was while the Greeks were in Poseidonis that, within one day and one night, powerful earthquakes and devastating tides destroyed Atlantis. The prospering continent sank beneath the Atlantic Ocean. Both armies and all the people perished. And, according to the description that Sonchis gave Solon, all that was left where once plains and mountains stretched to the horizon, was a huge morass and swamp, something like today's Sargasso Sea.

This detailed and dramatic story is probably one of the greatest recollections of mankind; but until recently it was very hard to take it for anything but legend. Today, however, we know many things not known until relatively recently. We know that human beings have been around for much more than 100,000 years and highly civilized people existed for at least 12,000 years. We know that our continents drift, that the poles shift, that ocean levels change, and that islands emerge and sink. It is no longer possible to say the legend of Atlantis is plain myth because the events it describes were impossible. To the contrary, the disappearance of Atlantis is now known to have been quite possible, geologically as well as historically.

But there is still serious argument as to where Atlantis was located before it disappeared, and for a while it was even believed that Atlantis was the Aegean island of Thera (now called Santorin); and that the great earthquake that made Atlantis disappear into the sea was actually the eruption in 1521 BC of the volcano on Thera.

The Thera argument won't stand up for several reasons. First, if Atlantis really disappeared in 1521 BC, how come the Bible doesn't say anything about it? This was 700 years after the death of Abraham and about 100 years before the birth of Moses, when the Hebrews undoubtedly had mastered the art of keeping written records.

Next, if the disappearance of Atlantis had taken place in the Aegean Sea only 940 years before Solon lived, everybody in Greece would have known it, especially Solon, who was a very learned man. He would have known it just as most educated people today know that England was invaded by the Normans in 1066, even though it happened more than nine hundred years ago.

Equally improbable is the possibility that Atlantis, being larger than all of North Africa and the Near East together, could have been anywhere in the Mediterranean. And certainly a small island like Thera could never have mobilized 750,000 men. Nor have any remains of elephants been found in Thera. Finally we know that Atlantis disappeared after a series of earthquakes, not in a volcanic eruption, which is completely different.

Another much more likely theory postulates that Atlantis was the continents of North and South America together. Now, this total area is indeed as big as North Africa and the Near East together, and indeed there were elephants roaming the plains in America 12,000 years ago. Also, both Americas are rich in metal ores as Atlantis was, and there are many islands along both coasts.

Finally, this new theory is partially based on recent discoveries that Hindus and Phoenicians had agricultural colonies in eastern Mexico where cotton and jute were cultivated 2,900 years ago. Even older are the Sumerian and Phoenician copper and tin mines in Peru and

Bolivia, which also produced gold and silver as long as 4,300 years ago. Inscriptions resembling the Cretan linear writing have been found in cliffs of the Upper Amazon, indicating that sailors from the Aegean passed that way on regular trade routes.

However, even these finds don't seem quite old enough to fit the mystery of Atlantis. They only go back to about l,700 years before Solon, which is not the time of disappearance of the fabled island. Therefore it seems much more likely that, instead of covering both Americas, Atlantis was only located in the central part of the area, from Florida to the estuary of Amazon, which would be southwest of Gibraltar, or the Pillars of Hercules.

The Tibetan bible, the Book of Dzyan, which goes back to the very farthest past, records that in the year 9564 BC a very large part of the land sank into the ocean in what is now the Caribbean and the Gulf of Mexico. History does not tell us how the Tibetans of that time, on the other side of the world, learned about this cataclysm; but they probably got it from the best source - refugees from Atlantis, who went all the way to Tibet to make sure they were on firm ground that wouldn't disappear beneath the waves again. The point is that the date of the catstrophe was exactly recorded and preserved, and the Tibetan record of Atlantis dovetails nicely with Solon's account; so we have no reason to doubt it.

As for the location of Atlantis, if one studies a map of the waters surrounding the American continents, none could be more probable. It is easy to trace the coast of the sunken Atlantis along the line drawn from Florida to the Bahamas, Hispaniola, Puerto Rico, the Antilles, Trinidad, and the north coast of South America from the estuary of the Orinoco to that of the Amazon. And now new discoveries made at the centre of this region offer indisputable proofs and final evidence that Atlantis really existed.

The actual rediscovery of Atlantis began in l967, when Robert Brush, an American pilot, flying at low altitude near Bimini in the Bahamas, noticed a huge rectangular form a few feet below the water. He photographed it right away. Now, the first law of underwater archaeology states that water and waves can create all kinds of strange forms from the sand or rocks on the bottom, but never a rectangle with four right angles. The second law states that any such form invariably belongs to an ancient temple, usually surrounded by

176

smaller rectangles or circles, which were the habitats of the priests, servants, or pilgrims.

Brush called in Dimitri Rebikoff, a professional diver and archaeologist, who had spent twenty years in underwater exploration in the Mediterranean and was considered the most experienced and qualified scientist in this category. He recognized the importance of the discovery right away. He himself had photographed from a plane an immense submerged rectangle 400 m long off the Grand Bahama Bank, as well as other remnants of human construction along a straight line or grouped in circles in an area covering over thirty miles between Orange Cay and Bimini in the Bahamas. Rebikoff in turn asked Professor Manson Valentine, who had discovered important Mayan ruins in the Yucatan, to join in an expedition to Bimini and the surrounding islands.

In August 1968, this expedition discovered a 75-by-90-foot temple of very great age off the coast of Andros, the largest island in the Bahamas. But the most important discovery came on 2 September, 1968, when at the northwest extremity of North Bimini, under only fifteen feet of water, Valentine found a vast expanse of pavement made of flat, rectangular or polygonal stone slabs. All were obviously man-made. These stone slabs had been submerged for many thousands of years, as evidenced by their edges, which had been rounded by the movement of sand over a very, very long time. The biggest slabs were nine to fifteen feet long and formed the whole width of the paved avenues, and in some spots more than one layer of stones could be seen.

The size and form of these slabs, as well as the precise cuts and joints, reminded one of the stone slab ruins on both sides of the Atlantic - the Giza and Baalbek monuments and the temples of Cuzco and Tiahuanaco. Along the coast of Andros at a depth of 150 ft. the French undersea explorer Jacques Cousteau has found a huge stalactite and stalagmite cave, a type of cave that could only have been formed by drops of lime water falling over long periods of time in free air, not under water. And the sediment in this cave is about 12,000 years old.

During the same expedition Cousteau explored the Blue Hole, a deep abyss near the coast of Belize, in Central America, where he discovered a labyrinth of stalactite and stalagmite caves, all at an

177

angle, which is contrary to the way these formations can grow. The only explanation is that a strong earthquake tilted these caves and their formations of calcite deposits. Again, the analysis of the stalactites showed their age to be about 12,000 years.

This is clear evidence that some 12,000 years ago a large part of the American continent, now under the Caribbean Sea and the Gulf of Mexico, was submerged during a seismic catastrophe so that only the highest mountain peaks remained above water. These are, of course, the Caribbean islands of today.

All this sounds strangely similar to what the Book of Dzyan tells us about Atlantis. Everything is there, including the right date, 9564 BC. The location, too, is the same - the Gulf of Mexico, the Bahamian area of the Atlantic, and the Caribbean Sea. Is it still possible to assume that the authors of the Tibetan bible invented it? Personally I do not think so. I sincerely believe the ruins of human constructions on the submerged plateau off the Bahamas are indeed offering us the first indisputable evidence that Atlantis really existed and that at least part of this sunken continent was in that very area.

Also, if Atlantis had never existed, we would have to invent it to explain several mysteries that are otherwise totally unexplainable. First, there is the mythological mystery. How is it that the gods of nearly all civilizations around the world came from the sea, after they had descended from the skies, like the Mayan god Kukulkan? His sarcophagus, which has been discovered in Palenque, in southern Mexico, has the shape of a fish. The god Oannes emerged every day from the deep sea to teach the Sumerians assembled on the shore in order to listen and learn. We could also ask how come the gods arriving on the American continent always came from the east, while the gods coming to Europe always arrived from the west, all indications of one central Atlantic origin long since forgotten.

Then we have the mystery of the Atlantic dialects different from those of the Mediterranean: a group of rough, guttural dialects still spoken, from the Guanche dialect of the Azores and the Canary Islands to the many tongues of unknown origin spoken between Morocco and Ireland. And the impossible-sounding names, even more difficult to write in our Greek-Latin alphabet, consisting of letters that we use very little, like x and z, found in places inhabited by the Bretons, the Basques, the Gaels, the Andalusians, and the Berbers. All of these

178

mysterious languages are related to the Guanche dialect, all the way across the Azores and the Canary Islands to the Mayan land of the Yucatan with its ancient religious centres like Chichen Itza, Iszamal, Tzebtun, Uxmal, Uxul, Yaxuna or Oxkintok.

There is the story of the Basque missionary, who arrived in the Yucatan and discovered that the best way to make himself clear to the local Indians was to talk to them in his native dialect! Some day, when we decipher the mysterious ancient inscriptions found in the Azores and the Canary Islands, we might learn more about these languages, too. Even the Basques themselves are an unsolved enigma. Tall and strong, they have all of the characteristics of the Cro-Magnon people who emerged suddenly about 65,000 years ago, while the lesser Neanderthal man continued to exist for a while longer. Could the Cro-Magnons have been colonists from Atlantis, who established their new homes in Europe and survived there the destruction of their land of origin, continuing the culture that they had brought along?

Besides, the Basques have a blood type and Rh factor combination that is extremely rare and can be found only along the shores of the Atlantic Ocean in people speaking the strange dialects. The same blood types are found in Egyptian and Inca mummies. That could explain why the Incas and the pharaohs married between brothers and sisters - in order to preserve the rare blood that was not of this world, so it seems, because no other humans have it in such pure form.

In 1952 two British scientists analyzed the blood of five Inca mummies discovered at Cuzco and lent to the British Museum in London. One showed a blood group with an Rh factor that no one had seen anywhere in this world before. Another mummy had a blood group that was very rare among other American Indians. Unfortunately, the experiments cannot be repeated because all five mummies were destroyed when a water pipe burst in the basement of the British Museum. But it does look as if both the Egyptians and the Basques on one side of the Atlantic, and the Incas on the other, had blood that was different from that of the people living next to them. Was that the blood of the inhabitants of the sunken continent of Atlantis?

Another mystery is the similarity of customs on both sides of the Atlantic. Sumerians and Egyptians used the same art of mummification that was practiced by the Mayas and the Incas. They did this out of their belief in either a life after death or reincarnation, and they constructed pyramids to preserve and protect the departed. Now we have scientific proof that somehow the shape of the pyramid preserves and sterilizes organic matter, an effect that can be observed even in small pyramid-shaped containers made of plastic or cardboard. On both sides of the Atlantic, pyramids were also constructed in ancient times as astronomical observatories, but that, probably, was not the primary reason for building them.

Above all, the similarity between each of these cultures is demonstrated by the way they did their astronomical calculations and by the systems of measurement they developed. Obviously, they all observed the same stars and planets. Yet the fact that they made the calculations in exactly the same way and that from among so many other possible combinations in the movements of the celestial bodies, they chose the very same conjunctions of the same planets, is more than striking. It just could not have happened unless the Sumerians, the Egyptians, the Aztecs, and the Mayas had either evolved from one central civilization, or were in constant contact with each other. If there was a common centre, it had to be a land in between the two sides of the Atlantic Ocean, the sunken continent of Atlantis.

Another equally striking similartity was the Sun worship of the Egyptians and the Mayas, both of whom believed that their kings were sons of the Sun god, even though the Egyptians, being more civilized, did not practice human sacrifice. Since the Egyptians did not colonize the Mayas or vice versa, the only logical explanation is that both cultures developed from a Sun cult in a land of common origin, probably an island in the Atlantic.

Finally, on both sides of the Atlantic we find identical huge stone block edifices, built of cut pieces so heavy that even our present-day equipment could not move them. If anyone doubts this, let him remember what happened only a few years ago, when an international task force helped save the gigantic Abu Simbel statues before completion of the Aswan Dam in Egypt. The statues had to be cut into pieces for lifting and transportation.

On the west side of the Atlantic, similar huge blocks were used at Cuzco and Tiahuanaco and also at the newly discovered underwater constructions near Bimini. On the east side we have the pyramids of Egypt and the gigantic stone slabs of Baalbek in Lebanon, a temple of totally unknown origin. The ruins of Baalbek, at an altitude of 3,800 feet, stand on a platform built of enormous stone blocks weighing more than 800 tons each. None of today's machines could move these megaliths or even lift them. Such blocks must have been put into place either by giants or by beings of a civilization that knew the secrets of levitation and antigravity.

Three giant blocks from Baalbek now serve as the base of a Roman temple dedicated to Jupiter. The largest of these blocks measures 21 by 4 by 4m exactly; the two others are each 19.50 by 4 by 4m. Together all three represent 60 m in length and 960 cu m in volume. *These exact measurements make it nearly impossible to believe that the ancients who built Baalbek didn't know our metric system.* Evidently they did not use our standard metre, but a cubit of 500 mm and a foot of 333 mm which is exactly the same. For them, the length of one latitude degree was equal to 222,222 cubits and one minute of latitude measured 5,555 feet. The same foot of 333 mm, also called Carolingian foot, was used by Emperor Charlemagne for the construction of his cathedral at Aix La Chapelle in AD 798.

For the constructors of this ancient site, the polar circumference of our globe was 80 million cubits, or 120 million ft; and these units of length seem to have common ground with Sakkara, where metric dimensions were discovered and even a double metre standard was found engraved on a wall. The huge stones of Baalbek were cut out from bedrock 400 m away from the edifice and the quarry was set at a much lower level than the building site. It is there that another unfinished block was found, measuring 21.33 by 4.66 by 4.33 m; obviously, a block that would eventually have been cut to the exact size of 21 by 4 by 4 m, like the largest stone of the temple foundation. We will probably never know what caused the constructors of Baalbek to leave suddenly without finishing what they had begun, just as the statue carvers of Easter Island did, probably at the same time and for the same reason.

There is another group of stones that is probably related to the catastrophe of Atlantis. These are the megalithic monuments found only near the shores of the Atlantic in Europe and North Africa in the areas where people still speak the strange dialects. This is another confirmation of the theory that they all came from the same race of

181

Atlanteans, at one time spoke the same language, practised the same Sun cult, and constructed very similar megalithic monuments, at one time in the past.

It appears now that as a group of refugees survived the sinking of the continent and landed first on the West African coast, a majority of them moved north and reached first Morocco, then Spain, Portugal, France, and finally the British Isles. Others went around Africa to Ceylon and the occidental part of India, where they constructed more than 2,000 megaliths. Some went farther on and reached Tibet, which explains how the authors of the Tibetan bible knew with such certainty the date of the great disaster of Atlantis and all the other precise details.

A very interesting book was published some time ago by Glyn Daniel that registers the distribution of megalithic monuments all over the world and tells us that an enormous dolmen with a stone table weighing 600 tons stands in eastern Korea; so it seems that refugees from the sunken Atlantis even got as far as that.

Until recently the general opinion was that the megalithic monuments of Europe were no more than about 3,000 years old, so nobody associated them with Atlantis that disappeared 12,000 years ago. But now, when we have the first proofs that Atlantis really existed, we also have discoveries indicating that some of the dolmens and menhirs are at least 10,000 years old or older. Colin Renfrew threw out all the old traditions and came up with a book proving that the megaliths of France, Spain, and Wales are much older than the tombs of Myceneae, the ziggurats of Mesopotamia, or even the pyramids of Egypt.

In other words, our civilization was not born in the Middle East, to be brought north into Europe. Just the opposite - it started in Western Europe and went down southeast towards Greece, Crete, Egypt, Mesopotamia, and western India.

Some who do not believe that Atlantis really existed might ask how come no artifacts have ever been found from the lost continent that could have been brought to Europe or the Mediterranean basin before the destruction of Atlantis. I have wondered about this question myself and I think that I have found an answer. No material except solid rock, which is not easily transported, and maybe solid gold, can last for 12,000 years. Most other materials oxidize and turn to dust. It is quite possible that some objects that fill our museums as unidentified primitive art and pagan idols are indeed remnants of Atlantis. The pure gold tablets in the museum of Cuenca are one example of such possibility. So were the many hieroglyph-covered gold statues and tablets that the Spanish conquistadors melted into ingots, destroying for ever the great archaeological value of these relics. Much of the evidence we now seek may have been destroyed centuries ago.

Luckily, however, there is one object, the only one that I know, that in my opinion comes from Atlantis. It is unique at this moment and the only one of its kind in the whole world. It is the ceramic disc of Phaistos, thousands of years old, discovered by Sir Arthur Evans in the 1890's in the southern part of Crete under a thick layer of volcanic ashes. This ceramic disc, about twenty centimetres in diameter, is covered on both sides with hieroglyphs that no one so far has been able to decipher.

The characters are displayed in a spiral form, starting in the centre and turning anticlockwise. The signs are clustered in groups of one to seven, separated by a stroke. These strokes, as well as the spiral line that encloses the characters, are engraved. The signs themselves have been impressed in the soft clay with a stamp or a seal. Judging by the fine detail of these seals, they must have been made of metal; and so immediately one is reminded of the mysterious gold tablet of Cuenca with its fifty-six hieroglyphs struck in the soft gold before it solidified, in order not to alter the standard weight.

Thirty of the undeciphered sign groups on the Phaistos disc are on one side, thirty-one on the other, which could suggest that it is a calendar based on alternating thirty- and thirty-one-day months, coming into phase every four years with the solar year. The cycle of such a calendar would be 1,461 days or twenty-seven months of thirty days each and twenty-one months of thirty-one days each. The hieroglyphs for each day could represent either the name of the day or what had to be done that day. Some scientists even think the disk may have been a navigational table. But so far no one has been smart enough to decipher and explain its use and significance. Neither can I, despite my conviction that this artifact comes from Atlantis and is proof of that continent's existence, as are the stone pavements found under water near Bimini.

The discovery near Bimini, in the Bahamas, incidentlly, occurred just as predicted by the famous American seer Edgar Cayce, who in 1923 said that a temple of Atlantis would be found underwater near Bimini in 1968. Even for someone who is no adept of occult sciences, it is difficult to abstain from the belief that indeed Cayce must have had some contact with extraterrestrials who knew exactly where the vestiges of Atlantis were to be found, and who may therefore some day give us *all* the information about the sunken continent and its lost civilization.

EXTRATERRESTRIAL CIVILIZATIONS

Early in 1961, Otto Struve, the director of the National Science Foundation's radio astronomy observatory at Green Bank, West Virginia, and Frank Drake, his assistant, initiated Project Ozma to search for radio signals from outer space, in order to determine if there were other civilizations in space trying to contact us. No one was prepared for what was going to happen, even those who had worked so long and so hard to finally get the authorization to perform the experiment.

There are several stars located at a reasonable distance from the Earth, only a few light-years away, suspected of having a planetary system comparable to ours. For some reason, it was decided that the most favorable of these stars at that time was the star Tau Ceti, in the constellation of Cetus, the Whale, which is located close to the celestial equator and next to the constellation of Aries, the Ram.

The huge parabolic antenna of the observatory was aimed in the direction of Tau Ceti. The mechanism of compensation for the rotation of the Earth was set in motion; then the receiver, maser amplifier, and recorder were turned on. The only thing left to be done was to wait, but those attending the experiment did not have to wait too long.

Almost immediately, the needle of the recorder began indicating strong signals which, for any specialist in space communications, could mean nothing but a coded message from an intelligent correspondent on a planet orbiting Tau Ceti. The signals lasted for about two minutes, then stopped, leaving those attending stupefied and unable to say a word. Finally, the whole thing was classified 'secret' and that was the end of Project Ozma; it had lasted little more than two minutes.

However, there was a general feeling in the scientific circles of that time that a message from outer space had been received and deciphered but that, for some reason, it was decided that it could not be disclosed to the public. Since then a new Project Ozma has been initiated, but by military personnel this time.

The second case of communications with a space civilization, which was reported in *Paris-Match,* 21 April, 1973, occurred in the Soviet Union. Two Russian specialists in space communications, Vsevolod Troitsky, director of the Radiophysics Research Institute of Gorki, and Nicolai Kardashev, director of the Space Research Institute in Moscow, were absolutely convinced that they had received radio signals from an extraterrestrial civilization.

They initiated their space listening program in 1970, with four radio frequency receiving stations located far apart from each other. This allowed them, by comparing the signals received, to eliminate terrestrial interferences and keep only the space signals, those that were identical from the four receiving stations. These signals from outer space whose duration varied from two to ten minutes, were repeated at regular intervals, following a regular pattern. For these scientists this indicated, without any doubt, that they had an artificial origin and that they were transmitted by intelligent beings whose culture was at least as advanced as ours.

The two Russian scientists have not succeeded so far in establishing the exact origin of these signals, but they are positive that they must originate from our solar system, either from another planet or from one of its satellites or even from an alien spacecraft from another solar system. The third case of radio communications with outer space was that of the Izarian astronauts deciphered by Duncan Lunan and already discussed in this book.

There is another case history which links extraterrestrial civilizations and flying saucers. Everyone knows the story of Barney and Betty Hill who disclosed under hypnosis that they had been kidnapped in a flying saucer in 1961 and had undergone a physical examination. They had been shown a celestial map of the stars as seen from the planet of origin of the astronauts.

To tell you the truth, I did not believe a word of it at first. I only became interested in 1964 when Betty Hill was able, again under hypnosis, to reproduce the star map shown to her by the astronauts; but

I was still skeptical about the whole thing. I thought that maybe she was really going too far.

But then I became fascinated when an amateur American astronomer named Marjorie Fish discovered that the celestial map shown to Betty Hill corresponded exactly to the one that could be seen from the star Zeta Reticuli, which is located in the southern hemisphere of the celestial vault, between the two bright stars Achernar and Canopus.

I had good reasons to be excited because the main star drawn by Betty Hill on her map was a double star; and no one on Earth at that time, in 1961, or even in 1964, knew that Zeta Reticuli was a double star. This was only discovered in March 1973 by the American astronomer Peter van de Camp, who specializes in that kind of research, especially the stars that move in spirals instead of straight lines, which indicates stars with a planetary system or double and triple stars.

Then I knew that Betty Hill had been telling the truth all the time, because there was no way she could have known that Zeta Reticuli was a double star when she was drawing the star map. Also, that map was drawn in a way that I have never seen anywhere on Earth. The Reticulian astronauts, who were practical people rather than poets, linked their stars with traffic lines (double, single, or dotted), depending on the intensity of their traffic, instead of trying to draw bulls, lions, or even virgins as our ancestors used to do.

About thirty years ago, an incredible phenomenon happened in France that is very little known (it was reported in the September 1959 issue of *Aerospace Engineering*) but could very well have been a signal from an outer-space civilization for the purpose of informing us about their existence.

For almost five years, from 1953 to 1957, Maurice Allais, director of the French National Centre of Scientific Research, performed in his underground laboratory of Saint Germain on the west side of Paris experiments in terrestrial gravitation with a 7,500 g pendulum at the end of an 830 mm rod weighing 4,500 g, or, in other words, a total pendulum weight of 12 kg.

187

As proven by the 1851 experiments of Leon Foucault, a pendulum always oscillates in the same plane with respect to outer space, in such a way that its plane of oscillation seems to rotate relatively to the surface of the Earth.

The constant observation and recording of this apparent rotation and its variations, relative to the theoretical rotation that has been computed from astronomical data, allows a very accurate study of the different motions of the Earth and, especially, of the regularity of its rotation around its polar axis.

On 30 June, 1954, Maurice Allais was watching his pendulum with particular attention, for a total eclipse of the Sun visible in Europe was to happen that day around noon, which eventually could slightly modify the plane of oscillation of the pendulum. But he certainly did not expect what did happen during that eclipse.

When the eclipse started, the plane of oscillation of the pendulum suddenly shifted by 15 degrees, from 170° to 185°. It stayed at 185° for the duration of the eclipse, but finally came back to its original position when the eclipse was over. As far as we know, this had never happened before and it has never happened since.

The announcement of this fantastic phenomenon made a lot of waves in scientific circles at the time, and Allais was almost accused of having made up the whole story; but he was a very conscientious scientist, and the angular shift of the pendulum was recorded by several of his instruments. It was indisputable. In the thirty years which have elapsed, numerous tentative explanations have been proposed without success.

Many scientists have been thinking for some time that outer space civilizations could very well have discovered a long time ago the secrets of gravitation, which they would thereafter know how to control and could use for the propulsion of their flying saucers. That would explain the incredible maneuvers flying saucers perform in our skies, which have never been explained by the classical theories of official science.

Let us now suppose that they had decided some day to use gravitational forces to catch our attention and give us scientific proof of their existence. They would evidently have many different ways to do it;

but one of the best would certainly be to use gravitational forces to disturb suddenly the observations made by our astronomers and physicists during a total eclipse of the Sun, which would naturally be watched by thousands of scientists. Moreover, that would have the additional advantage of being noticed only by scientists, without the risk of causing a panic in the general public.

Also, that phenomenon did not happen at the time of just any solar eclipse. It happened during one of those famous total solar eclipses that occur precisely on 30 June every nineteen years, like the last one on 30 June, 1973, or the next one on 30 June, 1992. Is it still really possible to believe that it was just another *coincidence*, especially during the year 1954, when there was an *invasion* of flying saucers in France?

For that reason or some other, French scientists seem to take the problem of flying saucers very seriously. A few years ago a young French scientist by the name of Claude Poher, director of the French National Centre of Space Research in Toulouse, decided to prove scientifically once and for all the actual existence of flying saucers and to establish their composite sketch, as reported in *Paris-Match,* 23 March, 1974.

Out of 35,000 UFO observation reports that he had been able to collect, he selected the thousand best, translated them on to IBM punch cards, and fed them to a computer. Then he fed to the same computer the apparent characteristics of everything that could be seen in the sky and be mistaken for a flying saucer, like the planet Venus or weather balloons so dear to the US Air Force, for the computer to compare with the UFO sightings and reach a final decision as to whether there was some correlation between the two kinds of data.

The verdict of the computer was that, first, flying saucers really do exist and cannot be confused with anything else in the sky. They have landed hundreds of times in deserted spots, far away from urban areas. They appear during the day as bright metallic objects reflecting sunlight and casting shadows, and during the night take on a yellowish or greenish-orange color. They can appear in the form of discs, spheres, or even cigars.

Seventy percent of the observations were made at night, one in ten involved landings, and one in twenty were cases when extraterrestrial astronauts were seen by or had contacts with humans. Very powerful magnetic forces were always present in any case, and these forces could cut the power of automobile or aircraft generators, disturb radio transmissions, and make all kinds of on-board electromagnetic instruments go completely crazy.

Moreover, flying saucers can fly at more than 25,000 km an hour and suddenly fly back in the opposite direction, a maneuver that no space vehicle of human construction could do at present without disintegrating on the spot. Also, Poher has investigated eleven landing sites in France and found impressions on the ground similar to those that would have been left by a three-ski aircraft landing gear. The depth of these impressions indicates a weight of from 50 to 100 tons and a length of 200 to 300 m for the spacecraft. Also, nothing can now grow in those impressions, as if the ground had been burned.

I am not going to retell the story of Ezekiel and the flying saucer he saw near Babylon in 592 BC because you can read it in the Bible or in a very interesting book published a few years ago by one of my colleagues at NASA, *The Spaceships of Ezekiel* by Joseph Blumrich. But it is the oldest flying saucer report that I know of. I think, however, that I should make a personal contribution. I think I know how flying saucers enter our solar system and, step by step, arrive near Earth. In other words, I think that I have discovered their flight schedule.

In April 1973, when I was computing the revolution and conjunction periods of all the planets to verify the validity of the Nineveh number as a constant of the solar system, I was puzzled by the fact that Mars was in conjunction with the Earth every 780 days, or every 2.135 years, while it was in conjunction with Jupiter every 816 days, or every 2.235 years, a difference of only 36 days.

Then I remembered reading a few months before that flying saucer invasions seemed to occur precisely every 800 days, or a little bit more than every two years. That was enough to put my computer in motion and I discovered that the dates of flying saucer invasions corresponded precisely with the dates of Mars-Earth or Mars-Jupiter conjunctions.

Arriving from a faraway stellar system with a very high velocity, these spaceships could use the enormous gravitational attraction of the four big planets of our solar system to slow down and settle into an orbit around Jupiter or one of its four largest satellites. There, like in an airport terminal, they could wait for their connecting flight, the planet Mars, to pass by and then settle into an orbit around that planet. There they could wait again for the Earth to pass by and then settle into an orbit around the Earth or the Moon.

In astronautics, passing from one planet to the next with a minimum of fuel consumption is called using a minimum energy orbit, and space astronauts might just do that. Anyway, for the fun of it, and before we know for sure, I have established a flight schedule for outer space travellers arriving on Earth and, believe it or not, it checks perfectly with the dates of the latest flying saucer invasions.

Of course, the interval between two flights will never be exactly 780 or 816 days, because of elliptical orbits, but do you know one single airline that is always on time? Anyway for optimal precision in arrival time, the Mars-Jupiter and Mars-Earth flights will coincide every 143 years.

MYSTERIOUS VISITORS

Thirty years ago, I did not believe in flying saucers. At that time I was working for NASA as a space scientist, on the Communications System of the Apollo spacecraft, which was to land on the Moon five years later. Then the UFO phenomenon was practically unknown; and anyway, none of us would have dared to mention it in NASA circles, because that would certainly have been the end of one's career.

Then I made several trips to France, where I learned from French scientists not only that the UFO problem was real, but also that it was seriously investigated by official agencies of several European countries including Russia. Unfortunately, I had to keep that for myself when I came back.

Now things have changed. First of all, I am not working for NASA any longer. Then NASA itself has been forced to recognize the existence of the UFO phenomenon, and even to admit that it did not know what it was or where it was coming from. Also, serious magazines now discuss the UFO problem with qualified scientists such as Jacques Vallee, for example. Moreover, according to recent astronomical discoveries, it is now very likely that there might exist other civilizations in outer space, and that some of them could even be far more advanced than we. It is therefore perfectly logical to try to establish a contact with these civilizations, first by listening to the messages that they might try to transmit to us, then by sending them simple messages ourselves with the primitive means at our disposal, such as radio and laser, for example.

We first have to determine the kind of message that would have the best chance to be received and understood by ourselves in the first case, or by them in the second case. Most information scientists now believe that the best message would be one made of simple numbers representing mathematical ratios, such as 22/7 for Pi or 89/55 for Phi, or prime numbers such as 7, 11, 13, for example, whose ratios have decimal values representing repetitions of figures that could not fail to attract attention.

As a matter of fact, it seems that we have already received several similar messages that went completely unnoticed, even by those who were supposed to notice and decipher them. But we are crossing a sacred and dangerous frontier between two different scientific worlds.

The first one is made of official scientists who might be willing to accept the possibility of extraterrestrial life in the universe, but would never accept the possibility of interstellar travel, or the idea that flying saucers could exist and carry astronauts from another world in outer space. The second one is made of independent or retired scientists like me, who can afford to discuss the UFO problem freely without the risk of losing their jobs, and very few official scientists who have the courage to take that chance. This is why interesting discoveries in the field of UFO research are always made by these independent scientists.

Since we are not accepted in scientific publications, we have to disclose our theories and discoveries in popular books, magazine articles, and television interviews. Personally, I first wrote a book which was published in French in Paris ten years ago and has now been translated into five languages, including two English editions here and in England. I also wrote a second book which has been published in French and Spanish, and will soon be published in English here. The publication of the first book has already resulted in several television interviews where I could discuss the UFO problem, and in my participation in "*In Search of Earth Visitors*", an episode of the popular television series of Alan Landsburg.

Personally, I am mostly interested in UFO landings, and especially in their landing patterns and in the tracks they leave on the ground. As you know, many UFO landings that have been reported in recent years have occurred in France, where the local gendarmes are instructed to go immediately onto the landing site to investigate and record everything. They determine the longitude and latitude, and make a drawing of the landing print, with exact measurements of angles and dimensions.

In 1954, for example, there was an invasion of flying saucers in France. There were 76 UFO landings in 25 days, from 24 September to 18 October of that year. As usual, the gendarmes recorded the time, longitude and latitude of each landing, as well as the shape and dimensions of the print left on the ground, and the estimated weight of the object, according to the depth of the tracks and to the condition of the ground at the time of the landing.

The landing sites were investigated at that time by several famous French experts such as Aime Michel and Paul Misraki, who plotted the landing sites on a large map of France. This allowed them to discover that straight lines could be traced on the map between a certain number of landing sites, such as between Bayonne and Vichy for example, over an amazing distance of 483 kms or about 300 miles.

They also noticed that some of these lines were parallel and separated by an average distance of 63 kms. These were the first numerical data ever obtained from UFO observations, and the only logical conclusion that could be derived from them was that both distances were exact multiples of a length of 21 cms, the wave length of hydrogen, which can be found anywhere in the universe and therefore could represent an ideal measuring unit for astronauts from another world wanting to establish a contact with us.

A few years later, a French scientist named Jean Charles Fumoux had a bright idea. He took a very large map of France and started tracing triangles between the 76 landing sites, in order to see if some of them had any particular characteristics that would give him a clue to the landing pattern of these mysterious alien spacecraft. He was then surprised to discover *that many of the triangles were isosceles with two equal sides*, and decided to push the investigation a little further to find out what the percentage could be, and if it was always the same for any number of triangles.

Our friend Fumoux knew that, with a set of 76 points and according to a well known formula, one can make 70,300 different triangles, which is an enormous number, but that did not discourage him because he already knew that he had discovered something really fantastic, which could be the first clue that he was looking for. It took him a few years to measure all the triangles, but he finally made it, and found that there were 1864 isosceles triangles or an approximate ratio of 264/7 or twelve times 22/7, and that ratio reminded him of something that he had seen some time before.

As a matter of fact, he had just read my original book which was published by Dell in 1979, where I indicated that our ancestors, who probably had a cosmic origin, were using a Pi factor of 22/7 for the construction of Stonehenge and for that of the Great Pyramid, for example. However, Fumoux could not understand why the percentage of isosceles triangles indicated by the UFO landing sites should be an inverse function of the Pi factor that was used a long time ago by our prehistoric ancestors.

He then wrote to me and asked me to check his calculations, which I found to be correct. I advised him to check all of his data once more and feed them to a computer, in order to see if the percentage would remain the same with any number of triangles, or if it was just a coincidence in that case. It took him some time to find a French computer scientist who would believe him and consider his theory seriously enough to agree to check it with his computer. He finally convinced Jean Francois Gille, a Director of Research at the CNRS or Centre National de Recherche Scientifique, who was convinced that the Fumoux theory was wrong, but accepted anyway to check it on his computer. It if could be proved wrong, it could be dismissed.

The computer showed that Fumoux was right and that Gille was wrong, which caused quite a shock to those who were watching the experiment. Gille was an honest scientist, however, and he sent me a telegram immediately, saying that the Fumoux theory was correct and that I would receive all of the details later.

He took the latitudes and longitudes of the 76 landing sites, transformed them into decimal coordinates and fed them to a computer in order to have the dimensions of all the triangles and find out how many of them were isosceles. He used several different combinations of points in order to prove that the results would be different, but on the contrary, the computer always gave him the same result.

There was an average of 1864 isosceles triangles, give or take a few. And 70,300 divided by 1864 gave Gille a ratio of 264/7 or twelve times 22/7, exactly the same as that which Fumoux had computed with his bare hands, a few nails, and a few hundred meters of string. Just to be sure, Gille then picked up 76 random points on the map, fed their geographic coordinates to the computer, in order to find out what the difference would be. He did that four times, with four different sets of 76 random points, and successively obtained 1613, 1621, 1631, and

196

l637 isosceles triangles, or about 250 less than with the actual UFO landing sites! Gille therefore concluded that, beyond any reasonable doubt, the UFO landing sites in France were not randomly distributed, but on the contrary, **seemed to have been carefully selected by our mysterious visitors**.

In my opinion, they were selected in such a way as to form a very particular geometric pattern representing a mathematical message based on the Pi factor, the oldest calculation tool in the world, discovered by our prehistoric ancestors when they first decided to trace a circle on the ground. All we have to do now is to try to find out who these mysterious visitors are who came from a distant planet especially to leave their marks on the soil of France and in 76 different locations.

To announce their discovery, Jean Francois Gille and Jean Charles Fumoux called a press conference at the Cercle Republicain in Paris with Philippe Schneyder, a friend who had press connections. Most French newspapers attended the conference, including the conservative Le Monde and Le Figaro, and the more liberal Liberation and Le Parisien Libere. Moreover, Agence France Presse issued a communique which was transmitted all over the world on ll December 79. So far, there has been no official reaction to the disclosure of the Fumoux theory; and French government officials are probably still wondering what they should do about it.

I have been puzzled for some time by the number 76. A multiple of l9, it was very seldom used by ancient astronomers and mathematicians, except for the standstill cycle of the Moon of 6802 days, the sidereal revolution period of Jupiter of 4332 days, or the Egyptian lunisolar cycle of 27,759 days which represented 76 solar years or 940 lunar months, and was used in the construction of the astronomical computer discovered in l900 at the bottom of the Aegean Sea near Antikythera.

In a book published in Paris in l975, the late French scientist Jean Sendy mentioned two units of time, the REGA and the HELEK, which were used by ancient Hebrews and mentioned several times in the Bible. There were l080 Rega in one hour, which was three times the sacred number 360 and therefore not too strange, and 76 Helek in a Rega, which is much more surprising since the Hebrews never used that number for anything else. As an example, the Book of

Enoch has an astronomical section based on the numbers 7, 13, and 364, but the number 19 is never mentioned there. It seems very likely that the Hebrews learned about that number during their captivity in Egypt, in Nineveh, or in Babylon.

Jean Sendy had also discovered that our ancestors probably knew about the velocity of light, which they estimated at 296,400 kms per second; in that case, one Helek would be the exact time necessary for light waves to travel thirteen million meters, a very important number for our ancestors. Moreover, light waves would take exactly 30 Helek to travel from the Moon to the Earth, and 150 Rega from the Sun to the Earth. So as one can see, there might be another mystery to solve in the use of the sacred number 76 by our mysterious visitors from outer space.

Of course I do not expect every one to believe that my theory is correct, but the facts are here to prove it; and the geographic coordinates of the 76 landing sites will be mailed upon request to any serious scientist who has a computer and the technical ability to program it correctly. Gille, Fumoux, and myself are still working on that mysterious problem, in France and in California.

On 10 May 1967, a French farmer of Marliens, near Dijon in Burgundy discovered in his field a deep print left by a UFO whose landing had been observed the night before by several witnesses from that village. The farmer called the local gendarmes who arrived immediately from their nearby headquarters in Genlis, and started to measure the landing print. They noticed that the print had the shape of an irregular star with six points and that there were six holes in the center that could make another smaller star. Considering also each of these stars as an irregular hexagon, one could obtain a series of twelve irregular triangles whose 24 sides were all different and whose surfaces were also different.

I had seen the drawing of that print in a French UFO magazine and had noticed its strange shape, but without giving it any particular attention at that time. It was only recently that I had the idea of investigating all of these dimensions and to feed them into a computer with different coefficients, in order to find out if there could be any relation among them or with other astronomical, mathematical, or nuclear numbers.

198

I was then surprised to discover that all of these dimensions were exact multiples of an inch of 25 millimeters which was used a long time ago by our Egyptian ancestors, and that they represented *indisputable mathematical ratios which certainly could not have happened by chance, but could very well represent a mathematical message that astronauts from another world might have tried to transmit to us.*

By transforming the metric dimensions of the print into ancient inches of 25 mms, I obtained a series of 24 different numbers from 19 to 118 which it would be fastidious to enumerate here, but will be sent upon request to any qualified investigator interested. I noticed immediately that these numbers were all multiples of thirteen prime numbers from 7 to 79 whose ratios correspond to well-known mathematical factors such as Pi and Phi, as well as to usual trigonometric functions. Then I noticed that five of these prime numbers, when they were combined with the other numbers, could produce repetitions of figures such as those already mentioned. I finally noticed that these thirteen prime numbers were precisely those that were used by our ancestors to compute their astronomical cycles, such as 364 - 365 - 378 - 399 - 584 - 780 days, which were related to the Moon and the Sun, Saturn and Jupiter, or Venus and Mars, respectively.

When I computed the surface of the large hexagon, I found that it was equal to 15,792 ancient square inches or 9.870 square meters, which did not seem to have any particular meaning, at least until I discovered that this metric value was the square of the Pi factor. In other words, the surface of the large hexagon was equal to that of a square with sides of 3.1416 metres! Then when I computed the surface of the small hexagon, I was not too surprised to discover that it was equal to 2836 ancient square inches or 1.7725 square meters, which is exactly the square root of the Pi factor!

Of course it could be just a fantastic array of coincidences and again, I cannot expect everyone to believe it, but some will and that is good enough for me. Whether my assumptions are correct or not, these cases of UFO landings in France are really puzzling and should be investigated. Could it be that extraterrestrial astronauts are really landing on the surface of the Earth just to try to communicate with us by means of a very simple mathematical message that we could understand? I agree that it must be very difficult to believe for most

199

people, and especially for official scientists; but it could very well be true and we cannot afford to miss such a wonderful opportunity to get acquainted with our cousins from outer space.

Many UFO observers are convinced that our extraterrestrial visitors, with their fantastic maneuvers in the sky, are trying to show us what we could do ourselves if we were not so stupid as to waste the limited natural resources of our planet for rocket propulsion, when there are at our disposal several unlimited sources of power, such as solar or electromagnetics, and the nuclear fusion of hydrogen whose supply is unlimited anywhere in the universe.

Solar energy is not very practical on the surface of the Earth, since it only works for a few hours during the day when it does not rain; but it is already used efficiently in space, where all our satellites and space vehicles are now powered with solar cells. Scale models of flying saucers have already been flying at fantastic speeds in magnetic fields in Toulouse, France. British scientists have finally realized the fusion of a hydrogen nucleus enclosed in an electromagnetic field, at a temperature of one million degrees centigrade, but only for a few seconds.

Other UFO observers believe that our extraterrestrial visitors want us to consider them as brothers and sisters and not as enemies trying to conquer our planet by force. As a matter of fact, there is so far no example of aggressive behavior from our visitors, either on the Earth, in our atmosphere, in outer space, or even on the Moon. They were often very close to our spacecraft, probably out of curiosity, and certainly scared our astronauts, but always managed to avoid them at the last second.

The most interesting part of the UFO mystery is not so much what they are or where they come from, but how they can manage to travel at fantastic velocities of twenty thousand miles an hour in our atmosphere, and suddenly turn at ninety degrees or fly in the opposite direction. There is no terrestrial spacecraft that could even try to reach that velocity or performing such incredible maneuvers without disintegrating on the spot. Therefore, there are only two possible explanations. Either flying saucers do not really exist and are just an optical illusion, or they are extraterrestrial and come from another world somewhere in outer space.

200

Along with several French scientists, such as Claude Poher for example, I think that the UFO propulsion system could very well be based on a combination of electric, magnetic, and gravitic forces, or in other words, on the Unified Field Theory, which could provide a fantastic amount of power out of a small mass of matter such as hydrogen, for example. That theory was first suggested by Albert Einstein in 1925, but it was based on experiments performed a few years before by another genius of physics named Townsend Brown, when he was still in high school!

About seventy years ago, Brown was doing some research on Roentgen radiations which had just been discovered at that time. He was not so much interested in X-rays for themselves, but he thought that a key to space flight might be found there. He set up an experiment to determine whether there might be a useful force of some sort exerted by the rays from his Coolidge tube.

Brown mounted his X-ray tube in extremely delicate balance and began testing for results. He was unable to detect any measurable force exerted by the X-rays but suddenly, he became aware of a very strange reaction of the tube itself. Every time it was turned on, the tube seemed to exhibit a motion of its own, a thrust of some sort, just as if it was trying to move.

Brown had discovered a new physical phenomenon resulting from the combination of electric, magnetic, and gravitic forces, very similar to that which seems to be used by flying saucers. He had designed an anti-gravity device which he called a GRAVITOR, and that had nothing to do with X-rays. It was caused by the high voltage being used to produce the rays, which resulted in magnetic and gravitic forces. Brown was still in high school; and in spite of the fact that there were a few accounts of his work in local newspapers, no serious scientist expressed any interest in his fantastic discovery.

It took more than twenty years, and the genius of Albert Einstein, for the scientific world to finally see the unlimited possibilities offered by Brown's gravitor. His device looked like nothing more than a bakelite case some 12 inches long and 4 inches square; but when it was placed on a sensitive scale and connected to a 100,000 volt power source, it proceeded to either gain or lose about one percent of its weight, depending on the polarity used.

Finally, the Navy performed in 1943, in the unmagical surroundings of the Philadelphia Navy Yard, nothing less than a successful experiment in invisibility which looks to me like a manifestation of pure magic. Of course the experiment was immediately classified TOP SECRET by the Naval Office of Scientific Research, but there were some leaks as usual.

According to the witnesses, a Navy destroyer escort was surrounded by powerful magnetic and gravitic fields which made it vanish temporarily, appear in another place for a few seconds, then reappear exactly where it was before. Of course no one will believe it, but it now seems almost certain that it really happened.

Unfortunately, there are now very few witnesses left. Some of them died in the experiment, many went completely crazy, which was not surprising after such an experience, some died mysteriously after the experiment, probably because they knew too much, and a few managed to disappear forever in Canada or Mexico, probably because they thought that their lives were in danger. Only a few had the courage to talk before they died.

Personally, I am convinced that the UFO propulsion system is based on the same physical principle as Brown's gravitor and the Philadelphia experiment, which must be the Unified Field Theory of Albert Einstein. Einstein always claimed that his research in that field was not completed; but I am convinced that it was, that he asked the Navy to test it, and then got scared when he saw the fantastic results and the tremendous military power that could be obtained with it, for which he would be responsible.

I am also convinced that scientific research in that field is still going on here and in other countries, and that it is probably the best kept military secret of all times. This is also probably why official government agencies do not want independent scientists to play with the UFO propulsion system and do everything they can to discourage them. If the Navy could perform such an experiment forty years ago, just imagine what an advanced extraterrestrial civilization could do with the same principle and a few thousand years of research and development.

Actually, what is important is not whether flying saucers actually exist physically, or whether they are just an illusion of our minds. Even if they did not really exist, the result would now be the same because of the tremendous impact they have already made in our social, religious, political, and scientific lives. As someone said before, if they did not exist, we would have to create them to justify their incredible effects.

Personally, I believe that they really exist and I keep trying to find out exactly what they are, where they come from, and why they come and visit us at this particular time in the history of human evolution. Maybe they are just trying to warn us that we are on the eve of a terrible cosmic cataclysm that will destroy almost everything on the surface of the Earth, as it has already happened several times before, a very long time ago. In that case, it might be a good idea to listen to them.

CONCLUSION

Years ago, when I decided to write this book, I wanted to prove the accuracy of three of my favorite theories that would help explain many great mysteries of the past. Long before I tried to present my ideas, many other men had attempted to explain the same phenomena, but they did not quite succeed, I think, because they started from the wrong assumptions.

The first of my theories states that even tens of thousands of years ago our ancestors possessed amazingly precise scientific knowledge, especially in astronomy and mathematics. But if we accept the official scientific views of today, such advanced knowledge was quite impossible, because at that time man barely knew how to make a crude flint axe and had not even invented the wheel.

My second theory states that this astounding knowledge was given to mankind by extraterrestrial astronauts who came from outer space, with a much higher civilization and culture. It states that, little by little, these astronauts created modern man by insemination and mutation. Our primitive ancestors were thus slowly transformed from Neanderthal men into Cro-Magnon men, the strong and intelligent beings that appeared on Earth about 65,000 years ago.

My third theory states that this unbelievably high scientific knowledge of our ancestors, as well as their religious beliefs and their social customs, almost identical in all four corners of the Earth, had to come from one common source that in relatively recent times seemed to have been situated somewhere in the middle of the Atlantic, but in a more distant past was located in the Pacific.

These centres disappeared without a trace in cosmic cataclysms, leaving only distant memories, inherited from a few survivors, which were reflected in ceremonies, sagas, and some sacred texts.

I have tried to prove the accuracy of these theories by using numbers, even though I know that many people dislike numbers and figures. To these readers I offer my apologies, but I had no choice. For the benefit of those who may still doubt the accuracy of the evidence presented in the preceding chapters of this book, I will summarize my facts.

The scientific knowledge of astronomy shown by our ancestors tens of thousands of years ago was far superior to that of astronomers only 300 years ago. Our prehistoric ancestors knew that the celestial dome is fixed and that the Sun, the Moon, and the planets revolve. They had noticed that the triangle formed by the stars Sirius, Procyon, and Betelgeuse is fixed, while other constellations, like the Great Bear, change their relative positions imperceptibly over many thousands of years. That was why the ancient astronomers chose the star Sirius as the base for their long-range calculations.

They knew without doubt that the Earth revolves around the Sun and that the Moon revolves around the Earth. They knew about the existence of the planets Uranus and Neptune even though it is very rarely possible to see Uranus with the naked eye and impossible to see Neptune at all. They also knew that Mars has two satellites, Jupiter four, Saturn seven, and Uranus two. They knew that comets reappeared at fixed intervals. Some astronomers of the past knew about the existence of the planet Pluto, which we *discovered* only very recently, and even suspected the existence of another planet beyond Pluto, which they named Proserpine. We still have not found this distant planet, but many present-day astronomers are quite sure that it does exist.

The ancient astronomers also knew that the two points where the equator intersects the ecliptic at the equinoxes shift in a westerly direction by 1° every 72 years, or by 360° in 25,920 years. This phenomenon, which for thousands of years was known in many parts of the Earth, was forgotten for a long time; and the Christian Church ignored it until only three hundred years ago.

Our ancestors also knew that the period of 25,920 years was the time elapsed for one rotation of the terrestrial axis at 23 1/2° around the celestial axis, and they called this period of time the Great Year. They knew that this rotation explained why the polar star was not always the same and why some circumpolar stars were sometimes visible and sometimes not.

Finally, our ancestors knew that all the planets and satellites in our solar system return to the same position on the celestial vault after

206

2,268 million days, or after 6.3 million years of 360 days each, a timespan that for modern astronomy equals 6,209,578 years of 365.2422 days each.

In mathematics instead of the decimal system, our ancestors used fractions which were much more precise than our decimals. They did not use the decimal system and had no need for it since they did not have decimal calculators. The use of fractions instead of decimal values allowed them to resolve, for instance, the squaring of the circle, which is the computation of a square with the same perimeter as a given circle. This is considered impossible by our modern mathematicians, who use a value of Pi with an infinite number of decimals. For our ancestors, Pi was the ratio 22:7. Therefore, a circle with a radius of 7 had a perimeter of 44, the same as a square with a side of II.

The golden section, or factor Phi, which allowed them to construct triangles or rectangles having the same surface area as a given circle, was expressed by the ratio I96:I2I. The square root of this number used by our ancient ancestors is I4:II, which equals 4:Pi, or 28:22. Consequently, a circle with a radius of I4:II has a surface of 56:II, the same square area as a rectangle with sides of 22:7 and I96:I2I, or a triangle with a base of 44:7 and a height of I96:I2I.

Angles too were expressed as fractions. These could, depending on the case, represent the functions of sine, cosine, or tangent of the angles. So, sine of 30° was I/2, sine of 60° was equal to I3/I5, and the tangent of the base angle of the Great Pyramid was I4/II, the square root of the Golden Section.

The angle of inclination of the Earth's rotational axis with the axis of the ecliptic was defined by its cosine value, or the fraction II/I2, found in the dimensions of the Kalasaya Temple in Tiahuanaco, which measures 264 x 288 cubits, and in those of many other temples around the world.

But this temple in Tiahuanaco was probably constructed 27,000 years ago, as can be seen by its astronomical layout; and, if nothing else testifies about its age. It is the condition of the ruins which prove to us that much more than I0,000 years have elapsed since it was built. It is therefore evident that our ancestors of I0,000 or more years ago possessed a level of mathematical and astronomical knowledge so superior that they could not have developed it by themselves.

With this conclusion, we arrive at my second theory, namely, the intervention of some extraterrestrial source in human affairs many thousands of years ago. This theory is already generally accepted by the public and also is considered a possibility by part of the scientific community. But it is difficult to get the official scientific establishment to accept it because that could turn upside down all traditional scientific beliefs.

Nevertheless, this theory must be correct, because there is none other that would better explain the sudden appearance of intelligent man and his very advanced scientific knowledge so long ago. Also, there are many proofs of ancient technical knowledge that could only have reached our ancestors by direct transmission from a more highly developed culture. Let me cite a few examples.

Our ancient ancestors knew and used static electricity, electric current, wet-cell batteries, electroplating, and powerful light projectors fed by high-voltage cables. They used platinum, a metal that melts only at 1,753° C, and aluminum, which allegedly wasn't discovered and produced until the nineteenth century.

Our ancestors knew optics. Possibly they even used telescopes and microscopes, because perfectly polished optical lenses, made out of glass or quartz, have been found in various archaeological sites.

It is also very likely that they knew the secret of gravitaion and used it to perform levitation - something we cannot even explain today. Without this knowledge of gravitational control, our ancestors could not have built edifices of enormous stone slabs, which have been found all over the world. No modern construction cranes could lift the huge stones of the temple at Baalbek, once the ancient town of Heliopolis, northeast of Beirut, Lebanon.

In several places on the globe somebody traced gigantic figures and geometric designs like those in Nasca, the Maltese cross in the Aegean Sea, or the triangle of France. None of these figures and designs could have been created by humans standing on the ground. Flying machines and possibly electromagnetic navigation devices were needed to trace these huge markers, which could be seen and recognized only from high up in the sky. Humans of that period did not have the technology needed to fly nor the neccesssary electromagnetic distance-measuring equipment. It seems that the only valid explanation is that these machines were built somewhere else in space and brought here by astronauts to improve and to educate the human race.

My third theory, which states that all terrestrial civilizations evolved from the same source, is probably the easiest to prove. With the exception of some reference in ancient legends, there are no remaining traces of the mysterious Land of Mu, the continent that existed perhaps only 100,000 years ago in the middle of the Pacific Ocean and that certainly will be found some day on the ocean floor. But many clues exist today which prove the existence of Atlantis and its culture that linked east with west, the Eurasian continent with the Americas, until it too disappeared some 12,000 years ago.

We have found some of the ruins of Atlantis underwater in the Bahamas. Also, there is no better explanation than the common source of Atlantis to make us understand the astounding similarities between ancient civiliztions on both sides of the Atlantic Ocean, like the Mayan and Egyptian, both of which had pyramids, mummies, close intermarriage, the same basic measurement and calculation techniques, and many other things in common. A large number of serious people do not doubt that Atlantis existed. What is still left for us to find out is its exact location on the map and the exact dates of creation and destruction of the famed civilization.

As one could see from this book, I did succeed in solving some of the problems that were submitted to me during my visit at the astronautical congress in Paris some years ago. Since my speciality was space communications, it seemed logical for me to start by trying to solve the mysteries of flying saucers and extraterrestrial civilizations. But I am also a mathematician, and I had a vague feeling that at least some of these assumptions were correct. One single number - the constant of the solar system - solved more than one of my mysteries and only the first three problems were really difficult to solve. The rest were resolved in a much simpler way because I had developed an efficient calculation technique.

I started with the mysterious number of fifteen digits found in Nineveh and soon discovered that it was the esoteric form, expressed in

209

seconds, of the much simpler number of 2,268 million days, or just about 6.3 million years. When I discovered later that this time span represented exactly 240 equinoctial cycles, which always played a prominent role in ancient astrology, I immediately realized that by sheer luck I had found the great constant of the solar system, lost for many centuries, and it happened without my even looking for it. My discovery that this solar, or Nineveh, constant had been calculated 64,800 years ago, at the time when Cro-Magnon man suddenly appeared on the Earth, made me feel that I had hit the jackpot.

Up to now, none of our classic theories could satisfactorily explain the sudden appearance of the Cro-Magnon man on Earth. No one using the classic theories of evolution will ever explain how the Cro-Magnon, immediately upon arrival, could calculate the Nineveh constant based on the planets Uranus and Neptune, which he couldn't even see, and the imperceptible displacement of the equinoctial point that shifts west by only one degree every seventy-two years.

In my opinion, both these mysteries have just one explanation - the intervention of astronauts from another world, who came, just as the Bible tells us, to create, educate, and civilize a new human race in their own image.

Thus, once upon a time, about 65,000 years ago, extraordinary visitors came from another civilization in space, discovered the Earth was a wonderful place to live on, and decided to establish a colony here. But in the beginning they did not like our air and water, and they weren't used to the Earth's gravity. So, these visitors decided to create a hybrid race, so that by cross breeding with humans after a few generations the new race would be perfectly adapted to life on Earth and would carry on at least part of the intelligence and technical know-how of its ancestors from space. To achieve this, the most attractive and the most intelligent young females were inseminated, and this procedure continued with their daughters and granddaughters until the results were acceptable for life on Earth; and the education and civilization of the new race could start.

Another mystery I tried to solve was that of the Mayan calendar. Once I knew the Nineveh constant and the exact periods of revolution and conjuction of planets, it didn't take long to find the only astronomical period that had a duration of about twenty years. I had more trouble with the starting date of the Mayan calendar, but I knew

210

that it too had to be a date of conjunction between two planets other than Jupiter and Saturn. So I tried Uranus and Neptune and discovered the cycle of quadruple conjuction of 4,627 years that is hardly known. After that came the realization that the Mayas, who were obsessed with calculations using enormous numbers, used the number 34,020 million days - a number fifteen times greater than the Nineveh constant - and that this number corresponded exactly to 3,600 Sumerian cycles of precession of the equinoxes.

Then we had the mystery of the Great Pyramid of Cheops, which was based on three differnt mathematical principles, incompatible if expressed in decimals, but compatible when expressed as fractions. The pyramid was at the same time and astronomical observatory, a standard of weights and measures, and a standard of time. Both its volume and the length of the coffer in its royal chamber were based on the solar constant.

The Maltese cross, the Rhodes calculator, and the navigational systems of the ancient seafarers did not give me much trouble. I found the solutions by accident while trying to solve other problems. As for the signs of the zodiac, the polar rounds, and the universal calendar, I was greatly helped by the research work done by others before me. I have listed their publications in the bibliography at the end of this book.

The last three puzzles - those of the four moons, of Atlantis, and of the extraterrestrial visitors - really fascinated me, because they were at the outer limits between science and complete mystery; and I need more than numbers and computers to solve them. I needed intuition, just as I needed intuition in discovering the Nineveh constant, the secrets of the Mayan calendar, and the mystery of the Great Pyramid of Cheops. *I am convinced that to resolve all this in a few weeks' time would not have been possible without the help of some occult power source that is unknown to me now and will probably remain unknown to me for ever.*

I have been helped in my research just as our ancestors were aided tens of thousands of years ago. Can anyone really think that all that fantastic knowledge in astronomy, mathematics, geodesy, and many other sciences was acquired by mankind without outside help? Frankly, is it not much more logical to accept the idea that all this knowledge was brought by astronauts who came from another world, just as many legends and the Bible tell us, or that the advancement of mankind was stimulated by some very highly developed cultures located in the Land of Mu or Atlantis, which were visited even earlier by outside civilizations from within the solar system or even from distant galaxies?

About thirty years ago one could question and dismiss such theories as incredible. But in the last three decades we ourselves walked on the moon and drove a jeep on its surface; and our space probes have flown at low altitudes over Venus, Mars, and Mercury and have taken magnificent photographs of the latter two planets. We have a space probe under way that will make a tour of the solar system beyond Saturn and Uranus. And the hypothesis that our ancestors were visited from space by extraterrestrial beings does no longer seem so impossible. Indeed, it now seems very logical. A few more years and a few more space explorations from now, and our children will wonder why such theories seemed so implausible to previous generations.

It is evident that all the theories and hypotheses that I have proposed here are subject to further verification, and it is possible that some will be proven inexact, as is often the case in this kind of research, touching on the outer limits of exact sciences. But that seems to be of lesser importance to me, at least as far as we are concerned now. *What is important is to launch and set into motion new ideas, so that these can inspire subsequent generations to make their own discoveries and formulate new theories.*

In the past, most men who came up with new thoughts and concept were dismissed as fools, provided they were lucky enough not be be burned alive, as the Roman Catholic Church did to Giordano Bruno in the year 1600, because he was so naive as to believe that the universe was infinite and that many other worlds similar to ours existed, where the inhabitants could live in peace because the Inquisition didn't exist there.

In our times, the honest search for truth is less likely to lead to violent death, but the risk still exists. There are quite a few American UFO researchers who have complained about death threats received either by phone or by mysterious visitors demanding that they cease their activities. Some have actually died under strange circumstances, and all of their archives have disappeared without a trace. That

212

could explain why we will never know the complete truth about all the riddles of the universe.

San Diego, June 1988

BIBLIOGRAPHY

Bailey, James, *The God Kings and the Titans.* St. Martin, 1973.
Barry, Georges, *Les Nombres Magiques Nucleaires.* Dervy, Paris, 1975.
Bellamy, Hans, *The Calendar of Tiahuanaco.* Faver, London, 1956.
Bergier, Jacques, *Extraterrestrial Visitations.* Regnery, Chicago, 1973.
Bibby, Geoffrey, *Looking for Dilmun.* Knopf, New York, 1970.
Biraud, Francois, *Civilisations extraterrestres.* Paris, 1970.
Bleeker, Sonia, *The Maya.* Morrow, New York, 1961.
Blumrich, Joseph, *The Spaceships of Ezekiel.* Corgi, London, 1974.
Brainerd, George, *The Maya Civilization.* Los Angeles, 1968.
Bronowski, Jacob, *The Ascent of Man.* BBC, London, 1973.
Bushnell, George, *The First Americans.* Thames and Hudson, 1968.
Carnac, Pierre, *Les Conquerants du Pacifique.* Laffont, Paris, 1975.
Ceram, C. W., *Gods, Graves, and Scholars.* Gollancz, 1971.
Charroux, Robert, *Lost Worlds.* Fontana, 1974.
Chatelain, Maurice, *Le temps Et l'espace.* Laffont, Paris, 1979.
Chubb, Mary, *City in the Sand.* Crowell, New York, 1957.
Cottrell, Leonard, *Lost Cities.* Pan Books, 1971.
Cousteau, Jacques, *Diving for Sunken Treasure.* Cassell, 1971.
Daniel, Glyn, *The Megalith Builders.* Penguin, London, 1968.
Daniken, Erich von, *The Gold of the Gods,* Corgi, 1975.
Davidson, Basil, *Old Africa Rediscovered.* Gollancz, 1959.
Davies, Nigel, *The Aztecs.* Macmillan, 1973.
De Santillana, Giorgio, *Hamlet's Mill.* Gambit, Boston, 1969.
Downing, Barry, *The Bible and Flying Saucers.* Avon, New York, 1970.
Flemming, Nicholas, *Cities in the Sea.* Doubleday, New York, 1971.
Flindt, Max, *Mankind Child of the Stars.* Coronet, 1976.
Gallant, Roy, *Astrology: Sense or Nonsense.* Doubleday, NY, 1974.
Gauquelin, Michel, *Cosmic Clocks.* P. Owen, 1969.
Giddings, Louis, *Ancient Men of the Arctic.* Knopf, New York, 1967.
Granger, Michel, *Extraterrestres en exil.* Michel, Paris, 1975.
Guerrier, Eric, *La Cosmogonie des Dogons.* Laffont, Paris, 1975.
Guingamp, Maurice, *Notre Dame de Paris.* Laffont, Paris, 1972.
Hapgood, Charles, *The Path of the Poles.* Chilton, Philadelphia, 1970.

Hawkes, Jacquetta, *Prehistoric Britain*. Penguin, London, 1944.
Hawkins, Gerald, *Beyond Stonehenge*. Arrow Books, 1977.
Hutin, Serge, *History of Astrology*. Pyramid, New York, 1972.
Hynek, Allen, *The UFO Experience*. Abelard-Schuman, 1972.
Irwin, Constance, *Fair Gods and Stone Faces*. St. Martin, 1963.
Keller, Werner, *The Bible as History*. Hodder and Stoughton, 1956.
Keyhoe, Donald, *Flying Saucers, Top Secret*. Putnam, New York, 1960.
Kolosimo, Peter, *Timeless Earth*. Sphere, 1974.
Lunan, Duncan, *Man and the Stars*. Souvenir Press, London, 1974.
MacNeice, Louis, *Astrology*. Aldus, 1964.
Mazel, Jean, *Avec les Pheniciens*. Laffont, Paris, 1968.
Misrakl, Paul, *Des Signes dans le ciel*. Labergerie, Paris, 1968.
Mooney, Richard, *Colony Earth*. Panther, 1976.
Moreau, Marcel, *Civilisations des etoiles*. Laffont, Paris, 1973.
Niel, Fernand, *The Mysteries of Stonehenge*. Avon, 1975.
Pauwels, Louis, *Morning of the Magicians*. Mayflower, 1971.
Pearson, Kenneth, *The Dorak Affair*. Atheneum, New York, 1968.
Pochan, Andre, *L'enigme de la grande pyramide*. Paris, 1971.
Poesson, Paul, *Le Testament de Noe*. Laffont, Paris, 1972.
Rackl, Hans, *Diving into the Past*. Scribner, New York, 1968.
Renfrew, Colin, *Before Civilization*. Cape, 1973.
Sagan, Carl, *The Cosmic Connection*. Coronet Books, 1975.
Sanderson, Ivan, *Invisible Residents*. Tandem, 1974.
Saurat, Denis, *Atlantis and the Giants*. Faber, London, 1957.
Sendy, Jean, *The Coming of the Gods*. Berkley, New York, 1973.
Silverberg, Robert, *Before the Sphinx*. Nelson, New York, 1971.
Soustelle, Jacques, *Daily Life of the Aztecs*. Stanford, 1961.
Steinhauser, Gerard, *Les Chrononautes*. Michel, Paris, 1973.
Tarade, Guy, *Les Dossiers de l'etrange*. Laffont, Paris, 1971.
Thompson, Eric, *The Dresden Codex*. Philadelphia, 1972.
Tomas, Andrew, *We Are Not the First*. Souvenir Press, 1971.
Tompkins, Peter, *Secrets of the Great Pyramid*. Harper & Row, 1971.
Vallee, Jacques, *Passport to Magonia*. Tandem, 1975.
Velikovsky, Immanuel, *Worlds in Collision*. Gollancz, 1950.
Vieux, Maurice, *Les Secrets des batisseurs*. Laffont, Paris, 1975.
Walsbard, Simone, *Tiahuanaco*. Laffont, Paris, 1971
Wooley, Leonard, *Ur of the Chaldees*. Penguin, London, 1954.